CAKE POPS

BIZCOCHOS CON PALITO PARA CELEBRACIONES Y FIESTAS

BLUME

Helen Attridge y Abby Foy

BLUME

Título original *Cake pops*
Edición Sara Ford, Leanne Bryan, Nicole Foster
Diseño Eoghan O'Brien, Clare Barber
Fotografía Lis Parsons
Estilismo Laura Fyfe
Traducción Remedios Diéguez Diéguez
Revisión de la edición en lengua española
Ana María Pérez Martínez
Especialista en temas culinarios
Coordinación de la edición en lengua española
Cristina Rodríguez Fischer

Primera edición en lengua española 2013

© 2013 Naturart, S.A. Editado por BLUME
Av. Mare de Déu de Lorda, 20
08034 Barcelona
Tel. 93 205 40 00 Fax 93 205 14 41
e-mail: info@blume.net
© 2012 Octopus Publishing Group, Londres

I.S.B.N.: 978-84-15317-23-4

Impreso en China

www.blume.net

Preservamos el medio ambiente. En la producción de nuestros
libros procuramos, con el máximo empeño, cumplir con los requisitos
medioambientales que promueven la conservación y el uso responsable
de los bosques, en especial de los bosques primarios. Asimismo, en nuestra
preocupación por el planeta, intentamos emplear al máximo materiales
reciclados y solicitamos a nuestros proveedores que usen materiales de
manufactura cuya fabricación este libre de cloro elemental (ECF)
o de metales pesados, entre otros.

CONTENIDO

INTRODUCCIÓN

Cuando Verónica, la cuñada de Helen, se trasladó de Estados Unidos al Reino Unido y preguntó dónde podía comprar *popcakes*, no teníamos ni idea de qué estaba hablando. Después de buscar en la red, nos enamoramos.

Siempre hemos trabajado en catering y nos encanta la creatividad, de manera que experimentamos con diferentes sabores y diseños. Nos divertimos tanto, y las reacciones a nuestras primeras creaciones fueron tan buenas, que decidimos crear Popcake Kitchen.

Este libro incluye *cake pops* que implican habilidad decorativa. Esperamos que todos se animen a probar los diseños «avanzados», pero nosotras disfrutamos igual con las creaciones más sencillas.

Lo único que nos gusta más que hornear (¡y comer!) nuestros *pops* es ver la reacción de los demás cuando descubren las creaciones únicas que hemos preparado para ellos. Estamos seguras de que después de probar nuestros *pops* también disfrutará mimando a su familia y a sus amigos. ¡FELICES CREACIONES!

ELABORAR *CAKE POPS*

Lo bueno de los *cake pops* es que el bizcocho horneado no tiene que parecer perfecto. Con nuestra receta, los *cake pops* apenas requieren esfuerzo y pueden adaptarse a diferentes sabores deliciosos.

RECETA BÁSICA DE *CAKE POP* DE VAINILLA

Con esta receta se obtienen algunos *cake pops* más que con la que se indica en las individuales, de manera que dispondrá de masa para experimentar... ¡o para preparar más, porque no durarán mucho!

CON ANTELACIÓN Precaliente el horno a 180 ºC. Forre una placa de 20 cm con papel sulfurizado.

PARA PREPARAR EL BIZCOCHO Ponga la mantequilla y el azúcar en el robot y mezcle a velocidad media, hasta que obtenga una pasta blanca y esponjosa. Añada el extracto de vainilla e incorpore de nuevo.

Agregue la mitad de los huevos batidos y la harina, y mezcle bien. Repita con el resto de huevos y harina.

Vierta la masa sobre la placa y hornee unos 30-35 minutos. Para comprobar si el bizcocho está listo, introduzca un tenedor en el centro: si sale seco y limpio, significa que ya está cocido. Déjelo enfriar sobre una rejilla.

PARA PREPARAR EL GLASEADO Bata la mantequilla, el azúcar y el extracto de vainilla en un cuenco hasta conseguir una textura homogénea.

VARIACIONES DE SABOR

CHOCOLATE INTENSO Sustituya 25 g de harina por 25 g de cacao amargo en polvo. Para el glaseado, añada 1 cucharadita de cacao amargo en polvo a la mezcla.

LIMÓN ESTIMULANTE Agregue el zumo y la ralladura de un limón a la preparación de mantequilla y azúcar, y remueva. Para el glaseado, añada el zumo de ½ limón.

PARA EL BIZCOCHO

Se obtienen aproximadamente 25 *cake pops* del tamaño de una pelota de golf

200 g de mantequilla, ablandada
200 g de azúcar superfino
1 cucharadita de extracto de vainilla
3 huevos batidos
250 g de harina con levadura, tamizada

PARA EL GLASEADO

125 g de mantequilla, ablandada
200 g de azúcar de lustre
1 cucharadita de extracto de vainilla

PREPARAR LAS BOLAS DE BIZCOCHO

Parta o corte el bizcocho ya frío en trozos manejables. Desmenúcelos a mano, o si prefiere un material más suelto, utilice el rallador del robot.

Con las manos, mezcle el glaseado con el bizcocho desmenuzado. Añada una cucharada cada vez (es posible que no lo necesite todo). Si se excede con el glaseado, las bolas quedarán demasiado húmedas y no se conservarán en los palitos cuando las bañe. La mezcla está lista cuando se mantiene homogénea al hacerla rodar en las manos.

Divida la preparación y forme bolitas del tamaño de pelotas de golf (de un peso aproximado de 25 g), o la forma necesaria para el diseño de *pop cake* que vaya a elaborar.

Ponga las piezas en una fuente y tápelas. Consérvelas en la nevera una hora como mínimo (hasta que la mezcla esté firme). Puede reservar la masa tapada en la nevera hasta 2 días.

NECESITARÁ

1 bolsa de *Candy melts* (pastillas de chocolate para fundir)
Cuchara y cuenco apto para microondas
Aceite vegetal
20 bolas de bizcocho
20 palitos para piruletas
1 palillo

BAÑAR LOS *CAKE POPS*

Cuando las bolitas estén firmes al tacto, ya están listas para bañarlas.

Ponga las pastillas en un cuenco para microondas a temperatura media durante 2 minutos. Remueva cada 20 segundos para asegurarse de que se rerritan homogéneamente y no se quemen.

Añada un poco de aceite vegetal (una cucharada cada vez) al chocolate fundido. De ese modo se diluirá un poco y conseguirá una textura sedosa y manejable. Debe quedar suelto.

Saque las bolas de bizcocho de la nevera. Sumerja 1 cm de un palito para piruleta en el chocolate e introdúzcalo en el centro de una bola, más o menos hasta la mitad. Tenga cuidado y no haga demasiada fuerza, pero asegúrese de introducir el palo lo suficiente para que la bola quede fija (un bloque de poliestireno resulta de gran ayuda en este paso).

Sumerja el *cake pop* en el chocolate fundido.

Dé unos golpecitos suaves con el palo en el borde del cuenco para eliminar el exceso de chocolate. Gire el *cake pop* y repita los golpecitos por el otro lado para conseguir una cobertura homogénea. Utilice el extremo de un palillo para eliminar las burbujas que podrían aparecer.

Deje secar en vertical. Los *cake pops* ya bañados se conservan 3-4 días en un lugar fresco y seco.

DECORAR LOS *CAKE POPS*

¡Ha llegado el momento de ser creativos! Puede añadir todo tipo de decoraciones comestibles a sus *pops* para crear diseños sencillos pero efectivos. Algunos de los *pops* más complicados requieren un poco más de trabajo, pero los resultados son espectaculares. Veamos algunas técnicas básicas.

- Añada la decoración en forma de bolitas mientras el chocolate todavía esté húmedo. Tome una pizca entre los dedos y repártalos cuidadosamente sobre el *cake pop*.

- Agregue las decoraciones comestibles cuando el *cake pop* esté seco. Aplique un poco de chocolate fundido en la superficie con un palillo y «pegue» la decoración elegida.

- Corte la decoración de *fondant* extendido, que es muy fácil de trabajar. Cuando lo trabaje, espolvoree la superficie de trabajo con un poco de harina o maicena para evitar que se pegue.

- Añada un toque elegante con adornos. Llene una manga pastelera de plástico con chocolate fundido, gire el extremo y apriete la manga para producir una línea uniforme.

CAKE POPS CON FORMAS

Convierta sus *cake pops* en formas sorprendentes y maravillosas utilizando alguna de las siguientes técnicas:

- Amase la bola sobre la superficie de trabajo hasta obtener una forma de salchicha (una base estupenda para muchos diseños).

- Desplace las manos mientras amasa para conseguir una forma ovalada.

- Apriete la bola contra la superficie de trabajo para conseguir bordes planos.

POPS DE CHOCOLATE

Estos *cake pops* sencillos, pero deliciosos, le permitirán aprender las técnicas básicas de elaboración y utilizar ingredientes fáciles de conseguir.

NECESITARÁ

20 bolas de bizcocho
  (*véanse* págs. 5-6)
20 palitos para piruletas
Poliestireno
Cuenco
Cuchara
Palillo

DECORACIÓN

1 bolsa de pastillas de chocolate
  blanco para fundir
Bolitas crujientes de chocolate,
  mariposas o estrellitas de
  chocolate blanco

NIVEL DE DIFICULTAD

CON ANTELACIÓN Refrigere las bolas de bizcocho durante 1 hora.

PARA PREPARAR LOS *CAKE POPS* Derrita las pastillas (*véase* pág. 6), sumerja un palito en el chocolate ya fundido e insértelo en una bola. Repita la operación con todos los palos y las bolas. Bañe los *cake pops* en el chocolate fundido y elimine el exceso con unos golpecitos en el borde del cuenco.

PARA DECORAR Espolvoree las bolitas de chocolate, si las utiliza, sobre los *cake pops* antes de que cuaje el chocolate.

Si usa estrellitas o mariposas, deje que el chocolate se seque, aplique un poco de chocolate fundido con la punta de un palillo y pegue las estrellas.

CONSEJO

Cuando espolvoree las bolitas de chocolate, hágalo sobre un cuenco para recoger las que caigan. Podrá aplicarlas después sobre los *cake pops* con una cuchara.

POPS VARIADOS

Estos *cake pops* sencillos, pero vistosos, ofrecen otra oportunidad
de aprender las técnicas básicas utilizando ingredientes
para decorar pasteles.

NECESITARÁ

20 bolas de bizcocho
  (*véanse* págs. 5-6)
20 palitos para piruletas
Poliestireno
Cuenco
Cuchara
Palillo

DECORACIÓN

1 bolsa de pastillas de chocolate
  blanco
Flores, mariposas o bolitas
  de glaseado real

NIVEL DE DIFICULTAD

CON ANTELACIÓN Refrigere las bolas de bizcocho durante 1 hora.

PARA PREPARAR LOS *CAKE POPS* Derrita las pastillas (*véase* pág. 6),
sumerja un palito en el chocolate derretido e insértelo en una bola. Repita la operación
con todos los palos y las bolas. Bañe los *cake pops* en el chocolate fundido y elimine
el exceso con unos golpecitos en el borde del cuenco.

PARA DECORAR Reparta las bolitas sobre los *cake pops* antes de que el chocolate
cuaje.

Si utiliza mariposas o flores, aplique un poco de chocolate fundido sobre el *cake pop*
ya seco con la punta de un palillo y pegue la decoración elegida.

CONSEJO

Cuando espolvoree las bolitas, hágalo sobre un cuenco para recoger las que caigan.
Podrá aplicarlas después sobre los *cake pops* con una cuchara.

PORCIONES DE TARTA

Su sabor es tan delicioso como su aspecto, sobre todo si se preparan con bizcocho de chocolate y glaseado intensos.

NECESITARÁ

20 bolas de bizcocho
   (*véanse* págs. 5-6)
20 palitos para piruletas
Poliestireno
Rodillo de plástico
Cuchillo
Manga pastelera de plástico
Palillo

DECORACIÓN

1 bolsa de pastillas de chocolate
   al cacao
250 g de *fondant* rosa claro extendido
Maicena
¼ de bolsa de pastillas de chocolate
   blanco
Flores de glaseado real rosa

NIVEL DE DIFICULTAD

CON ANTELACIÓN Convierta las bolas de bizcocho en triángulos. Utilice la superficie de trabajo o un cuchillo de lado para formar bordes rectos. Refrigere los triángulos durante 1 hora.

PARA PREPARAR LOS *CAKE POPS* Derrita las pastillas de chocolate (*véase* pág. 6), sumerja un palito en el chocolate ya fundido e insértelo en un triángulo. Repita con todos los palos y los triángulos, y deje que cuaje. Bañe los *cake pops* en el chocolate derretido y elimine el exceso con unos golpecitos en el borde del cuenco. Déjelos secar boca abajo sobre poliestireno.

PARA DECORAR Espolvoree la superficie de trabajo con maicena y extienda el *fondant* hasta conseguir una lámina de 2,5 mm, aproximadamente. Coloque un *cake pop* seco sobre el *fondant* y corte alrededor del vértice con un cuchillo. Levante el *cake pop* sobre el borde exterior y corte el *fondant* (le quedará una forma parecida a un cohete). Haga un agujero en el triángulo de *fondant* (asegúrese de que quede en el lugar correcto para que el *fondant* encaje perfectamente sobre el *cake pop*). Pase la forma de *fondant* por el palito y «péguela» con chocolate derretido, que aplicará con un palillo. Decore todos los *cake pops* de la misma manera.

Derrita las pastillas de chocolate blanco (*véase* pág. 6) y rellene la manga pastelera. Decore cada *cake pop* con una línea, que imitará el relleno de un pastel.

PARA TERMINAR Aplique chocolate fundido sobre los *cake pops* utilizando un palillo y coloque una flor de glaseado real en cada uno.

CONSEJO

Cuando golpee ligeramente los *cake pops* para eliminar el exceso de chocolate, deje que gotee desde el vértice para conseguir un acabado uniforme.

FRESAS CON CHOCOLATE

¡Sí, está viendo cake pops, no fresas de verdad!

NECESITARÁ

20 bolas de bizcocho
(*véanse* págs. 5-6)
20 palitos para piruletas
Palillo
Poliestireno
Rodillo de plástico
Cortapastas redondo de 2,5 cm
Cuchillo
Papel sulfurizado

DECORACIÓN

1 bolsa de pastillas de chocolate
rojas
100 g de *fondant* verde extendido
Maicena
½ bolsa de pastillas de chocolate
claro

NIVEL DE DIFICULTAD

CON ANTELACIÓN Para dar forma de fresa a las bolas de bizcocho, incline las manos cuando las trabaje y aplane ligeramente la parte superior. Refrigere durante 1 hora.

PARA PREPARAR LOS *CAKE POPS* Derrita las pastillas de chocolate rojas (*véase* pág. 6), sumerja un palito en el chocolate fundido e insértelo en la parte superior de un *cake pop*. Deje que cuaje. Bañe todos los *cake pops* en el chocolate fundido y elimine el exceso dando unos golpecitos en el borde del cuenco. Para crear la textura de una fresa, dé unos toquecitos ligeros en el chocolate húmedo con un palillo. Deje secar los *cake pops* sobre poliestireno.

Para crear el pedúnculo verde, extienda el *fondant* sobre la superficie de trabajo espolvoreada con maicena hasta conseguir una lámina de aproximadamente 1,2 mm de grosor. Corte 20 círculos con un cortapastas de 2,5 cm y abra un orificio en el centro de cada uno con un palito para piruleta. Utilice un cuchillo para crear la forma de estrella, empezando por el centro del círculo, y dejando aproximadamente 1 cm alrededor del orificio. Aplique chocolate fundido en la parte superior de cada fresa usando un palillo, pase el pedúnculo por el palo y sujételo a la fresa.

PARA TERMINAR Derrita las pastillas de chocolate y sumerja cada fresa hasta la mitad. Elimine el exceso y coloque las fresas inclinadas sobre el papel sulfurizado; sujételas hasta que cuajen.

CONSEJO

Apoye los palos en algún objeto para asegurarse de que todas las fresas formen el mismo ángulo.

FLORES PRIMAVERALES

Un ramo de flores de primavera es perfecto como regalo para el día de la madre.

NECESITARÁ

20 bolas de bizcocho
  (*véanse* págs. 5-6)
20 palitos para piruletas
Cuenco
Cuchara
Poliestireno
Rodillo de plástico
2 cortadores ovalados de 5 x 3,5 cm
Palillo
Cortador de 10 cm con forma
  de flor
Cuchillo

DECORACIÓN

1 bolsa de pastillas de chocolate
  amarillas
1 bolsa de pastillas de chocolate
  rosas
Decoración de azúcar amarilla
500 g *fondant* de varios colores
  extendido
Maicena

NIVEL DE DIFICULTAD

CON ANTELACIÓN Cuando prepare las bolas de bizcocho, trabaje la mitad para darles forma de tulipán; para ello, incline las manos mientras las trabaja (se trata de conseguir una forma de fresa invertida). Refrigere las piezas durante 1 hora.

PARA PREPARAR LOS *CAKE POPS* Derrita las pastillas de chocolate amarillas (*véase* pág. 6), sumerja 10 palitos en el chocolate fundido e insértelos hasta la mitad en las bolas. Funda las pastillas rosas, sumerja el resto de palitos e introdúzcalos hasta la mitad en las formas de tulipán (desde el extremo ancho). Deje que cuajen. Bañe los *cake pops* de tulipán en el chocolate fundido rosa y elimine el exceso con unos golpecitos en el borde del cuenco. Déjelos secar en vertical. Para el resto de las flores, sumerja los *cake pops* en el chocolate fundido amarillo y espolvoree con la decoración de azúcar amarilla antes de que el chocolate cuaje (hágalo sobre un cuenco para recoger el exceso, que podrá aplicar después con una cuchara).

Sobre la superficie de trabajo espolvoreada con maicena, extienda el *fondant* en una lámina de unos 2,5 mm de grosor.

PARA LOS TULIPANES Corte seis óvalos de *fondant* para cada *cake pop*. Aplique chocolate rosa en los dos tercios inferiores de cada óvalo utilizando un palillo. Pegue tres óvalos alrededor de cada tulipán, y después coloque los tres restantes encima. Doble ligeramente la parte superior de los pétalos.

PARA EL RESTO DE FLORES Corte 10 formas grandes de flores. Con un cuchillo, realice un corte en el fondo de cada pétalo. Con un palito para piruleta abra un agujero en el centro. Utilice un palillo para aplicar chocolate fundido amarillo alrededor del orificio e introduzca una forma de flor de *fondant* a través del palito de cada *cake pop* amarillo, pegando los pétalos a la parte inferior. Ponga el *cake pop* boca abajo y superponga los pétalos; asegure los dos tercios inferiores con *fondant* de caramelo. Abra la parte superior de los pétalos para crear la forma de la flor.

VESTIDOS DE VERANO

Convierta su vestido de verano favorito en un *cake pop*. Puede cambiar los colores de las pastillas de chocolate y del *fondant* al gusto.

NECESITARÁ

20 bolas de bizcocho
 (*véanse págs. 5-6*)
20 palitos para piruletas
Poliestireno
Rodillo de plástico
Cortador de 1 cm con forma
 de corazón
Cuchillo
Palillo

DECORACIÓN

1 bolsa de pastillas de chocolate
 amarillas o rosas
100 g de *fondant* rosa o lila extendido
Maicena
Decoración de flores

NIVEL DE DIFICULTAD

CON ANTELACIÓN Para convertir las bolas de bizcocho en vestidos, trabájelas hasta obtener una forma de salchicha gruesa y aplánelas ligeramente. Forme la cintura con los dedos y cree un poco de vuelo en la parte inferior de los vestidos. Si le resulta más fácil, apriete el borde inferior contra la superficie de trabajo o con la hoja plana de un cuchillo para aplanarlo. Defina un poco la parte superior añadiendo una pequeña ranura. Refrigere los *cake pops* durante 1 hora.

PARA PREPARAR LOS *CAKE POPS* Derrita las pastillas de chocolate amarillas o rosas (*véase pág. 6*), sumerja 1 palito en el chocolate fundido e insértelo en la parte inferior de un vestido. Repita con todos los *cake pops*. Deje que cuajen. Bañe los *cake pops* en el chocolate derretido y elimine el exceso con unos golpecitos en el borde del cuenco. Déjelos a secar en vertical.

PARA DECORAR Sobre la superficie de trabajo en la que haya espolvoreado maicena, extienda el *fondant* dándole unos 2,5 mm de grosor. Para crear el cinturón, corte una tira fina con un cuchillo y sujétela alrededor de la cintura utilizando chocolate fundido aplicado con un palillo. Para el lazo, corte dos formas de corazón de *fondant* y forme una bolita para el nudo. De nuevo, sujete las piezas con *fondant* y un palillo. Añada la decoración elegida utilizando el mismo método.

CONSEJO

Para eliminar el posible exceso de maicena del *fondant*, añada un poco de vodka cuando la pasta se haya endurecido. Éste se evaporará y obtendrá un acabado limpio.

GLOBOS DE COLORES

Son muy vistosos y muy sencillos de preparar.

NECESITARÁ

20 bolas de bizcocho
(*véanse* págs. 5-6)
20 palitos para piruletas
Poliestireno
Palillo

DECORACIÓN

Bolsas de pastillas de chocolate
de varios colores
200 g de *fondant* de los mismos
colores que los chocolates
Laca comestible en aerosol

NIVEL DE DIFICULTAD

CON ANTELACIÓN Para crear los globos, incline las manos con el fin de conseguir un extremo en punta. Refrigere los *cake pops* durante 1 hora.

PARA PREPARAR LOS *CAKE POPS* Derrita las pastillas de chocolate (*véase* pág. 6), sumerja un palito en el chocolate ya fundido e insértelo en el extremo de un globo. Repita la operación con todos los palos y los globos. Deje que cuajen. Bañe los *cake pops* en el chocolate derretido y elimine el exceso con unos golpecitos en el borde del cuenco. Déjelos secar en un bloque de poliestireno.

PARA TERMINAR Tome trocitos de *fondant* del color elegido y del tamaño de un guisante para hacer los nudos de los globos. Trabájelos con las manos para darles forma cónica y sujételos a cada *cake pop* pasando el palito desde abajo. Asegure los nudos a la parte inferior de los *cake pops* utilizando chocolate fundido, que aplicará con un palillo. Páselo por el *fondant* para crear el efecto de un nudo, dejando un borde redondeado en la parte inferior.

Vaporice con laca comestible en aerosol para conseguir un acabado brillante.

CONSEJO

Puede decorar los globos con números o nombres para darles un toque personal (por ejemplo, para una fiesta infantil). Utilice la técnica de la aplicación con manga pastelera o pinte la decoración con pintura comestible o en polvo.

SOMBREROS DE FIESTA

Son unos sombreros vistosos, coloridos y divertidos. Los niños se lo pasarán en grande.

NECESITARÁ

20 bolas de bizcocho
   (*véanse* págs. 5-6)
20 palitos para piruletas
Bloque de poliestireno
Palillo
2 mangas pasteleras de plástico
Rodillo de plástico
Cuchillo

DECORACIÓN

Bolsas de pastillas de chocolate
   de colores
50 g de *fondant* de colores
Lentejuelas de azúcar
Estrellas de azúcar
Maicena

NIVEL DE DIFICULTAD

 o

CON ANTELACIÓN Para crear las formas cónicas, trabaje las bolas de bizcocho con las manos sobre la superficie de trabajo. Aplane la parte inferior de cada forma aplastándolas sobre la superficie de trabajo. Refrigérelas durante 1 hora.

PARA PREPARAR LOS *CAKE POPS* Derrita las pastillas de chocolate (*véase* pág. 6), sumerja un palito en el chocolate ya fundido e insértelo por el extremo plano de un cono hasta la mitad. Repita la operación con todos los palos y los conos. Deje que cuajen. Sumerja los *cake pops* en el chocolate fundido y elimine el exceso con unos golpecitos en el borde del cuenco. Déjelos secar en vertical clavándolos en un bloque de poliestireno.

PARA DECORAR Forme bolitas pequeñas con el *fondant* y colóquelas en el extremo de cada sombrero; sujételas con chocolate fundido, que aplicará con un palillo. Decore con las lentejuelas y las estrellas utilizando el mismo método.

Para el diseño de rayas, más complejo, llene dos mangas pasteleras con pastillas de chocolate derretido de colores que contrasten. Aplíquelo en líneas rectas de arriba abajo. Acabe con una banda alrededor de la base del sombrero; para ello, extienda el *fondant* dándole 1,2 mm de grosor sobre una superficie espolvoreada con maicena y corte una tira fina con un cuchillo. Sujétela en el borde con chocolate fundido aplicado con un palillo.

JUEGO DE TÉ

¿A quién le apetece un té?

NIVEL DE DIFICULTAD

CON ANTELACIÓN Divida las bolas de bizcocho según las tazas y las teteras que desee preparar. Reserve las bolas para las teteras. Para las tazas, aplane la parte superior de las bolas aplastándolas contra la superficie de trabajo, y repita con la parte inferior, pero más ligeramente, para que las tazas se aguanten de pie. Refrigere todas las formas durante 1 hora.

PARA PREPARAR LOS *CAKE POPS* Derrita las pastillas de chocolate (*véase* pág. 6), sumerja un palito en el chocolate ya fundido e insértelo en la parte superior de una pieza. Repita la operación con todos los palos y las formas. Deje que cuajen. Sumerja los *cake pops* en el chocolate derretido y elimine el exceso con unos golpecitos en el borde del cuenco. Colóquelos con el fondo plano sobre papel sulfurizado para que se sequen. Cuando hayan cuajado, retire los *pops* del papel con cuidado para no dañar el material.

PARA ELABORAR LOS PLATITOS Extienda el *fondant* sobre la superficie de trabajo espolvoreada con maicena dándole un grosor aproximado de 2,5 mm. Corte círculos de pasta con el cortador más grande y déjelos secar en el fondo de un cuenco pequeño para crear una forma curva.

PARA PREPARAR LA DECORACIÓN Extienda un poco más fino el resto del *fondant*. Para las asas, corte con un cuchillo tiras de 5 mm × 6 cm. Doble cada una formando un bucle y asegure los extremos con chocolate fundido.

Con el cortador redondo más pequeño, corte círculos de *fondant* para las tapas de las teteras. Haga un agujero en el centro de cada tapa con un palito de piruleta. Forme bolitas para la parte superior de cada tapa y pase el palito por el centro. Para los pitorros de las teteras, haga salchichas con la pasta, deles la forma adecuada y espere a que se endurezcan ligeramente antes de sujetarlas a los *cake pops*. A continuación, corte los corazones. Necesitará cinco para cada taza y dos para cada tetera.

PARA TERMINAR EL JUEGO DE TÉ Sujete la decoración utilizando chocolate fundido con un palillo. Empiece con las asas, los corazones y los pitorros, y después pase los elementos de la tapa por el palito para asegurarlos a la parte superior de las teteras. Sujete la base de cada taza a un platito con chocolate fundido.

CÓCTELES

Convierta su bebida favorita en su *cake pop* predilecto.

CON ANTELACIÓN Trabaje las bolas de bizcocho con las manos en ángulo para crear conos. Alise los lados haciendo rodar las piezas en la superficie de trabajo y aplane la parte superior de cada cono aplastándolos contra la misma. Refrigere durante 1 hora.

PARA PREPARAR LOS *CAKE POPS* Reserve 20 pastillas de chocolate. Derrita el resto de pastillas rosas o blancas (*véase* pág. 6), sumerja un palito en el chocolate fundido e introdúzcalo en un cono hasta la mitad desde el extremo en punta. Repita la operación con todos los palitos y los conos, y deje que cuajen.

Realice un agujero en el centro de cada uno de los círculos de *fondant*; hágalo con un cuchillo, como si usara un destornillador. Le resultará más fácil si empieza por el lado curvado y después le da la vuelta al disco y trabaja por el otro lado. Utilice un palito de piruleta para terminar el agujero y asegurarse de que es del tamaño adecuado. Pase el disco por el palito hasta un tercio. Sumerja el *cake pop* en el chocolate fundido, cubriendo un tercio del palito. Elimine el exceso mediante unos golpecitos en el borde de un cuenco, e inserte rápidamente el disco para unirlo al chocolate. Deje secar en un bloque de poliestireno. Una vez seco, aplique cola comestible con un pincel en las zonas donde desea añadir la decoración de azúcar, y espolvoréela (hágalo sobre un cuenco para recoger lo que caiga, y después aplique el resto con una cuchara).

PARA LA DECORACIÓN Use *fondant* de diferentes colores.

Para la fresa, prepare una forma de pasta roja con los dedos y córtela por la mitad. En el lado curvo, realice las marcas de las semillas con un palillo y sujete una pieza de pasta verde oscuro para el pedúnculo. Para la lima, forme un círculo plano de *fondant* de color verde lima con los dedos y retire una sección con un cuchillo para que encaje en el lado de la copa. Utilice un palillo y el chocolate fundido blanco para añadir las líneas que salen del centro. Para el limón, forme un círculo plano con la pasta amarilla y retire una sección con un cuchillo para que encaje en el lado de la copa. Para la cereza, forme una bola con un poco de pasta roja.

Sujete la decoración a las copas con chocolate fundido aplicado con un palillo.

SOMBREROS VAQUEROS

Perfectos para una fiesta de chicas. ¡Vamos, chicas!

CON ANTELACIÓN Trabaje las bolas de bizcocho para realizar la parte superior del sombrero; empiece por crear formas ovaladas. Aplane la parte superior e inferior contra la superficie de trabajo y cree un hueco en el extremo más estrecho (será la parte superior). Refrigere las piezas durante 1 hora.

PARA PREPARAR LOS *CAKE POPS* Derrita las pastillas de chocolate (*véase* pág. 6), sumerja un palito en el chocolate fundido e introdúzcalo hasta la mitad de la pieza desde el extremo plano. Repita la operación con todos los palitos y las formas, y deje que cuajen. Sumerja cada *cake pop* en el chocolate derretido, elimine el exceso mediante unos golpecitos en el borde del cuenco y deje secar en un bloque de poliestireno.

Para las alas de los sombreros, extienda el *fondant* dándole un grosor aproximado de 5 mm; hágalo sobre una superficie espolvoreada con maicena y corte 20 círculos con un cortador redondo. Trabaje los círculos para que sean más grandes, hasta unos 2,5 mm de grosor. Haga un agujero en el centro de cada uno y pase el palito hasta llegar al *cake pop*. Utilice chocolate fundido, que aplicará con un palillo para sujetar los círculos, y coloque los sombreros boca abajo para que el *fondant* se curve un poco mientras se seca. De ese modo, las alas de los sombreros parecerán levantadas cuando coloque los *cake pops* hacia arriba.

PARA TERMINAR Sujete un corazón de caramelo con chocolate fundido en la parte delantera de cada sombrero. Pincele el corazón y el borde del ala con purpurina comestible mezclada con un poco de vodka (el alcohol se evaporará y obtendrá un acabado limpio).

EL SEÑOR Y LA SEÑORA POPS

Encantadora alternativa a las figuritas de los pasteles de boda.

NECESITARÁ

20 bolas de bizcocho
    (véanse págs. 5-6)
20 palitos para piruletas
Papel sulfurizado
Bloque de poliestireno
Manga pastelera de plástico
Rodillo de plástico
Cuchillo
Palillo

DECORACIÓN

1 bolsa de pastillas de chocolate
    blancas
1 bolsa de pastillas de chocolate
    negras
1 pieza pequeña de *fondant* blanco
1 pieza pequeña de *fondant* negro
Perlas de caramelo
Lustre comestible en aerosol

NIVEL DE DIFICULTAD

CON ANTELACIÓN Refrigere las bolas de bizcocho durante 1 hora.

PARA PREPARAR LOS *CAKE POPS* Funda las pastillas de chocolate blanco (*véase* pág. 6), sumerja un palito en el chocolate derretido e introdúzcalo en una bola (estos *cake pops* quedarán de pie, con la bola en la parte inferior del palo, que al introducirlo en la parte superior del *cake* creará una parte inferior plana). Repita la operación con todos los palitos y las bolas, y deje que cuajen. Sumerja cada *cake pop* en el chocolate derretido y elimine el exceso mediante unos golpecitos en el borde del cuenco.

Para la «Señora Pop», ponga la mitad de los *cake pops* sobre una lámina de papel sulfurizado y deje que cuajen (es posible que tenga que sujetarlos para evitar que se caigan). Para el «Señor Pop», deje que el resto de *pops* se seque boca abajo sobre un bloque de poliestireno. Derrita las pastillas de caramelo negro. Incline el cuenco para sumergir cada «Señor Pop» en ángulo con el fin de crear el traje. Elimine el exceso, gire y repita por el otro lado. Deje secar, junto a las «Señoras Pop», sobre el papel sulfurizado. Retire los *pops* del papel con cuidado cuando estén listos para no dañar la cobertura.

PARA TERMINAR LAS «SEÑORAS POP» Ponga un poco de chocolate fundido blanco en una manga pastelera. Retuerza la parte superior y aplique una forma en V en cada «Señora Pop». Para las flores, añada el caramelo en bucles partiendo de un punto central. Conseguirá un efecto de encaje. Reparta unos puntos de chocolate derretido alrededor del cuello y coloque las perlas de caramelo. Rocíe con el lustre.

PARA TERMINAR LOS «SEÑORES POP» Extienda el *fondant* negro y corte una corbata con un cuchillo. Sujétela a la pieza con chocolate fundido blanco aplicado con un palillo. Para el cuello, extienda el *fondant* blanco y corte dos pequeños triángulos con un cuchillo. Sujételos a cada pieza con chocolate blanco derretido.

CONSEJO

Los *pops* se pueden adaptar al color de boda deseado utilizando perlas de caramelo de diferentes tonos para el collar y de distintos colores para la corbata.

PASTELES DE BODA

Se trata de una gran alternativa al tradicional pastel de boda y a los recuerdos para los invitados.

NECESITARÁ

Bizcocho y glaseado para preparar
  los *cake pops* (*véanse* págs. 5-6)
Rodillo de plástico
Cortapastas acanalados de 2,5,
  3 y 3,5 cm
20 palitos para piruletas
Bloque de poliestireno
Palillo
Plato para mezclar la pasta en polvo
Pincel pequeño

DECORACIÓN

1 bolsa de pastillas de chocolate
  blancas
Decoración de corazones
Flores de glaseado real
Colorante alimentario en polvo,
  de colores bonitos, para formar
  una pasta con vodka

NIVEL DE DIFICULTAD

CON ANTELACIÓN Divida en dos partes la mezcla de bizcocho y glaseado (así será más fácil trabajarla). Amase cada pieza hasta conseguir una lámina de 1,5 cm de grosor, y utilice los cortadores para cortar las capas de los pasteles. Necesitará 20 círculos de cada tamaño. Refrigere durante 1 hora.

PARA PREPARAR LOS *CAKE POPS* Derrita las pastillas de chocolate (*véase* pág. 6), sumerja un palo en el chocolate fundido e introdúzcalo en el centro de un círculo grande de manera que asomen 5 mm por la parte superior. Utilice un palillo para aplicar chocolate derretido sobre el palo y en la parte inferior de un círculo mediano, y colóquelo sobre la capa inferior. Repita la operación con un círculo pequeño, que será la capa superior. Prepare todos los *cake pops* siguiendo esos pasos y deje que cuajen.

Sumerja los *cake pops* en el chocolate derretido y elimine el exceso mediante unos ligeros golpecitos con cuidado para no desmontar las capas. Déjelos secar en vertical.

PARA DECORAR Añada las decoraciones elegidas cuando los *cake pops* estén secos. Para sujetar los corazones y las flores, aplique chocolate fundido con un palillo. Para pintar las flores, prepare una pasta con el colorante alimentario y el vodka, y utilice un pincel pequeño para añadir los detalles.

CONSEJO

Cuando monte los *cake pops*, es posible que quede un pequeño hueco entre cada capa del pastel. Puede rellenarlo con chocolate fundido, que aplicará con un palillo; así se asegurará de conseguir un acabado uniforme cuando los bañe.

COCHECITOS DE BEBÉ

Estos encantadores carritos de bebé serán un verdadero éxito en una *baby shower* o un bautizo.

NECESITARÁ

20 bolas de bizcocho
(*véanse* págs. 5-6)
[como se elimina un cuarto
de la bola, hágalas un poco
más grandes]
Cuchillo
20 palitos para piruletas
Bloque de poliestireno
Manga pastelera de plástico
Palillo

DECORACIÓN

1 bolsa de pastillas de chocolate
blancas
Perlas de azúcar o lentejuelas
comestibles de colores

NIVEL DE DIFICULTAD

CON ANTELACIÓN Para preparar los carritos, aplaste las bolas de bizcocho. Utilice un cuchillo para eliminar un cuarto de cada disco y conseguir la forma de la capota. Refrigere durante 1 hora.

PARA PREPARAR LOS *CAKE POPS* Derrita las pastillas de chocolate (*véase* pág. 6), sumerja un palo en el chocolate fundido e introdúzcalo en un carrito. Deje que cuaje. Repita la operación con todos los palitos y los carritos. Sumerja cada *cake pop*, elimine el exceso con unos golpecitos y deje secar en vertical.

PARA DECORAR Llene la manga pastelera con el resto de chocolate fundido y retuerza el extremo para cerrarla bien. Abra la punta con un pequeño agujero para aplicar el chocolate (si es demasiado grande, le resultará difícil controlarlo).

Apriete suavemente la manga pastelera para empezar a aplicar la decoración. Disponga una línea horizontal alrededor del *cake pop*, empezando por la esquina de la abertura del carrito. A continuación, aplique una línea siguiendo el borde superior de la abertura y tres líneas más para crear la capota del carrito.

Aplique unos puntitos de chocolate debajo de la línea horizontal y coloque encima las perlas o las lentejuelas.

BOTELLAS DE CHAMPÁN

Con estas apetitosas botellas de champán, cualquier día festivo será un éxito.

NECESITARÁ

20 bolas de bizcocho
    (*véanse págs. 5-6*)
20 palitos para piruletas
Rodillo de plástico
Bloque de poliestireno
Cuchillo
Palillo
Plato para mezclar la pasta
    en polvo
Pincel pequeño

DECORACIÓN

1 bolsa de pastillas de chocolate
    verdes
150 g de *fondant* blanco
Maicena
Pintura dorada comestible
Colorante alimentario negro en
    polvo mezclado con vodka

NIVEL DE DIFICULTAD

CON ANTELACIÓN Para convertir las bolas de bizcocho en botellas de champán, trabájelas hasta conseguir una forma de salchicha gruesa y aplane la parte inferior aplastándola contra la superficie de trabajo. Para dar forma al cuello de la botella, reduzca el borde superior y trabájelo con los dedos hasta obtener la longitud adecuada. Refrigere las botellas durante 1 hora.

PARA PREPARAR LOS *CAKE POPS* Derrita las pastillas de chocolate (*véase* pág. 6), sumerja un palo en el chocolate fundido e introdúzcalo en el fondo plano de una botella. Repita la operación con todos los palitos y las botellas. Deje que cuaje. Sumerja cada *cake pop* en el chocolate derretido, elimine el exceso con unos golpecitos y déjelos secar en vertical.

Para el tapón, extienda el *fondant* sobre la superficie de trabajo espolvoreada con maicena, dándole unos 2,5 mm de grosor. Utilice un cuchillo para cortar tiras finas y rodee la parte superior de cada botella con una tira (sujételas con chocolate fundido).

PARA TERMINAR Corte una etiqueta de *fondant* para cada botella, de aproximadamente 2,5 × 1,5 cm, y sujételas a las botellas con chocolate fundido, que aplicará con un palillo.

Pinte la parte superior de la botella y el cuello con pintura dorada comestible, la misma que usará para el corazón de la etiqueta. Acabe pintando una línea negra alrededor del cuello con la pasta negra.

CORAZONES BRILLANTES

Un capricho para regalar a alguien especial el día de san Valentín.

NECESITARÁ

20 bolas de bizcocho
  (*véanse* págs. 5-6)
  [hágalas un poco más grandes
  que el tamaño normal de una
  pelota de golf]
Cortapastas de 5,5 cm con forma
  de corazón
20 palitos para piruletas
Bloque de poliestireno
Cuenco
Cuchara

DECORACIÓN

1 bolsa de pastillas de chocolate
  rojas
Bolitas de azúcar rojas
Purpurina roja comestible (añada
  un toque a la decoración
  de azúcar para conseguir
  un brillo extra)

NIVEL DE DIFICULTAD

CON ANTELACIÓN Tome las bolas de bizcocho (un poco más grandes que el tamaño normal para asegurarse de que los corazones tengan el grosor necesario para poder introducir el palo) y páselas por el cortapastas con forma de corazón. Asegúrese de que llega a todas las zonas de la cara inferior. Alise las superficies lo mejor que pueda para conseguir un acabado plano y saque el *cake* del cortador con cuidado. Refrigere las piezas durante 1 hora.

PARA PREPARAR LOS *CAKE POPS* Derrita las pastillas de chocolate (*véase* pág. 6), sumerja un palo en el chocolate fundido e introdúzcalo en un corazón hasta la mitad por el vértice. Sujete con cuidado las piezas por los lados durante esa operación para evitar que el *cake* se rompa. Repita con todos los palitos y los corazones. Deje que cuajen.

Sumerja cada *cake pop* en el chocolate fundido, elimine el exceso con unos golpecitos y espolvoréelos inmediatamente con las bolitas de azúcar y la purpurina comestible mezcladas (hágalo sobre un cuenco para recoger el exceso, que después podrá aplicar con una cuchara). Déjelos secar en un bloque de poliestireno.

CONSEJO

Si aparecen grietas en los corazones antes de sumergirlos, rellénelas con chocolate fundido, que aplicará con un palillo.

HUEVOS DE PASCUA

Prepárelos con bizcocho de chocolate y glaseado como alternativa a los huevos de Pascua tradicionales.

NECESITARÁ

20 bolas de bizcocho
  (*véanse* págs. 5-6)
20 palitos para piruletas
Papel sulfurizado
Palillo

DECORACIÓN

1 bolsa de pastillas de chocolate
  con leche
Lentejuelas de azúcar de colores

NIVEL DE DIFICULTAD

CON ANTELACIÓN Dé forma ovalada a las bolas de bizcocho inclinando las manos mientras las trabaja. Refrigere durante 1 hora.

PARA PREPARAR LOS *CAKE POPS* Derrita las pastillas de chocolate (*véase* pág. 6), sumerja un palo en el chocolate fundido e introdúzcalo en la parte superior de un huevo. Repita la operación con todos los palitos y los huevos. Deje que cuajen. Bañe cada *cake pop* en el chocolate derretido, elimine el exceso mediante unos golpecitos en el borde del cuenco y colóquelos sobre papel sulfurizado hasta que estén secos.

PARA DECORAR Coloque las lentejuelas de azúcar en los huevos de manera aleatoria utilizando chocolate fundido, que aplicará con un palillo.

CONSEJO

Estos *cake pops* también pueden prepararse de manera que el huevo quede en la parte superior del palo. Si los envuelve en bolsitas de celofán serán deliciosos regalos de Pascua.

CALABAZAS BRILLANTES

Estas calabazas relucientes son perfectas para Halloween.

20 bolas de bizcocho
    (*véanse* págs. 5-6)
Cuchara
20 palitos para piruletas
Bloque de poliestireno
Cuenco

DECORACIÓN

1 bolsa de pastillas de chocolate
    naranjas
Confites de azúcar naranja
Gominolas verdes con forma de
    huevo, cortadas por la mitad

NIVEL DE DIFICULTAD

CON ANTELACIÓN Añada estrías a cada bola de bizcocho pasando el borde del mango de una cuchara de arriba abajo. Tienen que ser profundas para que resulten visibles una vez bañados los *cake pops* en el chocolate fundido. Refrigere durante 1 hora.

PARA PREPARAR LOS *CAKE POPS* Derrita las pastillas de chocolate (*véase* pág. 6), sumerja un palito en el chocolate fundido e introdúzcalo en una bola de bizcocho. Repita la operación con todos los palos y las bolas. Deje que cuajen.

Sumerja cada *cake pop* en el chocolate derretido y elimine el exceso mediante unos golpecitos en el borde del cuenco. Mientras todavía estén húmedos, espolvoree con confites de color naranja (hágalo sobre un cuenco para recoger el exceso, que podrá aplicar después con una cuchara). Coloque una gominola en el centro a modo de pedúnculo. Deje secar los *cake pops* en vertical.

CONSEJO

Para crear una calabaza fantasmagórica, puede omitir la decoración de azúcar y cubrir los *cake pops* con el chocolate fundido naranja para conseguir un acabado liso. Si desea crear un rostro terrorífico, utilice colorante alimentario en polvo mezclado con un poco de vodka y aplique con un pincel pequeño.

MURCIÉLAGOS

Encantadores y al mismo tiempo terroríficos, estos divertidos *pops* serán un éxito en cualquier fiesta de Halloween.

NECESITARÁ

20 bolas de bizcocho
  (*véanse* págs. 5-6)
20 palitos para piruletas
Bloque de poliestireno
Rodillo de plástico
Cortador de 3 cm con forma
  de corazón
Cuchillo
Palillo

DECORACIÓN

1 bolsa de pastillas de chocolate
  negras
325 g de *fondant* negro
Maicena
40 lentejuelas comestibles blancas
20 lentejuelas comestibles naranjas,
  pequeñas

NIVEL DE DIFICULTAD

CON ANTELACIÓN Refrigere las bolas de bizcocho durante 1 hora.

PARA PREPARAR LOS *CAKE POPS* Derrita las pastillas de chocolate (*véase* pág. 6), sumerja un palito en el chocolate fundido e introdúzcalo en una bola de bizcocho. Repita la operación con todos los palos y las bolas. Deje que cuajen. Sumerja cada *cake pop* en el chocolate derretido y elimine el exceso mediante unos golpecitos en el borde del cuenco. Déjelos secar en vertical.

PARA LAS ALAS Y LAS OREJAS Sobre la superficie de trabajo espolvoreada con maicena, extienda el *fondant* hasta obtener un grosor aproximado de 2,5 mm. Corte 40 corazones, y de cada uno de ellos corte una forma de media luna para que el ala encaje en el lado del murciélago. Deje que los corazones se sequen y estén más firmes.

Para las orejas, aplaste conos pequeños de *fondant* negro.

PARA MONTAR LOS MURCIÉLAGOS Utilice pastillas de chocolate fundido negro y un palillo para sujetar las alas a cada lado de la bola y las orejas entre la parte superior de las alas. Coloque lentejuelas blancas a modo de ojos y una de color naranja para la nariz. Aplique una pequeña cantidad de chocolate negro fundido en el centro de las lentejuelas blancas para acabar los ojos.

CONSEJO

Sujete el *cake pop* de lado mientras coloca las alas para que estén rectas.

CALCETINES DE NAVIDAD

Utilice su creatividad para incluir estos *pops* en su decoración navideña.

CON ANTELACIÓN Convierta las bolas de bizcocho en calcetines formando una salchicha con cada una y doblando el extremo para crear la punta. Aplane el borde superior presionando contra la superficie de trabajo. Refrigere durante 1 hora.

PARA PREPARAR LOS *CAKE POPS* Derrita las pastillas de chocolate del color elegido (*véase* pág. 6), sumerja un palito en el chocolate fundido e introdúzcalo por el talón del calcetín. Repita la operación con todos los palos y los calcetines. Deje que cuajen. Sumerja cada *cake pop* en el chocolate derretido y elimine el exceso mediante unos golpecitos en el borde del cuenco. Déjelos secar en vertical.

Funda el chocolate del color que contraste. Tome un poco de chocolate derretido con una cuchara y sumerja el borde de cada calcetín; a continuación, espolvoree con la decoración de azúcar correspondiente mientras todavía esté húmedo (hágalo sobre un cuenco para recoger el exceso, que podrá utilizar después con una cuchara). Repita con la punta del calcetín y deje secar.

PARA DECORAR Coloque las decoraciones elegidas en los calcetines usando el chocolate fundido correspondiente aplicado con un palillo.

NECESITARÁ

20 bolas de bizcocho
    (*véanse* págs. 5-6)
20 palitos para piruletas
Bloque de poliestireno
Cuchara
Cuenco
Palillo

DECORACIÓN

1 bolsa de pastillas de chocolate
    rojas
1 bolsa de pastillas de chocolate
    verdes
¼ de bolsa de pastillas de chocolate
    blancas
Bolitas de azúcar rojas, verdes
    y blancas
Estrellas grandes para decorar
Copos de nieve para decorar
20 lentejuelas de azúcar naranjas,
    pequeñas

NIVEL DE DIFICULTAD

PETARDOS NAVIDEÑOS

Añada un toque festivo a su mesa de Navidad y disfrute
de un capricho delicioso después de la cena.

NECESITARÁ

20 bolas de bizcocho
  (*véanse págs. 5-6*)
20 palitos para piruletas
Bloque de poliestireno
Pincel pequeño
Palillo

DECORACIÓN

1 bolsa de pastillas de chocolate
  rojas
Pintura dorada comestible
40 estrellas grandes
  para decorar

NIVEL DE DIFICULTAD

CON ANTELACIÓN Convierta las bolas de bizcocho en petardos (se
asemejan a caramelos con sus envoltorios) formando salchichas. Utilice un palito
de piruleta para crear ranuras a 1 cm de cada extremo, y extienda un poco los
extremos para conseguir la forma del petardo. Refrigere durante 1 hora.

PARA PREPARAR LOS *CAKE POPS* Derrita las pastillas de chocolate
(*véase* pág. 6), sumerja un palito en el chocolate fundido e introdúzcalo en el centro
de un petardo. Repita la operación con todos los palos y los petardos. Deje que cuajen.
Sumerja cada *cake pop* en el chocolate derretido y elimine el exceso mediante unos
golpecitos en el borde del cuenco. Déjelos secar en vertical.

PARA DECORAR Pinte un motivo en zigzag alrededor de los extremos de cada
petardo. Utilice pintura dorada comestible.

Sujete una estrella en un lado de cada petardo usando chocolate fundido y un palillo.
Pinte las estrellas con pintura dorada.

CONSEJO

¿Por qué no intenta decorar este diseño con diversos colores y motivos festivos?

OSITOS

Estos preciosos ositos encantarán a todo el mundo.

NECESITARÁ

20 bolas de bizcocho
  (*véanse* págs. 5-6)
20 palitos para piruletas
Bloque de poliestireno
Rodillo de plástico
Cortapastas redondos de
  1 y 1,5 cm
Cortador de 5 mm con forma
  de corazón
Cuchillo
Palillo
Plato para mezclar la pasta
  en polvo
Pincel pequeño

DECORACIÓN

1 bolsa de pastillas de chocolate
  con leche
40 pastillas recubiertas
  de chocolate
50 g de *fondant* marrón claro
25 g de *fondant* negro
Maicena
Colorante alimentario negro
  mezclado con vodka para
  obtener una pasta

NIVEL DE DIFICULTAD

CON ANTELACIÓN Refrigere las bolas de bizcocho durante 1 hora.

PARA PREPARAR LOS *CAKE POPS* Derrita las pastillas de chocolate (*véase* pág. 6), sumerja un palito en el chocolate fundido e introdúzcalo en una bola de bizcocho. Para sujetar las orejas, sumerja una pastilla de chocolate hasta la mitad y colóquela en la bola ejerciendo un poco de fuerza. Sujétela hasta que se asiente y repita con la otra oreja. Haga lo mismo con todos los palos, las bolas y las pastillas recubiertas de chocolate.

Sumerja cada *cake pop* en el chocolate fundido y elimine el exceso mediante unos golpecitos en el borde del cuenco. Déjelos secar en vertical.

PARA TERMINAR Extienda el *fondant* marrón hasta conseguir un grosor de 2,5 mm; hágalo sobre la superficie de trabajo espolvoreada con maicena. Utilice los cortapastas redondos para cortar dos círculos pequeños y uno más grande por cada oso. Corte los círculos pequeños con un cuchillo, dejando un borde recto para que encajen dentro de las orejas; colóquelos utilizando chocolate fundido, que aplicará con un palillo.

Sujete el círculo más grande en el centro de cada oso; utilice chocolate fundido.

Extienda el *fondant* negro hasta obtener una lámina de 2,5 mm de grosor; hágalo sobre la superficie de trabajo espolvoreada con maicena. Use el cortador con forma de corazón para obtener 20 corazones. Colóquelos dentro del círculo utilizando chocolate fundido.

Pinte los ojos, la nariz y la boca empleando la pasta negra.

CONSEJO

Estos ositos también quedan perfectos en otros colores.

PINGÜINOS

¡Nos encantan estos pingüinos!

20 bolas de bizcocho
(*véanse* págs. 5-6)
20 palitos para piruletas
Bloque de poliestireno
Cuchara
Rodillo de plástico
Cortadores de 1 y 3 cm
con forma de corazón
Cortador pequeño con forma
de triángulo
Cuchillo
Palillo

DECORACIÓN

1 bolsa de pastillas de chocolate
negras
¼ bolsa de pastillas de chocolate
blancas
150 g de *fondant* negro
150 g de *fondant* naranja
Maicena
40 lentejuelas de azúcar blancas

NIVEL DE DIFICULTAD

CON ANTELACIÓN Refrigere las bolas de bizcocho durante 1 hora.

PARA PREPARAR LOS *CAKE POPS* Derrita las pastillas de chocolate negro (*véase* pág. 6), sumerja un palito en el chocolate fundido e introdúzcalo en una bola de bizcocho. Repita con todos los palos y las bolas. Deje que cuajen. Sumerja cada *cake pop* en el chocolate derretido y elimine el exceso mediante unos golpecitos en el borde del cuenco. Déjelos secar en vertical en un bloque de poliestireno.

Funda las pastillas de chocolate blanco y tome una cucharada grande. Sumerja la parte delantera de cada *cake pop* en la cuchara para crear el vientre del pingüino. Elimine el exceso con unos golpecitos y dé la vuelta al *pop* para repetir los golpecitos y conseguir una tripa plana. Deje que se sequen.

PARA LAS ALAS, LOS PIES Y LOS PICOS Extienda el *fondant* negro, dándole un grosor aproximado de 2,5 mm; hágalo sobre la superficie de trabajo espolvoreada con maicena. Corte 40 formas de corazón grandes para las alas.

Extienda el *fondant* naranja y corte 40 corazones más pequeños para los pies. A continuación, corte 20 triángulos pequeños para los picos (trabaje con un cuchillo para conseguir el tamaño adecuado).

PARA MONTAR LOS PINGÜINOS Utilice el chocolate fundido negro y un palillo para sujetar el pico, los pies y las alas. Deje las alas sueltas por abajo y dóblelas ligeramente hacia arriba. Coloque las lentejuelas blancas para los ojos y aplique un punto de chocolate fundido negro en el centro.

CONSEJO

Añada un poco de tragacanto (aproximadamente 2 cucharaditas por puñado de *fondant*) a la pasta y mezcle bien. De ese modo conseguirá una textura más firme, lo que hará que la forma deseada se mantenga mejor.

FAMILIA DE PATOS

Deje volar su imaginación y cree su propia selección de patitos disparatados y divertidos.

NECESITARÁ

20 bolas de bizcocho
  (véanse págs. 5-6)
20 palitos para piruletas
Rodillo de plástico
Bloque de poliestireno
Cortapastas redondo de 1,5 cm
Cuchillo
Palillo
Plato para mezclar la pasta
  en polvo
Pincel pequeño
Cortadores con forma de corazón
  de 5 mm y 1, 1,5 y 2,5 cm
Cortador con forma de flor
  de 1,5 cm

DECORACIÓN

1 bolsa de pastillas de chocolate
  amarillas o rosas
200 g de *fondant* naranja, y trozos
  pequeños de otros colores
Maicena
Colorante alimentario negro en
  polvo mezclado con vodka
  para formar una pasta
Lentejuelas de azúcar amarillas
Decoraciones con forma de corazón

NIVEL DE DIFICULTAD

CON ANTELACIÓN Divida cada bola de bizcocho en dos partes; una de ellas debe ser tres veces más grande que la otra. Trabaje cada pieza pequeña para formar una bola, que será la cabeza, y cada pieza grande para el cuerpo (aplane el fondo y cree un extremo en punta para la cola). Refrigere durante 1 hora.

PARA PREPARAR LOS *CAKE POPS* Derrita las pastillas de chocolate amarillas o rosas (*véase* pág. 6), sumerja un palito en el chocolate fundido e introdúzcalo en el fondo plano del cuerpo. Sumerja la parte inferior de una bola para la cabeza en el chocolate derretido y sujétela al cuerpo (manténgala en su lugar hasta que se asiente). Repita la operación con todos los palos, los cuerpos y las cabezas. Bañe cada *cake pop* en el chocolate fundido y elimine el exceso mediante unos golpecitos en el borde del cuenco. Déjelos secar en vertical.

PARA AÑADIR LOS PICOS Y LOS OJOS Extienda el *fondant* naranja dándole de 2,5 mm de grosor; hágalo sobre la superficie de trabajo espolvoreada con maicena y corte 20 círculos. Corte cada uno por la mitad, con la ayuda de un cuchillo, para crear el pico. Coloque los picos con chocolate fundido, que aplicará con un palillo. Pinte los ojos con la pasta negra.

PARA TERMINAR Añada la decoración elegida para completar el diseño. Utilice chocolate fundido, que aplicará con un palillo para sujetarla.

Para los lazos y las pajaritas, use *fondant* extendido de colores. Corte dos corazones pequeños (los más pequeños para la pajarita) y forme una bola para el nudo.

Corte las flores a partir del *fondant* y coloque una lentejuela en el centro.

Para la cresta, corte la punta de tres corazones y sujételos con chocolate fundido.

Para las alas, corte cuatro corazones (dos de 1,5 cm y dos de 2,5 cm) de *fondant* y sujételos a cada lado del pato con chocolate fundido.

BALLENAS

Se lo pasará en grande preparando estos *cake pops*.

NECESITARÁ

20 bolas de bizcocho
(*véanse* págs. 5-6)
20 palitos para piruletas
Bloque de poliestireno
Cuchillo
Palillo
Plato para mezclar la pasta
en polvo
Pincel pequeño

DECORACIÓN

1 bolsa de pastillas de chocolate
azules
100 g de *fondant* azul
40 lentejuelas de azúcar blancas
Colorante alimentario negro
en polvo mezclado con vodka
para formar una pasta

NIVEL DE DIFICULTAD

CON ANTELACIÓN Para crear las ballenas, haga huevos con las bolas de bizcocho. Para la cola, pellizque cada *cake* desde el extremo más estrecho, tire ligeramente hacia fuera y aplánelo un poco. Divida el final de la cola por la mitad y cúrvela un poco hacia arriba. Refrigere durante 1 hora.

PARA PREPARAR LOS *CAKE POPS* Derrita las pastillas de chocolate (*véase* pág. 6), sumerja un palito en el chocolate fundido e introdúzcalo por la parte inferior de una ballena. Repita la operación con todos los palos y las ballenas. Deje que cuajen. Sumerja cada *cake pop* en el chocolate derretido y elimine el exceso mediante unos golpecitos en el borde del cuenco. Déjelos secar en un bloque de poliestireno.

PARA TERMINAR Para el chorro de agua, tome un poco de *fondant* azul, forme una salchicha y divídala hasta la mitad con el cuchillo. Doble los extremos hacia fuera y coloque el chorro en la parte superior de cada ballena utilizando el chocolate fundido y un palillo.

Añada dos lentejuelas blancas en los lados de la cabeza (utilice para ello chocolate derretido) y pinte los ojos y una amplia sonrisa con pasta negra.

CONSEJO

No se preocupe si la cola se agrieta cuando la trabaje, ya que puede rellenar las fisuras con chocolate fundido, que aplicará con un palillo antes de sumergir los *cake pops*.

LOROS

Buen gusto con un toque tropical.

NECESITARÁ

20 bolas de bizcocho
  (*véanse págs. 5-6*)
20 palitos para piruletas
Bloque de poliestireno
Pincel pequeño
Rodillo de plástico
Cortador de 5 mm con forma
  de corazón
Palillo
Plato para mezclar la pasta
  en polvo

DECORACIÓN

1 bolsa de pastillas de chocolate
  azules
1 bolsa de pastillas de chocolate
  rojas
¼ de bolsa de pastillas de chocolate
  amarillas (sólo para los loros
  rojos)
1 pieza pequeña de *fondant* negro
Maicena
40 lentejuelas de azúcar blancas
Colorante alimentario negro en
  polvo mezclado con vodka
  para obtener una pasta

NIVEL DE DIFICULTAD

CON ANTELACIÓN Retire una pieza del tamaño de un guisante de cada bola de bizcocho para el pico. Para conseguir el loro, convierta las bolas en salchichas gruesas. Hunda el dedo pulgar en un extremo para formar la cola y haga que el final de la cabeza quede ligeramente más estrecho que el centro del loro. Con las piezas retiradas forme un pico curvado y puntiagudo, con el fondo plano para encajarlo en la cabeza del loro. Refrigere durante 1 hora.

PARA PREPARAR LOS *CAKE POPS* Derrita las pastillas de chocolate azules o rojas (*véase pág. 6*), sumerja un palito en el chocolate fundido e introdúzcalo en una pieza por debajo del estómago. Sumerja la parte plana del pico en el chocolate derretido y colóquelo en la parte delantera de la cabeza. Repita la operación con todos los palos, los cuerpos y los picos. Deje que cuajen. Sumerja cada *cake pop* en el chocolate fundido y elimine el exceso mediante unos golpecitos en el borde del cuenco. Déjelos secar en un bloque de poliestireno.

PARA TERMINAR Funda el chocolate amarillo y pinte un ala en cada lado del cuerpo del loro rojo. Deje secar y pinte la sección inferior con el chocolate azul.

Para los pies, extienda el *fondant* negro hasta conseguir un grosor aproximado de 2,5 mm de grosor; hágalo sobre la superficie de trabajo espolvoreada con maicena y corte 40 corazones. Sujételos, junto con las lentejuelas blancas de los ojos, utilizando chocolate fundido y un palillo.

Use la pasta negra para pintar los elementos negros (los picos, los ojos y las alas del loro azul).

CERDITOS

Perfección sabrosa.

NECESITARÁ

20 bolas de bizcocho
  (*véanse* págs. 5-6)
20 palitos para piruletas
Bloque de poliestireno
Palillo
Plato para mezclar la pasta
Pincel pequeño

DECORACIÓN

1 bolsa de pastillas de chocolate
  rosas
100 g de *fondant* rosa
Colorante alimentario negro
  en polvo mezclado con vodka
  para obtener una pasta

NIVEL DE DIFICULTAD

CON ANTELACIÓN Refrigere las bolas de bizcocho durante 1 hora.

PARA PREPARAR LOS *CAKE POPS* Derrita las pastillas de chocolate rosas (*véase* pág. 6), sumerja un palito en el chocolate fundido e introdúzcalo en una bola de bizcocho. Repita la operación con todos los palos y las bolas. Sumerja cada *cake pop* en el chocolate derretido y elimine el exceso mediante unos golpecitos en el borde del cuenco. Déjelos secar en vertical.

PARA LAS OREJAS Y LOS HOCICOS Forme conos pequeños con 40 piezas pequeñas de *fondant* rosa y aplástelas ligeramente para crear las orejas. Tome una pieza mayor para crear los hocicos: forme una bola, aplástela un poco y trabájela sobre el lado para conseguir una forma cilíndrica plana. Sujete las orejas y los hocicos con chocolate fundido, que aplicará con un palillo.

PARA TERMINAR Pinte los ojos, las fosas nasales y las sonrisas con la pasta negra.

ORUGAS

Esta oruga es perfecta para una fiesta infantil porque permite añadir un mensaje, como, por ejemplo, «Feliz cumpleaños».

CON ANTELACIÓN Refrigere las bolas de bizcocho durante 1 hora.

PARA PREPARAR LOS *CAKE POPS* Derrita las pastillas de chocolate azules y amarillas (*véase* pág. 6), sumerja un palito en el chocolate fundido del color elegido e introdúzcalo en una bola de bizcocho. Repita la operación con todos los palos y las bolas. Deje que cuajen. Sumerja cada *cake pop* en el chocolate derretido y elimine el exceso mediante unos golpecitos en el borde del cuenco. Déjelos secar en vertical en un bloque de poliestireno.

PARA LA CABEZA Pegue dos malvaviscos mini en la parte superior de uno de los *cake pops* utilizando chocolate fundido, que aplicará con un palillo. A continuación, coloque una bola de chocolate verde en la parte superior de cada malvavisco. Añada los dos discos de azúcar blancos a la parte delantera de la cabeza y coloque una perla de caramelo negra en el centro de cada disco; sujételas con chocolate fundido. Por último, pinte una gran sonrisa con la pasta negra.

CONSEJO

Para personalizar la oruga con un mensaje de cumpleaños o un nombre, utilice una manga pastelera (*véase* pág. 7) o pinte con colorante alimentario en algún tono alegre mezclado con un poco de vodka.

NECESITARÁ

20 bolas de bizcocho (*véanse* págs. 5-6), o las que necesite según la longitud que desee

20 palitos para piruletas

Bloque de poliestireno

Palillo

Plato para mezclar la pasta

Pincel pequeño

DECORACIÓN

1 bolsa de pastillas de chocolate azules

1 bolsa de pastillas de chocolate amarillas

2 malvaviscos mini

2 pastillas de chocolate de color verde

2 discos de azúcar duro blanco (como los de las pulseras de caramelo)

2 perlas de caramelo negras

Colorante alimentario negro en polvo mezclado con vodka para obtener una pasta

NIVEL DE DIFICULTAD

CONVERSIONES

1 cucharadita = 5 ml
1 cucharada = 15 ml

Si cocina con gas, la conversión de temperatura para hornear la receta básica del bizcocho es la siguiente:
180 ºC /gas 4

GLOSARIO

Azúcar de lustre = azúcar muy fino
Barniz comestible en aerosol = glaseado comestible en aerosol
Flor de glaseado real = flor de azúcar
Fondant = extendido listo para trabajar
Maicena = harina de maíz
Papel sulfurizado = papel resistente a la grasa

LISTA DE ESTABLECIMIENTOS

Consulte nuestra página web: www.popcakekitchen.co.uk. Vendemos palitos para piruletas, bolsas, lazos y *fondants*. También disponemos de kits para empezar a preparar *cake pops*.

En la red podrá encontrar ingredientes para decorar y equipo de repostería.

AGRADECIMIENTOS

Gracias a Veronica por introducirnos en el fantástico mundo de los *cake pops*, y también a mis padres, familia y amigos, especialmente a Kathryn y Nicole, por su apoyo continuo y su confianza en nosotras.
   Gracias a mi marido, que ha supuesto un gran apoyo y una fuente de inspiración durante todo el proceso, y que se ha prestado a probar todos los *pops* que le he ofrecido en la búsqueda del *cake pop* perfecto. **HELEN**

Deseo dar las gracias a mi familia y mis amigos por su amor, su apoyo y su inspiración, y especialmente a mis padres, que siempre me han inculcado la fuerza y la confianza en mí misma para lograr mis sueños.
   Un agradecimiento especial a mi novio, Matt. No habría hecho esto sin su apoyo, su inspiración y su comprensión, sobre todo durante las sesiones de elaboración de *pops* a altas horas de la noche. **ABBY**

Un último agradecimiento especial a Greg, que nos ha ayudado durante la creación y la evolución de Popcake Kitchen.

JUAN SCHOBINGER has a Ph.D. in Philosophy and Letters from the University of Buenos Aires, Argentina. He was a full professor of Archaeology and Prehistory at the University of Cuyo in Mendoza, Argentina, from 1957 until his retirement in 1994, when he became Professor Emeritus. Dr. Schobinger also taught courses in Anthropology and Ancient History of the East. His main research areas are South American pre-ceramic cultures, cave art, and Inca archaeology. He is the author of five books.

THE ANCIENT AMERICANS

A Reference Guide
to the Art, Culture, and
History of Pre-Columbian
North and South America

Volume II

JUAN SCHOBINGER

Translation: Carys Evans-Corrales
University of Pittsburgh at Bradford

Consultant: Susan Kart
Columbia University

SHARPE REFERENCE
an imprint of M.E. Sharpe, Inc.

SHARPE REFERENCE

Sharpe Reference is an imprint of ℳ.E. Sharpe INC.

ℳ.E. Sharpe INC.
80 Business Park Drive
Armonk, NY 10504

Original title
Arte prehistórico de América

The original volume was published
in collaboration with the
Mexican National Institute of Anthropology and History

Library of Congress Cataloging-in-Publication Data

Schobinger, Juan.
    [Arte prehistórico de América. English]
    The Ancient Americans : a reference guide to the art, culture, and history of
pre-Columbian North and South America / Juan Schobinger.
        p. cm.
    Includes bibliographical references and index.
    ISBN 0-7656-8034-3 (set : alk. paper)
        1. Rock paintings—America. 2. Petroglyphs—America. 3. Indians—Antiquities.
    4. Indian Art. 5. America—Antiquities. I. Title.

E59.P42 S3613 2000
970.01—dc21
00-056280

Printed in Italy - Nuova GEP, Cremona

The paper used in this publication meets the minimum requirements of
American National Standard for Information Sciences—Permanence of
Paper for Printed Library Materials,
ANSI Z 39.48.1984.

Translated from Spanish by
Carys Evans-Corrales

For ℳ.E. Sharpe INC.
Vice President and Director, Sharpe Reference: Evelyn M. Fazio
Vice President and Production Director: Carmen P. Chetti
Senior Reference Editor: Andrew Gyory
Reference Production Manager: Wendy E. Muto
Cover Design: Lee Goldstein

Table of Contents

Chapter V
CAVE ART OF EARLY FARMERS, EARLY POTTERS,
AND LATE HUNTERS: AN OVERVIEW OF THE REGION   **105**

General Information

A cruel trick of fate has caused the geographic region known today as Latin America—once the cradle of brilliant civilizations—to become a significant part of the sidelined, exploited part of the world, which, together with Africa and parts of Asia, is collectively known as the Third World. Controversies rage on this matter at every single level, and this is not the forum to expand on them. Long ago, the area was the cradle of a hunter art within a genuinely Paleolithic tradition, and in later periods a cave art flourished that is still little known in relation to the vastness of the territory. Its chronology also poses a problem, particularly considering that with the extension of the time lines for agricultural and pottery cultures (see Chapter IV) there is also a greater margin for the chronological and cultural placement of the paintings and petroglyphs attributable to these cultures. Three great geocultural regions divide the continent, each possessing specific characteristics of cave art. The first two were the agricultural communities occupying the humid tropical areas and the arid and semi-arid regions of the western strip of South America. The third was occupied by hunters and gatherers who were a late survival of those discussed in Chapter II.

Central-Southern Mexico

According to available data, a certain "family resemblance" can be perceived between Central America, the Caribbean, and northern South America. As we have seen, this was the region where Neolithic elements first appeared, both in regard to agriculture (Mesoamerica and the Central Andes) and to ceramics (Ecuador and the Amazonian region, with their ancient cultivation of tropical plants). The borders of this large region are imprecise. To the north they coincide with the demarcation accepted for the high Mesoamerican culture: a line roughly coinciding with the 25° North parallel and extending westwards to include a considerable part of Sinaloa. To the south the Amazon River forms a boundary, extending southwestward to the basins of the Madre de Dios and Beni rivers, and the headwaters of the Madeira—a line that is precise in geographical terms, but arbitrary in cultural ones.

The first of the areas under consideration, which coincides with the Mesoamerican Tradition (in the sense indicated by Gordon Willey, 1966) and covers El Salvador and western Honduras, presents its own special set of concerns. Its cave art not only shows "primitive" figures attributable to simple agricultural peoples, but it also presents (in certain areas) the technical and stylistic traits of the high cultures which developed after the Olmec expansion in the first millennium B.C.E. These works have the advantage of being assignable to certain cultures, and therefore dates for them are known. But the following question arises: should they be included in a book such as this? We have opted for a compromise: we will refer to works attributable to the Pre-Classic phases and, for practicality, exclude others that are direct expressions of later urban cultures.

But this latter group also poses a problem: does it correspond to ancient peoples—those lumped together as Late Preceramic (the Abejas de Tehuacán phase) and Early Pre-Classic (Purrón and Santa María phases of the same region)? Or are we discussing folk culture that existed at the same time as the more advanced Pre-Classic and Classic phases? Could we not think, even, in terms of survivals into the Colonial era, except where European influence is evident? For the moment the matter remains the subject of conjecture.

The first bibliographical listing of cave art in modern Mexican territory appeared only in 1987 (Casado, 1987). The section on the Mesoamerican area includes about 500 titles, but in very few cases do we find an exhaustive description of the sites. Furthermore, many of these are relatively inaccessible reports filed in the Technical Archives of the Office of Pre-Hispanic Monuments. Many others are just passing mentions in books devoted to other subjects. If matters concerning reliefs and paintings corresponding to the High Cultures are also subtracted, it is clear that a global overview based on extensive documentation is still an impossibility.

The subarea known as Western Mexico is rather rich in cave art sites. Sinaloa, for example, is home to a number of petroglyphs that include schematic anthropomorphs, at times associated with spirals and fret patterns. Fret patterns are generally a repeating set of lines intersecting at right or oblique angles. "Tecomate Hill features a set of engraved human footprints of different sizes, associated with feline prints, spirals, concentric circles, and human forms" (Ortíz de Zárate, 1973, p. 74). Animal-shaped figures are also to be found, as in the case of an open-jawed coyote associated with an apparently female figure at Quebrada de Amapal. The deer are reminiscent of some found in the southwestern United States, and the spiraled figures lead one to believe in a link with the Gila River

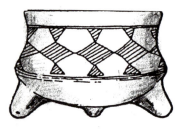

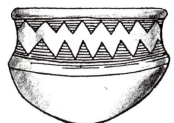

115. Early Pre-Classic ceramic vessels from the Valley of Mexico. Their decoration is incised and among their characteristic elements is the tripod-style bowl. They correspond to the village stage preceding the Olmec influence (approximately 1800–1000 B.C.E.) (after Alcina Franch, 1965).

style seen earlier. Irregular lines and curvilinear figures of all kinds abound. Engravings are predominant in the states of Nayarit and Jalisco.

To the southeast, also along Mesoamerica's northern border, the great engraved rock wall at Atotonilco, analyzed by Nadine Orloff (1982), deserves mention. There is an escarpment in northern Jalisco, which currently serves as the habitat of certain Huichol groups. The symbolism in Huichol art is very different from that of the Atotonilco site, indicating that the drawings precede this culture's arrival in the area. This is corroborated by the discovery of fragments of pottery which portray quadrupeds and human figures of the same style belonging to the Pre-Hispanic Chalchihuites culture. This represents one of the few cases of correlation between pottery and cave art: the figures, standing some 20 inches (50 centimeters) tall, are frontal and highly schematic. They wear typical headdresses angling out toward both sides, and carry large shields. A schematic eagle reminiscent of the North American Thunderbird dominates the central panel. Circles, vulvar signs, and irregular figures, along with some zoomorphs (concentrated on a panel which is possibly more recent) complete the set, which, despite its colorful variety, lacks (to our knowledge) a narrative or scenic character. This is found, however, at another site located deeper into Mesoamerica, in the Zamora region (Michoacan), specifically on petroglyphs located on the rocky edges of Curutarán Hill. Explorations by F. Horcasitas and F. Miranda identified about 200 stylized human and animal figures composed in dancing, chasing, and hunting scenes, the latter particularly involving deer. These scenes show a certain dynamism. One or two figures present circular heads with extensions like rays or crosses. Horcasitas and Miranda suggest hunting magic as underlying the expressions of cave art in the area. As for its age, once a post-Colonial origin is discarded, two choices emerge regarding attribution of the engravings: either a group of Chichimec hunters who invaded the area at various times, or Preceramic hunter-gatherers. The latter is not impossible, if it is remembered that there also exists a considerable series of red paintings, faded by exposure, which are of the same style as the petroglyphs. Here are found the first traces of a hunter style in Mexico, parallel to that of the Preceramic Andeans discussed in Chapter III.

Moving to the central plateau, John Greer (1990) has reported four newly found rock shelters with paintings and another with anthropomorphic and abstract engravings at the border between the states of Querétaro and Guanajuato, in the basin of the upper Ayutla River. Site Number 1 presents only irregular figures and a double circumference. Site Number 2 (El Cedro) features simple, frontal anthropomorphs in black with some red dots along their borders. There are also highly stylized zoomorphs and suns with dots in the center, as well as other abstract figures. A lateral section of the panel features more simply drawn small human figures—undoubtedly later attempts at copying the original ones. Site Number 5 features only a large "mask or the face of a deity." Site Number 4 (Rincón del Medio Día) is the most complete: it is a large rock shelter that was also employed as a dwelling, as indicated by fragments of rough pottery scattered on the floor. Here we find very diverse cave paintings. For example, there are three red negative handprints, one with a circle painted in its center (indicating a rather late variant), simple quadrupeds, and complex two-colored geometric paintings (for example, a sun with a triple circumference). Another group portrays symbols clearly inspired by Classic and Post-Classic cultures, such as a figure wearing a headdress formed by countless arrows, clusters of arrows lacking any other precise associations, and geometric symbolic clusters inside rectangles. Both sites are located near the "Basement"—a geological formation shaped like a wide well some 1,300 feet (400 meters) deep, which has still not been archaeologically investigated. It is possible that there are more of them in almost inaccessible reaches of the area's canyons, which are inhospitable and covered in overgrowth. The area was previously occupied by Otomí Indians.

Somewhat farther south, in the Mezquital Valley and its bordering regions (west of the state of Hidalgo), Carlos Hernández Reyes (1973) studied another area featuring numerous rock shelters containing cave paintings. Given that the city of Tula—the ancient capital of the Toltec kingdom—is not very far away, it is not surprising that some of these figures betray Toltec influence, such as fret patterns, symbolic-geometric figures, and the Plumed Serpent. But we also find handprints in white and black.[1] In the Tepeapulco area are found simple, small human figures like those of El Cedro. Peña de los Chivos has wild goats and white-painted deer. "We also notice traces of an early age of red paint with prints of hands, fingers, schematic human figures, etc." (Hernández Reyes, 1973, p. 78). We can therefore see the stylistic variety present in the area (which even contains a site with Colonial paintings of candelabra, a chalice, and other elements from the European tradition). We believe that in this case some of these examples of cave art predate the Toltec influence.

Nearer Tula, at Cerro de la Malinche, there are petroglyphs which can be identified directly as Quetzalcoatl and Cinteotl, the corn goddess (Zambrano, 1985).

In the humid woodland area of central Veracruz, near the Gulf of Mexico, is another recently studied example. Italian investigator Alberto Guaraldo (1987) reported two sites in the municipality of Vega de Alatorre featuring petroglyphs executed on large basalt blocks. Despite the existence of important ruins in the area, there are no specific analogies to be found with the art of the more sophisticated cultures. Among the varied motifs we find zoomorphs (even stylized jaguars) and bird-shapes with lines on their necks and bodies. Among these is the "line of the heart" (a shamanic motif observed in North America). There are also small schematic men engaged in a "praying" attitude, simple faces (two eyes and a mouth), irregular geometric motifs, a beautiful spiral crossed by a line associated with a schematic anthropomorph whose ribcage is represented (Death?), short linear designs, and so forth. Guaraldo also poses the possibility that we are dealing with a "popular" type of art, contemporary with the flowering of the elitist art of the ceremonial centers. We believe that in this case the works probably date to the Pre-Classic period (circa 2000 B.C.E. to the year 0).

A few words now follow on monumental cave art, which first appeared in the Olmec culture (Middle Pre-Classic, circa 1200–300 B.C.E.). These are sites far removed from the core area of this culture, near the Gulf of Mexico. The best known among them is the cluster of large rocks and reliefs from Chalcatzingo, southeast of Mexico City. The vertical walls of some large rocky outcroppings—located in a heavily wooded area—were used to execute a group of reliefs. The complexity and subject of these are in every way comparable to the works of La Venta and other centers of this remarkable prehistoric culture. In one section there is a seated personage, in profile, bearing complex insignia within a symbolic cave from which several volutes, or scrolls, are emerging ("the jaguar's jaws"?). Another section presents three masked figures wielding large weapons before a seated prisoner who is apparently about to be sacrificed. A unique scene appears on another: two nude figures, sexless or female, who are being pounced on by masked felines. While this appears to represent an attack, the scene could reflect the prototype of a legend that survived until the Spanish Conquest. This recounted how a woman had once been impregnated in distant times by a jaguar, and gave birth to a jaguar child or man. This were-jaguar figure (possessing qualities similar to the legendary werewolf) was a mythical character frequently depicted in Olmec art.[2] A similar figure, wearing a bird-shaped mask and bearing insignia, is carved on a formatted rock in San Miguel Amuco (Guerrero).

Several other sites can be found in the southeastern region. In Chiapas, among others, there is a relief of an isolated warrior at Xoc. There is also an Olmec-type character in relief seen from the front at a height of 50 feet (15 meters) over a rock wall facing Lake Miramar, and an important cluster called "the Soldiers" on large rocks in Pijijiapán, on the Pacific side of the southern Sierra Madre. Here we find figures standing almost 10 feet (3 meters) tall, with large heads with feline elements and representations of seeds about to burst on their foreheads and rears; a man with a headdress ending in volutes. These and other figures possessing remarkable symbols are engraved with a type of iguana measuring 10 feet (3 meters). The site contains Cuadros Phase pottery, dated between 1000 and 800 B.C.E., a date which could easily apply to this important set of monumental cave art (Navarrete, 1969). In Guatemala, human figures in relief can be found at San Isidro Piedra Parada, and El Salvador offers two warriors with "Jaguar-Man," or were-jaguar faces in Chalchuapa. This site represents the southeastern extreme of Olmec influence.

Returning to the western end of this influence, two notable caverns containing Olmec-style paintings should be mentioned. One of the caves is Juxtlahuaca, located in the mountainous region east of Chilpancingo, Guerrero, explored by Carlo Gay (1967). Its shape and depth are reminiscent of the Paleolithic caves of southern France. A large chamber located some 2,300 feet (700 meters) from the entrance served at some point as a burial site. Some 3,100 feet (940 meters) into the cave, a zigzagging gutter (presumably for drainage purposes) 250 feet (75 meters) long leads to the first hall containing paintings. The colors employed are red, yellowish ocher, and black. We find characters in ritual action (one of them seated), and somewhat later another man almost 3.3 feet (1 meter) tall clad in nothing but a loincloth, his forehead sloped forward in Olmec fashion, holding unidentifiable objects. A serpent's head and that of an open-mouthed feline menace him from behind. Not far away is a rectilinear drawing interpreted as the reproduction of a temple. Finally, 3,900 feet (1,200 meters) from the entrance and in front of several underwater lakes, is the Hall of the Serpent. The Serpent is a red figure some 6.5 feet (2 meters) long, which follows the natural arched seam lining the edge of a rocky projection. Its great head shows internal and external curved scrolls on either side of a long forked tongue. The rattlesnake would have been the model that inspired this representation, which would eventually metamorphose into the Plumed Serpent of the later Mesoamerican cultures. Facing it is a large, unidentified animal with feline-like characteristics. Gay supposes that an effort was made to represent a mythic struggle between these two beings. In my opinion, there is little doubt that this evocative site was employed for ritual purposes (as happened later on with the caves located underneath the Pyramid of the Sun at Teotihuacan and some caves in the Maya area).

The same could be said for the Oxtotitlán Cave, although it lacks the dimensions of Juxtlahuaca. It is near Chilapa, some 25 miles (40 kilometers) north of Juxtlahuaca. David Grove has directed studies of it (1970). Aside from other characters, in an example of a rather realistic-looking jaguar is a multicolored character seated on a bench or altar; he has a wide, stylized feline head, one arm upraised and the other tilted downward. His head looks to the right, and is covered by a large mask

116. Black and red cave art in a steep rock shelter known as El Cedro, near Río Blanco in Querétaro (approximately 125 miles (200 kilometers) north of Mexico City). Its age is unknown. (After Greer, 1990.)

representing a bird of prey (an owl?); more than an emblem, this raptor could represent his guardian and inspirational spirit. One leg dangles while the other is upraised. Even more significant is the arm placement: one upraised and the other tilted downward. What is this painting—worthy of the best Olmec artist—doing in the bowels of a cave? Is it of a prince, a shaman priest, an initiate? A mediator between heaven and earth? I share the bewilderment and amazement of Jacques Soustelle and other researchers regarding this highly symbolic cave art that predates that of the Mayas by more than 700 years.

Along with its jade and serpentine ceremonial axes and its stone and ceramic statuettes, Olmec cave art represents an important document of this culture's expansion. (This is not the place to discuss the origins of this Mesoamerican "mother culture," and we refer the reader to Roman Piña Chan's book on the subject (1989).) One petroglyph shows a probable indirect Olmec influence: a deer with schematic faces drawn on its body, from the Soteapan area (Veracruz). It is likely that other sites with cave art may be attributable to this kind of indirect influence, not only in their seemingly theocratic culture but also in other Olmec-like traits. Phase I of Monte Albán in Oaxaca could be one of these. The Dainzú Site offers an example of Phase II: its cliffs contain a series of engravings shaped like ball players' helmets, similar to the ones worn by the players depicted in the archaeological ruins at Monte Albán. The function of these stone depictions is unknown (Bernal, 1973).

There are cases associating simple or generalized motifs with others that are monuments. An interesting example would be the cluster of rocks found along the slopes of Cerro del Chivo on the Río Lerma valley near Acámbaro 112 miles (180 kilometers) northwest of Mexico City. Numerous rocks, decorated almost always on their horizontal surfaces, are painted with spirals shaped like classic pitted petroglyphs in no way different from the ones in Arizona, western Mexico, Nicaragua, and Colombia; others present mask-shaped reliefs and stairways with platforms imitating temples, which are datable to the Late Classic Period (approximately 700 C.E.) (Hyslop, 1975). It is possible that the first group corresponds to a Neolithic-type culture. This does not exclude the figure's reappearance at a later date, and its complex symbolism may have been included within that of the High Cultures.

The cave art engravings and reliefs also appear at the heart of the Post-Classical cultures (Toltec, Aztec, and Puebla-Mixteca). Depictions of deities in certain areas have already been mentioned. To these can be added animals and calendar dates, shields and weapons, temples with stairways, stairways (such as the deeply carved flight of steps in a rock near Chalco),[3] and complex works, such as the sculpted rock of Acalpixcan near Mexico City, interpreted as a kind of "cosmic plan" (Noguera, 1972). There are also paintings like the ones mentioned earlier in the Teotlalpan (Hidalgo) region, others discovered on the southern slopes of the Popocatépetl volcano depicting the god Tlaloc (of Aztec manufacture), the Toltec paintings of Ixtapanapa, etc. These could be considered stone variants of the known pictographic codices, or ancient manuscripts: in both cases there are very late derivations of prehistoric paintings.

117. *Left:* One of the Olmec-style bas-reliefs executed on the rock walls of the Cerro de la Cantera, Chalcatzingo (Morelos, Mexico), a monumental cluster of cave art from between 1000 and 500 B.C.E. Within a cave, a seated figure appears surrounded by symbolic figures. Above, the clouds send down drops of water which will fertilize the earth (after Piña Chan, 1989). *Right:* Two masked felines pouncing on two human beings, the upper one with a bird's head. This belongs to another section of the Chalcatzingo cave reliefs (after Soustelle, 1984).

One example of monumental cave art directly related to a temple cluster is at Tonalá, in the southern region of Chiapas. Large granite boulders scattered over the site were engraved with complex feline-like motifs; simpler human figures can also be found. This could be a substitute for the sculpted decoration absent in the buildings. The site is dated to the Late Pre-Classic period (Ferdon, 1951).

Northwest of this same state is an extensive group of petroglyphs (60 blocks), which on the whole are stylistically primitive, but are considered to be the product of classic influences. There is no ceremonial site in the immediate vicinity (the site, known as Finca Las Palmas, is located on the western border of the Maya cultural area), and its creators would have been members of an agricultural community not directly dominated by one of those centers. The engravings themselves are generally irregular and abstract, dotted with numerous circular or elongated holes, sometimes joined to one another through grooves. There are cases in which this occurs on a horizontal surface; in such instances the rocks could be altars. The existence of simple heads and at least one human figure with a set of curvilinear designs in lieu of a head, leads to the belief that the custom of beheading enemies was prevalent. (It is believed that the custom originated among the Olmecs.) Possible solar symbols, crosses, and a few spirals complete the holdings of this unique ceremonial site studied by Gertrud Weber and Matthias Strecker (1976).

Deeper into the Maya area, the most prominent characteristic of its early archaeology—aside from the large and small cities with high architectural and artistic development—are the hundreds of natural caves, or sinkholes formed by subterranean rivers, under the region's limestone crust, some of them small and others several miles in length. "The caves hold a special place in the relationship between the Maya and their landscape, like nodal points in the sacred geography. The perception that caves constituted something different from the secular world is frequent in Amerindian tribes, some of which would claim that their forebears had emerged from caves" (A. Stone, 1987, pp. 95–96). One example is Chicomoztoc among the Aztecs or Tampu-Toco among the Incas.

As well as certain objects and fragments of pottery from different ages, paintings and petroglyphs have been found in several of these caves. In one of them, Naj Tunich in Guatemala, is classical Maya art, with characters engaging in ceremonies, symbols, and glyphs, or symbolic figures, of their writing. Another is the richly clad "warrior" executed in bas-relief near one of the two entrances to the great cave of Loltún, near the Yucatán's Puuc Mountains, which correspond in style to the Late Pre-Classic period (circa 200 B.C.E.?). In other caves are figures of a type deemed primitive, such as in Actum Tziib in Belize, only 19 miles (30 kilometers) from Loltún. Here are spirals, combs, T-shapes, stylized individuals, frogs, and serpents. Another example is the Dzibichén Cave, at the site of Chichén Itza. This cave, 82 feet (25 meters) wide and 164 feet (50 meters) deep, has a water stream at its bottom, near which are found a ghostly set of line

118. *Left:* Olmec-style cave painting, remarkable for its location and symbolism. Found in the Oxtotitlán Cave (Guerrero). It probably depicts a shaman priest wearing an owl or raptor mask, seated on a jaguar-monster in a ritual pose appearing to seek union between heaven and earth. Probably embodying a deity (after D. Grove, reproduced in Soustelle, 1984). *Right:* Shaman priest/warrior in complex garb holding a large shield-shaped object in his arm. Cave art bas-relief of Olmec origin found in Xoc (Chiapas, southeastern Mexico)(from Soustelle, 1984).

paintings which include open-jawed serpents, frogs, a jaguar in a curious position, vulvar signs, and a seated character interpreted as the rain god Chac. The belief in water as a source of life is indicated here.[4]

In the preceding cases one might think in terms of an earlier chronological period, but we also have the juxtaposition of both styles in the same cave. For example, both occur in Loltún, with the added detail—already remarked upon in Chapter II—of positive and negative handprints. An interesting case in point is the Cave of the Petroglyphs near Dzibichén. This features simple faces reminiscent of those at Finca Las Palmas, skeletal figures holding a bowl at chest level, vulva-type figures (which also appear at the Dzibichén Cave and in other sites), stairways, circles with and without central dots, and circular and rectangular holes on horizontal spaces (another parallel with the site in question). Matthias Strecker, who first described it (1984), indicates that in spite of the limitations of these means of expression, the number of figures and their planned distribution is impressive. Skeletal representations, which in various degrees of schematization appear in several Mesoamerican sites and in the Caribbean, would not be "Death Gods" but rather deities related to concepts and notions of fertility, earth, and rebirth. Of themselves, the caves—in their role as "wombs of the earth"—are dualistically perceived as places of death and rebirth, as mediators of the great transformation processes. According to the conclusions drawn by Andrea Stone,[5] this may be why they were chosen as sites in which to carry out rites of passage or initiation. (A depiction of this appears to have been painted on the Naj Tunich cave.) This question regarding the Olmec cave at Juxtlahuaca has been posed, and the same can be done for some stages of Maya culture as well.

The question of the existence of both styles of cave art and whether or not there is any chronological coincidence between them is yet to be solved. In any case, this ritual use of the deep caves represents a clear and notable survival from prehistoric times.

Aside from the Olmec-type reliefs already mentioned for Guatemala and El Salvador, few instances of cave art have been found in either country. The best known petroglyphs are in the environs of Santa Lucía Cotzumalhuapa, at the foot of a southern Guatemalan mountain. They are not related to Central American cave art. We also find some engraved figures in El Salvador which were also painted. A cave near the town of Corinto, also known as Sumcuyo or "Holy Spirit," has been visited by scholars for many years. This cave contains a variety of paintings in red and yellow, including two schematic figures of probable shamans with a bird between them. The negative handprints that appear at this site hardly correspond to the same time frame. Among the petroglyphs at Cueva del Toro in the southeastern part of the country are Maya hieroglyphs intermixed with other drawings (Strecker, 1982).

Central America

No unanimity exists regarding Mesoamerica's southern border, which some extend along the Pacific Coast down to the Nicoya Peninsula in northwestern Costa Rica. If influences traveled that far south, they are no longer noticeable in the cave art. This marks the start of the Central American or Isthmian Cultural Area, which runs along a line that crosses Honduras from the mouth of the Illua River on the Caribbean Sea to the Gulf of Fonseca in the south. We

119. Spirals and other abstract figures deeply engraved into a volcanic rock at Cerro El Chivo, near Acámbaro in Michoacán (some 155 miles (250 kilometers) west of Mexico City). While other bas-reliefs from the area date back to the High Classic and Post-Classic periods (700–1250 C.E.), these motifs correspond to an ancient agricultural and ceramic tradition (photograph: J. Hyslop).

will therefore refer in this section to the largely petroglyphic art of Honduras, Nicaragua, Costa Rica, and Panama.

This region, as with a large part of Colombia, has preserved the basic cultural characteristics of small tropical agricultural areas: their inhabitants were excellent potters and stone sculptors, and goldworking was added to their activities by the early first millennium C.E. This places the region at an intermediate level between the Mesoamerican and Andean civilizations. We have already seen that these originated in an expansion which, according to available data, started in southwestern South America around the third millennium B.C.E. Cave art must also be placed among these basic elements, which have, with some exceptions, a rather uniform family resemblance. Its cultural dating seems clear. On the other hand, a more detailed chronology within the 3,000 years that this tradition endured cannot yet be carried out. Nor have any clear stylistic subdivisions been made, and there are only examples in which some Mesoamerican ideological influence appears. (One would be the plumed serpent engraved in a rock shelter at Santa Elena de Izapa in southern Honduras, or the plumed serpent painted on the borders of Laguna de Nijalpa in Nicaragua. Here, the serpent is coiled into a spiral-shape, surrounded by four groups of three feathers each aside from the ones on its tail.)

In Honduras the snake motif is common, in combination with other sinuous or wavy lines, circles, spirals, and at times circular holes and straight-lined motifs that form lines imitating stairways (for example, at the La Pisila rocks west of Comayagua, where plume-headed personages can also be found).[6] Sometimes we find schematic quadrupeds and monkeys along with simple faces such as the ones appearing in the Miskito region (eastern edge of Honduras and Nicaragua).

The present territory of Nicaragua is one of the great centers of cave art in the Americas, with numerous petroglyphs concentrated particularly in the two islands of Lake Cocibolca or Nicaragua: El Muerto and Ometepe. These and other sites have been extensively surveyed by Joaquin Matilló Vila.[7] Almost always, the numerous rocks scattered throughout valleys and slopes were employed as a background, reminders of the ancient eruptions of this volcanic region. The general style of these petroglyphs, executed through controlled pitting, can be described as streaked with curvilinear tendencies. They attain their maximum point on the Isle of Ometepe, which is formed by two volcanoes, one still active and the other extinct and covered with vegetation. On the slopes of the latter volcano (called Maderas, at an elevation of 4,400 feet, or 1,340 meters) and in the vicinity of the coast, we find over 2,000 engraved figures, which were recorded by Matilló Vila. More than half of the figures constitute abstract signs: circles, spirals, parallel lines, different geometric figures, points, and small bowls. We also find stylized anthropomorphs, simple faces or masks, representations of probable priests, sorcerers and *caciques*, groups of dancers, and so forth, which are often juxtaposed. There is also an example in which the shape of the rock was employed to execute a relief of two intertwined felines, a motif reminiscent of Mesoamerican art. Some abstract and complex engravings, carved with greater precision (such as an exceptional mask-shaped figure with radial lines found on a vertical face at Hacienda El Porvenir) point in this direction. Also found is the framed cross that sometimes occurs in the Caribbean and more extensively in the Andes region. Some large-headed, large-eyed figures remind one of West Indian or Venezuelan figures. Are these convergences? There is no doubt that Ometepe was a sacred island, as is indicated by its paired volcanoes and its location on Central America's largest lake. The island also contains large statues of seated figures crowned by animal alter egos, either eagles, jaguars, or coyotes. These statues are related to others in Costa Rica and articulate a concept also present in Colombia (San Agustín).[8]

There is no certain basis for interpreting the Ometepe petroglyphs, but the obsession with circular and spiral figures suggests a symbolism of movement, which may indicate life and fertility. Here, as in other cases, whenever one comes across apparently phantasmagorical art it is conceivably a cave tradition that sprang from an effort to capture or represent psychic experiences achieved during trance states by the priests or shamans guiding these ancient village communities.

A singular stylistic group based on zoomorphic figures converted into geometric groups exists in the Sierra de Managua, located south of Managua. It has been attributed to the Chorotegas, a group that may have emigrated from the Maya region in the sixth century C.E.

Although research on Costa Rica is scarce, everything points to a continuation of the stylistic trend predominating in Nicaragua. Rounded blocks were used for the carvings, which at times cover the entire surface of the rock. This cave art is generally characterized by simple or concentric circles (either in isolation or interconnected), spirals, volutes, and rakes. There are also human heads, and—less frequently—entire anthropomorphs and an occasional association with owls and *morterillos* (circular holes). There is an important concentration along the Río Reventazón, which flows into the Caribbean Sea. At the locality of Las Mercedes, northeast of San José (where numerous stone objects have been discovered), are anthropomorphic and zoomorphic reliefs made on the rocks themselves. The Boruca region in the country's western half features petroglyphs in the vicinity of a

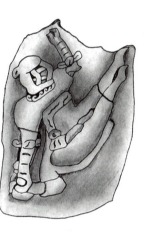

120. *Above:* A bas-relief of a ball player, Dainzú (from Whitecotton, 1984). *Below:* Bas-relief of a dancer. Monument 3 at San José Mogote (drawing by M. Orsen, after Blanton, Kowalewski, Feinman, Appel, 1987).

group of large stone spheres 3 to 5 feet (1 to 1.5 meters) in diameter. These spheres constitute one of the area's archaeological mysteries.

Cave art is scarce in Costa Rica and Panama. For the latter there is an extensive series of photographs with petroglyphs, some with rather deep lines, published by Neville Hartre (1961). These can be found in the western end of this isthmian nation. Taking a look at the distribution map, we notice that the petroglyphs form a chain along the Pacific Rim, although only a few are located near the sea. We do not know if this is indeed the case, or if it is a consequence of a lack of exploration of the Caribbean coast. The same can be said to apply to Panama's eastern half.

The general characteristics of the roughly fifty sites featuring petroglyphs (some of them made up of several closely situated blocks) are similar. There is a tendency toward the curvilinear, with single and double circles (sometimes with short external or internal rays) and often interconnected; spirals and volutes that are generally connected to other lines which sometimes form clusters of labyrinths, and a very few framed crosses. The style is no different from what can be seen in Costa Rica and Nicaragua; however, the themes are enriched by abstract motifs of clear and sometimes complex symbolism. These motifs include double volutes facing each other, generally encircled by small rays; two opposing "faces" (this sign, at times, lacks the three points representing the eyes and mouth); long-rayed wheels and suns; four-part signs; mask-shaped faces sometimes lacking an external border; and a reptile or frog with lines or dots on its body. The circular holes or dome-shaped holes appear to be lacking here. One significant aspect is the appearance of the haloed mask-shaped head, very schematic in this case (at Llano Colorado and Calobre, Veraguas Province), which will be prominent in certain Caribbean sites and in the Guyanas. A rock with rounded surfaces in Remedios (Chiriquí) presents an intricate network of lines in its entirety. It also shows some of the symbolic or emblematic motifs mentioned above. Some of the designs are hard to describe, and the art stands in contrast to the decoration of several types of pottery known in the region. For this reason, and because it is far from dwelling sites or tombs, there is no basis for a possible chronology and cultural attribution. The Panamanian petroglyphs may be a reflection of an important shamanic trend perhaps contemporary with that of the ceramic cultures, which also extended to the northern region of South America and to a lesser extent the Caribbean islands.[9]

Certain engraved blocks are located in flat, open regions, while others lie in the highland areas of the Chiriquí Province volcanoes. The majority exists in rainforest or densely wooded areas, contributing to the air of mystery that often surrounds these works.

The Caribbean

This island region is often included with central and eastern Venezuela and the northern Guyanas within the Caribbean Area in the tropical regions of the Americas. This is justified by the hypothesis—backed by archaeological and linguistic findings—that the ancient and modern peopling of the islands occurred from this area of the continent. For geographic reasons it deserves a section of its own.

There are no traces of Pleistocene hunting populations in any of the West Indian islands. A few workshops with stone chips, knives, and pins found in Santo Domingo and eastern Cuba (the Seboruco and Levisa Caves, dated to 3200 B.C.E.) indicate the late presence of gatherers of unknown origin. As of the second millennium B.C.E. the presence has been recorded of fishers and shellfish-gatherers forming part of a wide dispersion covering the coasts of the Central American isthmus, Colombia, Venezuela, and the Greater and Lesser Antilles up to Cuba. The phase known here as Guayabo Blanco is very similar to the Manicuare phase on the eastern coast of Venezuela, being archaeologically characterized by a varied conch-shell industry (i.e., gouges made with large seashells could be employed in the manufacturing of canoes). In certain sites stone elements have

121. A pair of petroglyphs from the Isle of Ometepe, Nicaragua. Curvilinear and spiral motifs are predominant (redrawn from Matilló Villa, 1973).

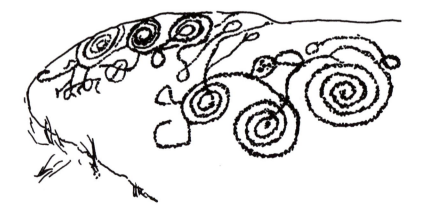

been found, such as long knives, *bolas,* and near-polished daggers, aside from pins, grindstones, and stone and conch-shell necklace beads. The inhabitants of western Cuba in the sixteenth century, known as the Ciboney ("Men of Stone") are distant descendants of this first wave of prehistoric Caribbean occupants.

By the beginning of the Common Era a second movement may be observed, bringing tropical crops (manioc, yams, maize) to the islands, as well as pottery. The Caribbean is known for its Salado-like pottery that originated in the lower Orinoco region. This pottery features painted decorations with a variety of geometric motifs—often curvilinear—with white lines on a red background being the customary detail. This probable migration of an ancient Arawak group reached the islands of Puerto Rico (Cuevas Phase) and Santo Domingo. On the other hand, Cuba's most ancient ceramic phase is the Mayarí in its eastern end, tentatively dated between 800 and 1100 C.E., which preserved much of the earlier stoneworking and conch industry. The decorations on these vessels are basically incised, geometric rectilinear patterns. Here polished axes began to be used, some shaped like petals. At this same time period, the Ostiones sub-tradition developed in Puerto Rico, with new variants in pottery and the development of stone art. The Ostiones sub-tradition extends to Santo Domingo, Jamaica, and Cuba, a cultural cluster usually known as sub-Taíno. As a result of a new movement from the continent, originating with the Barranca-like tradition of central and eastern Venezuela, the final pre-Hispanic cultural horizon—known as Taíno—was formed in the thirteenth century. It was named after the people whom the Spaniards found in the island of Santo Domingo, whose language belonged to the Arawak family. The artistic decoration of the Taínos reached its height in their pottery (with its incised, curved designs and adornments), their stone axes, and their sculpted deities, or *zemí.* Also of note are Mesoamerican influences such as the rectangular ceremonial plazas and ball courts. They indicate the existence of relatively complex and hierarchical social groups.[10]

The West Indian cave art landscape is rather complex. Some apparent hunting scenes (small-scale men surrounding highly schematic animals) painted on some caves in the Guara region of Cuba's northern coast could be the product of ancient hunters. However, since there is no trace of these in the entire region, it is likely more modern, and perhaps post-Conquest. Except through indirect indications, there is no way to date the numerous works found. These can be fundamentally divided into two large types: paintings within more or less deep caves in Santo Domingo and above all Cuba, and engravings that appear in some caves in both countries and particularly on large, rocky blocks in Puerto Rico and the Lesser Antilles.

Starting with the first group, it can be said that the numerous caves which burrow through the limestone surface of Cuba constitute another marvel of American cave art. The motifs depicted are indeed somewhat poor and monotonous, given that the representative drawings—when they exist—are very schematic. But could it not be that the ancient inhabitants who dared to become absorbed by them, and who were submerged in this evocative environment that they saw as sacred, must have felt the need to embellish them excessively? Irregular geometric signs and lines in red and black would have sufficed to mark the passage of proto-shamans in their evocation of divinities and as a probable reminder of their trance states. The most frequent motifs are simple and composite circles (three or more), sometimes with internal radial lines; triangular, rectangular, and rhomboidal figures; rectangles with lines or ladder-shapes; rake- or comb-shapes, two united circumferences or circumferences joined by a single line; zigzags; tree- and leaf-shaped figures; prints or drawings of hands; and schematic birds seen in profile, as well as the occasional fish-shape and stylized anthropomorph. In 1987, 130 rupestrian art sites were known, largely found in caves, of which 66 had been studied.

It is worth noting two exceptional sites in Cuba: Cave Number 1 at Punta del Este, and García Robiou Cave. The first is found on the Isle of Pines near its southeastern shore, and has an opening toward the east. It was first studied by René Herrera Fritot (1939) and subsequently by Antonio Núñez Jiménez (1975). It consists of a dome 82 feet (25 meters) in diameter with seven natural perforations in its roof that serve as skylights, allowing the light of the sun and the moon to shine in at their zenith. "The cave's domes and walls are literally covered in hundreds of pictographs," Núñez Jiménez has written. "Most of them represent series of concentric circles, generally alternating between black and red, sometimes separated by the natural white color of the limestone.

"Pictograph Number 1, known as the Central Motif and considered a masterwork of Cuban cave art, is slightly oval in shape. Its diameter is over 5.1 feet (1.54 meters) and the motif itself is formed by 56 concentric circles, 28 of which are red, the remainder being black. They symbolize, according to Fernando Ortíz, the computation of a lunar month as ancient priest-artists must have understood it. In other words, the red circles would represent days and the black circles, nights. Superimposed on this great pictogram we find a long, red arrow pointing directly toward the east, to the spring and fall equinoxes. Within the Central Motif we find a series of concentric circles whose meaning remains enigmatic. Seen as a whole, the Central Motif suggests to the viewer the image of a star map, a representation of constellations, but it could also mean something completely different" (Núñez Jiménez, 1986c, p. 9).

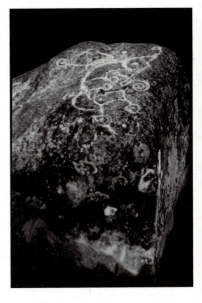

122. Curvilinear designs on a rock in the Central American rainforest in San Vito de Java, Costa Rica (photograph: L. Laurencich Minelli).

Following pages:
123. Panamanian petroglyphs with curvilinear and symbolic motifs (redrawn after N. Harte).

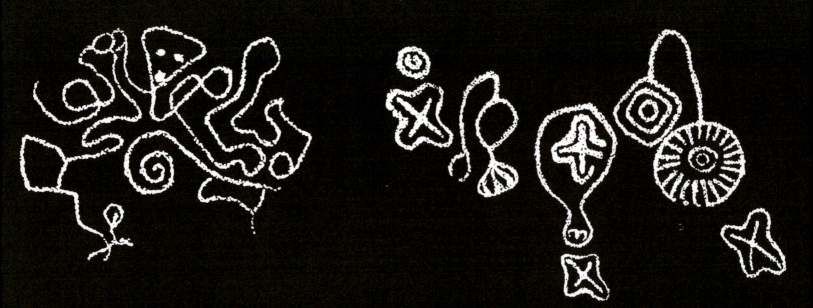

Preceding pages:
36. *Parque de La Venta, Villahermosa, Tabasco (Mexico). An Olmec sculpture representing a priest seated on the body of a rattlesnake (photograph: D. Domenici).*

37. Facing page, top: *Parque de La Venta. Side of an Olmec altar with a bas-relief of men carrying jaguar-children (photograph: D. Domenici).*

38. Facing page, bottom: *Parque de La Venta. Rock 3, detailing the face of a personage wearing an elaborate headdress (photograph: D. Domenici).*

39. *Monte Albán, Oaxaca (Mexico). Glyph on a stone reused in building J. The glyph, which should really be viewed upside down, indicates the conquest of a city (photograph: D. Domenici).*

40. Above: *Monte Albán. "The Dancers," a bas-relief illustrating a clear Olmec-like influence (photograph: Jaca Book).*
41. Right: *General view of Monte Albán (photogragh: D. Domenici).*

42. Above: *Tepeapulco, Hidalgo (Mexico). Abstract petroglyph in the vicinity of the Teotihuacán site (photograph: D. Domenici).*
43. Left: *Tepeapulco, the main pyramid (photograph: D. Domenici).*

44. *Panama. Petroglyphs representing faces and other abstract figures (photograph: G. Orefici).*

45. Panama. The great rock on whose surface the petroglyphs in the above photograph are engraved (photograph: G. Orefici.)

Preceding pages:
46., 47., 48., 49. La Chaquira, San
Agustín (Colombia).
Anthropomorphic figures engraved
on large rocks. An example of cave
art in the environs of the high
cultures (photographs: D.
Domenici).

50. Above: *Fuente de Lavapatas, San Agustín (Colombia). The ceremonial fountain features bas-reliefs among which some serpents are visible. The flowing water provides an evident sensation of dynamism among the figures (photogaph: D. Domenici).*

Preceding pages:
51. *Barinas (Venezuela). An example of the rich cave art of the eastern Andes (photograph: Grupo Arqueológico Kuayu).*

52. Above: *Pantiacolla (Peru). Great wall with hundreds of abstract engravings (photograph: G. Orefici).*

In the French Guianan hinterland near the source of the Marouini River, a large rock 49 feet (15 meters) long emerges from the ground, covered by anthropomorphs of the "praying" type, long-beaked birds, a fish, two axes, and two arrows or lances piercing a square filled with dots or small aligned bowls. This site appears to constitute its own local style, classifiable as stylized naturalism. According to Jean Hurault and his researchers, "It possesses a certain originality and elegance, and follows well-defined artistic concepts." On the other hand, however, "the arrangement of the cluster of engravings does not explain the rites—possibly shamanic in nature—with which they may well be associated." (Hurault et al., 1963, pp. 160–63.) Slightly to the north, amid the bare, rocky mountains which form the border between Suriname and Brazil, the same researchers discovered a curious set of geoglyphs. These are 15 figures created by means of aligning stones extracted from a rocky cliff located not far away. Human silhouettes, turtles, and serpents have been identified, each averaging about 16 feet (5 meters) in length. An oval-shaped enclosure has been demarcated through the use of large boulders (the petroglyphs can be found next to the borders), which can only be interpreted as a sanctuary or ceremonial complex. Given the dearth of further information, this can be ascribed to the ancestors of the Oyana Indians, who currently populate the area in small numbers (ibid., pp. 163–66).

Returning to Brazilian Guyana, there is one significant cave containing linear rubbed engravings, located on the Tütha-Cariwai River on the southern end of the Sierra de Tumuc-umaque. This strange type of petroglyph, already noted in two sites in French Guiana, appears scattered over the immense territory of Brazil. Aside from concentric rhomboids, cartouches with linear designs, and other abstract motifs, there are anthropomorphs with headdresses, a large bird with outstretched wings, and a sign which can be considered Amazonian: double volutes back-to-back.

The existence of petroglyphs in the upper basin of the Trombetas and Cuminá rivers, and of the Río Branco, have already been mentioned. The most important example of these is Pedra Pintada, blocks and rock walls seen on a large rock somewhat rounded by rain erosion, rising over the surrounding savanna together with a few others. Painted in different shades of red are vertical rows of rhomboids, filled-in triangles, grids (some of them 3 feet, or 1 meter, tall), concentric circles or circles with diagonals, suns, dots, and simple or complex irregular figures.[22] Pedra Pintada was, without a doubt, a sacred spot to the ancient inhabitants. A reminder of this can be found in the tradition retold in 1838 to explorer R. Schomburg by his native escorts: that this was the House of the Spirit of Macunaima. (The belief that this Carib cultural hero was the creator of the petroglyphs was rather widespread; he marked the rocks with his fingers as a reminder of his passage through our world.)[23] In some nearby rock shelters, burials with ceramics and other elements belonging to the late cultural Rupununi phase of the Guyanas were unearthed. Excavations directed by Pedro Mentz Ribeiro (1987) proved the existence of the two earlier phases, one with ceramics and the other pre-ceramic, for which we have radiocarbon dates of between 2000 and 1000 B.C.E. Mentz Ribeiro ascribes the paintings to the latter, since traces of paintings were discovered beneath the level that produced the dates in question. We believe that the abstract linear paintings of Pedra Pintada, the Pereyra rock shelter, and other sites close to the Parimé and Surumu rivers are related to what has come to be known as the Geometric Tradition much farther east (Piauí). The same applies to four or five sites in Guyana, particularly Tramen Cliffs on the upper Karowreeng River, a high rock wall with rectilinear geometric paintings, clusters of positive handprints, and some stylized zoomorphs (Dubelaar, 1986b, pp. 198–202).

Petroglyphs have also been discovered slightly farther south along the Río Branco, showing an abstract curvilinear tendency with the occasional zoomorph. As a curious variant we find broad and deep rectilinear and elliptical incisions, achieved through rubbing on certain horizontal rocks, distributed irregularly (Mentz Ribeiro et al., 1989). While they look similar to the grindstones found in many regions, their affiliation to perfectly made and polished circular holes suggests some kind of ritual function.

132. Archaeological and artistic elements of the Guyanas: a painted funeral urn with reliefs from Cunany (Brazilian Guyana); a funeral urn from Moracá; petroglyphs from the Upper Anumi (French Guyana).

The Northern and Western Amazon

Seen on the map, the Amazonian cultural area constitutes a broad rhomboidal shape that runs from the eastern edge of the Andes Mountains to the Atlantic Ocean. From the archaeological viewpoint, its northern half is better known from both banks of the Amazon River to its not very well-defined northern end. Modern research has concentrated largely on the east (the Amazon Delta region) and the west (the upper Napo, Marañón and Ucayali rivers). Chapter IV described the great antiquity of the settlements of both regions by farmer-potter peoples. The entire area has until recently been a true preserve of indigenous peoples who have preserved a lifestyle adapted to the tropical rainforest since pre-Columbian times. With the first European explorations and the discovery of engravings on the rocky outcroppings marking some of its rivers, a question emerged which has not been answered to this day: were their creators these modern tribes, or were they their immediate ancestors? If neither, would they be the product of "ancient

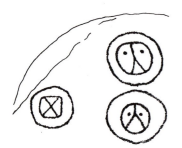

133. "Round Faces": petroglyphs on a rock beside the Lucie River, Seven Broeders Falls site (Suriname). Diameter of the upper figure: 20 inches (50 centimeters) (redrawn from Dubelaar, 1986).

vanished civilizations"? Both possibilities tend to be discarded in our times. Consideration is given on the one hand, to the ignorance and oftentimes great fear of modern native peoples of the petroglyph sites—though they do not have any mythological attributions, unlike in Venezuela and the Guyanas. On the other hand, there is the similarity of some rupestrian motifs to others on archaeological pottery, as evidenced by the Aristé Phase in eastern Brazilian Guyana, or in the Polychromatic Stylistic Area. This extends from the eastern Andean border to the Isle of Marajó and is dated at between 600 and 1300 C.E. However, pieces from the Incised Edge Area, placed at 0 to 900 C.E. (i.e., the Mangueiras Phase of Marajó), present incised decoration with parallel and spiraled lines. These also appear, albeit differently, in the pottery of the Shakimu Phases (circa 500 B.C.E.) and Hupa-iya (circa 200 B.C.E.) on Peru's Ucayali River, the latter having affinities with the Barranca style.[24]

This generic analogy of curvilinear and spiraled trends among certain types of Amazonian pottery and cave art does not fully explain the chronological and cultural context, nor the origin of this large stylistic group, represented almost entirely by petroglyphs. We must make do, then, with a broad characterization of this stylistic group, as exemplified in certain important areas or sites.

Theodor Koch-Grünberg's classic book of 1907 remains the basic reference work for Amazonian art in its "purest" expression. His surveys along the Uaupés and Izana rivers, and other tributaries of the Negro River on the border between Colombia and Brazil also show petroglyphs engraved at varying depths on the rocks bordering the cascades and rapids (cachoeiras) of those rivers. In this we find an analogy with sites from the Guyanas and some areas of Venezuela, also appearing on some of the motifs depicted. Nor can we speak of true "scenes" here, since even the depictions of natural elements appear juxtaposed haphazardly without a perceivable narrative.

Aside from concentric circles (sometimes with a central hole) and single or double spirals like volutes, there is the sign—already seen in Panama—of the double-backed volutes, wave- or snake-like lines, strange stylized figures of birds and perhaps fish, and above all, the human figure seen frontally in various schematized shapes. These range from the simple linear "praying" or elliptical-bodied figure (often three-fingered), to certain curious depictions of a triangular body formed entirely by holes, surmounted by a round face with eyes also made of holes. There are also some large mask-shaped faces (like one with spiraled ears on the Aiary River). Less frequent is the frog-shaped anthropomorph. Also exceptional are the anthropomorphs with a lower phallic extension—in one case, a line departing from the center of the face toward one side, which could be either a pipe or a tube employed for inhaling cohoba, a Caribbean-Amazonian drug prepared from the *cebil* plant.[25]

Helmut Schindler (1978) has detected several groups of similar petroglyphs along the neighboring Apaporis River in the Colombian Amazon, although here the human or human-like figure predominates.

One is a figure 3 feet (1 meter) long with deep lines and a row of dots on its body that has been classified as a scorpion. There are also rows of dots or circular holes, as well as some mask-shaped heads with upper extensions shaped like simple volutes. Here, as in other cases, the engraved rocks are in direct contact with the water; in other cases, part of the designs are underwater during high tide. Another important series of petroglyphs has been surveyed by Elisabeth R. von Hildebrand (1975) along the Caquetá River, toward the Brazilian border. Going upriver we find many sites photographed by F. Urbina, who has tried to relate them to Indian myths, such as the metamorphosis of the "serpent-man." The Caquetá River, which originates in the eastern

134. Petroglyphs with anthropomorphs (some of them double-headed) on a rock of the Sabana de Sipaliwini (Suriname), near the Brazilian border. The rock's height is about 6.5 feet (2 meters), while that of the figure on the left is 21 inches (53 centimeters) (redrawn from Dubelaar, 1986).

196

Andes and flows east of San Agustín, has served as a means of communication between the northern Andean area and the Amazonian forests. In 1962, at the foot of the mountains in the outskirts of the city of Florencia, aquatic erosion uncovered a long wall with a frieze bearing some broad engravings, 52 feet (16 meters) long by 3 feet (1 meter) tall. The human figure—always seen frontally, in some cases lacking lower extremities—with a round or almost rectangular head, lacks ornaments save a pair of lines issuing from a character depicted in the panel's center. Many figures are intertwined. There are few abstract signs. On the other hand, we also find an abundance of sinuous irregular lines and some groups of holes, particularly in the right sector, which appear to have been made more recently. A pair of birds and a monkey essentially complete the work. One of the figures has one arm extended upward and the other downward, while another is in a "praying" stance (both arms upraised at an angle). In the opinion of E. Silva Célis (1963), who studied them, the petroglyph from Florencia's El Encanto site "presents symbols related to ancestor worship and to agrarian and fertility rites, atmospheric phenomena, and ideas and problems related to human fertility." Although these details cannot be proven, one might suppose that at this site—perhaps one of the most remarkable in the Amazonian Basin—an attempt was made to tell a long mythical story.

Perhaps the same attempt was made on another large wall located on the Pantiacolla River, a tributary of the Madre de Dios in the Peruvian Amazon. The difference here is that human figures are more scarce and appear camouflaged in a veritable sea of curvilinear designs of all types. The importance of this site comes from its great extension (more than 66 feet (20 meters) of uninterrupted drawings, reaching heights of 10 feet (3 meters) in some parts) and the relatively elaborate technique in their execution as rather broad designs. Intricate and intriguing, it remains undeciphered.

The Keros River, another tributary of the Madre de Dios, features a large rock located in the middle of the waterway. Its horizontal face presents a good sampling of what is called the Amazonian stylistic group. Only human figures are lacking. We find the concentric circle, the double and triple circle joined by a line, the two spirals joined by a design, the S-shaped double spiral, and the elongated undulant serpent. Some geometric figures, two somewhat more complex ones, and the framed cross with its probable Andean origin complete the set. This rock, together with the one at Pantiacolla and a series of rocks engraved with irregular curvilinear sites existing in the province of La Convención northwest of Cuzco (the Urumbamba River and its tributaries), depict a concentration of petroglyphs belonging to this large rupestrian group.[26]

Another concentration can be found farther northeast between the junction of the Guaporé and Beni rivers and the city of Porto Velho on the Madeira River (Brazil). This concentration contains nearly 10 known sites, also associated here with the *cachoeiras,* and features the classic circular and spiral figures, sometimes quasi-rectangular ones and holes. I have discussed the most interesting of these sites: Tres Irmãos on the Madeira River (Grabert and Schobinger, 1969–1970). Deeply engraved on a tilted sandstone wall are triangular faces (one of them sporting a cap, the other with an extension ending in a spiral on its upper end), and "lizard-men" with extremities ending in three or four fingers (one of them with a considerably widened tail end). Curiously, more analogies can be made here with cave artworks from northern Venezuela than with the neighboring Andean region (the relationship between the Amazonian and Venezuelan petroglyphs have to be studied in detail, as they give the impression of an enriched Amazonian style).[27] This also should be done with the tiny southern Colombian area of the Department of Pasto (Nariño), which could be seen as an incursion of the Amazonian style into an Andean region. This is also evident farther south, at the source of the Putumayo and Napo rivers (the eastern edges of the Ecuadorian Andes). In this last area, Pedro Porras Garcés (1972) surveyed numerous sites with petroglyphs, which largely presented similarities with others of the Amazon Basin. Through the analysis of superimpositions and comparisons between some of the engraved motifs and the decorations of chronologically identified ceramic pieces, Porras Garcés has been able to determine four modes or styles in a probable succession over time (Porras Garcés, 1985).

A surprising transplant toward the eastern side of the Andes can be seen in the Ecuadorian province of El Oro, located between the Cordillera de Chilla and the Gulf of Guayaquil. Here, Celiano González has studied depictions similar to those appearing in the countries of northern South America and Brazil, such as the simple spiral and the S-spiral, the curvilinear E, linear anthropomorphs with open arms and legs and with three or four fingers, circular and quadrangular faces, and circular holes. This area that borders Peru is the only one in which work on cave art west of the Cordillera Septentrional has been published. It can be considered a clear case of diffusion from the Amazonian forests. No contextual or chronological data had previously been known.

There are almost no cave paintings within the area under consideration. There is some information on a site in the middle Amazon, and on another in the vicinity of the Apaporís River (Cerro Campana). In some limestone outcroppings near Monte Alegre, on the northern bank of the Amazon about 370 miles (600 kilometers) from its mouth, Mario Consens (1988) explored several walls and caves, which contain paintings corresponding to at least two different eras. Aside from an-

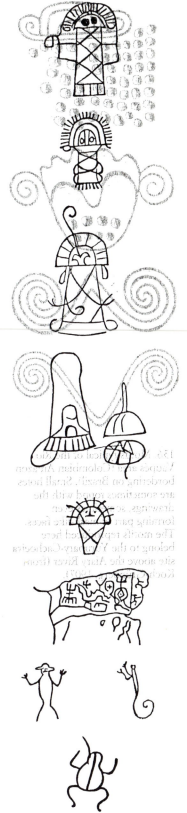

135. A selection of motifs engraved on the rocks of the Guyanas. The mask-shaped figures correspond to the shallow engraving technique, and the figures below to deep engraving. Various scales (from a plate by Im Thurn, reproduced by Dubelaar, 1986).

136. Motifs typical of the Río Vaupés area (Colombian Amazon bordering on Brazil). Small holes are sometimes found with the drawings, sometimes even forming part of mask-like faces. The motifs reproduced here belong to the Yurupary-Cachoeira site above the Aiary River (from Koch-Grünberg, 1907).

thropomorphic and zoomorphic figures whose schematization falls under the category of Amazonian, there are also simple faces, suns, and the branded hands which abound in eastern Brazil. In some sites are geometric-abstract clusters. The site yielding ancient Taperinha pottery almost faces this site on the great river's southern bank. Perhaps there is a correspondence between the two archaeological complexes.[28]

Peter Jackson (1982, p. 89) discovered headless linear anthropomorphs at the Umari site in the Uaupés River. Their insides were filled with a brownish-red pigment, which was preserved thanks to the fact that the rocks were located over the water level during the high-tide season. It is likely that these drawings are relatively modern.

There are very few sites with petroglyphs located east of the Madeira River group, and they are very isolated. Here we find an almost empty space until we reach the large eastern Brazilian rupestrian area.

I conclude this section with a mention of the southernmost site of the Amazon Basin's sub-Andean region, which constitutes a style all of its own: that of the Pachene River in Bolivia, a study of which was published by Karin Hissink (1955). These are two large rocks located on an ancient trail in the forested region, covered by representations of rather realistic vulvas executed in bas-relief. Some ghostly human figures and anthromorphized phalluses are associated with the site. Only in one other site in the Venezuelan Cassiquiare do we find an analogy (Koch-Grünberg, 1907, fig. 6). Chile also has two sites in which this style is repeated. Chronology, cultural context, and the ideological background of these works remain shrouded in mystery. We can only surmise that they have something to do with what is generically known as a fertility cult.

Although partly corresponding to the Amazonian Basin, the paintings and engravings of the southern Bolivian Oriente will be treated as part of the eastern Brazilian area.

The effect provided by the Amazonian petroglyphs, which also occur in southern Venezuela and the Guyanas, has to do more with their remote tropical environment than with their elaboration and symbolism, which are relatively simple. Referring to the engraved wall of Florencia, Silva Célis (1963, p. 13) has described "the loud and continuous noise of the waters, the dense vegetation which covers and conceals a considerable part of the rock, and the noises and squeals of the jungle animals [that] bring mystery, enchantment, and solemnity to the site where the monumental works sculpted by prehistoric man can be found."

PART 3: THE ANDEAN AREA

The Central Andes (Peru)

We now travel from the vast, damp, warm and forested tropical regions to the continent's western coast, which constitutes a great open rim toward the Pacific Ocean, presided over by the mountainous Andean ranges and the valleys and deserts that lie between them. In their northern reaches (Colombia and Ecuador) they tend to be separated along cultural lines, while from south-central Ecuador to the south the existence of two great subdivisions is accepted: the Central Andean Area and the Southern Andean Area. The first covers all of modern Peru (except for the eastern jungle plain) and northwestern Bolivia—in other words, the northern part of the great *Altiplano*. The second includes southern Bolivia, north and central Chile, northwestern and central-western Argentina. We shall now turn to the cave art attributable to the Ceramic cultures of the Central Andean Area.

This region presents particularities similar to those of Mesoamerica. After a thousand years of an early formative period (village culture, but with ceremonial complexes), there appears a more advanced cultural area centered around the temple complex of Chavín de Huantar in the central-northern Sierra. This complex has remarkable architecture, stone art, pottery, and textiles, dated approximately between 900 B.C.E. and 200 B.C.E. The first Pan-Peruvian area, also known as the Early Horizon, covers Peru's north and central sierra and the three coastal sectors (North, Central, and Southern) to the Paracas Peninsula. While there are no traces of a true state organization, this is a high culture possessing markedly religious artwork that in certain aspects presents notable evolutionary and chronological parallels to that of the Olmecs. As occurs in Mesoamerica in regard to the Olmecs, Peru has Chavín-style cave art as well as the Chavinoid style, which is either derived from it or is similar to it in certain ways. Some Peruvian art may thus be dated, but for the most part any relationship to other, more accurately dated art is purely hypothetical. In other words, even though it is found in the midst of areas characterized by well-defined cultures, rarely can one see motifs identified by one style or another. The only thing that can be proven is that within the imperial land of the Incas (circa 1400–1532 C.E.) cave art was not created. The question then arises: do Peruvian petroglyphs largely constitute an expression of ancient art, executed by village and herding cultures prior to Chavín (circa 2500–900 B.C.E.), or are they really a form of "popular art" paralleling the works of the Early Intermediate Period elites in the first millennium C.E.—Mochicas, Nazcas, Tiahuanacans, and so on? Or could they be late survivals, even from the colonial era? Only probabilities can be given as answers to these questions, aided to a certain extent and in specific cases by archaeological materials associated with the sites.

Until recently, data on Peruvian rupestrian art was scarce and scattered. The second International Symposium on American Rupestrian Art (Huánuco, 1967) represented a significant change of affairs, but its proceedings were never published. H. D. Disselhoff in 1955 and Eloy Linares Málaga in 1975 presented partial syntheses, preceded by Walter Krickeberg (1949), whose book on engravings and reliefs by the high cultures of the Americas listed only 10 petroglyph sites or clusters, and the existence of paintings was unknown. The situation changed drastically with the publication of the four-volume *Peruvian Petroglyphs* by Antonio Núñez Jiménez (1986). Taking advantage of his stay in Peru in his capacity as Cuban ambassador, the author visited 72 rupestrian sites, some of them with only a few engraved rocks, others with several dozen and even thousands, as in the case of Toro Muerto. Based on this considerable documentation, plus the few data available on paintings, a broad characterization can be made of Peruvian cave art of the farming-ceramic age, including two unique modes: the geoglyphs and the portable art of the rupestrian tradition.

Not knowing which sites and motifs may go back as far as the Initial period, let us start with those which may be located in its middle period, which, as already explained, is dominated by the Chavín cultural complex. Of particular note are the Udima Murals: multicolored paintings executed on rock walls near the community located on the Lambayeque River Basin in northern Peru. It deals with the Chavín personage or deity known as the Staff God—seen frontally—and other mythical creatures. Prominent colors include green and blue. These representations form part of the Monte Calvario archaeological zone, which aside from ruined structures contains petroglyphs depicting mythical Chavinoid entities on two large granite blocks (Mejía Xesspe, 1968). This is an interesting case of what is called monumental cave art. The same can be said about the petroglyphs of Alto de la Guitarra, at the foot of a mountain pass between the valleys of Moceh and Virú, through which an ancient road once passed, fragments of which can still be found. Among the many engraved rocks (largely through superficial sculpting or fine pitting), a "dancer" stands out that is very similar to the one depicted by fine incised lines on a large shell from the Chiclayo area of the Lambayeque Valley.[29] Another motif is that of the "fish-man" (?) in a horizontal position. It is nearly 5 feet (1.5 meters) long, with feline-like teeth, and holds a fish in one hand (a Mochica ceramic object has a depiction probably derived from this one). Two human figures with circular shields and serpents emerging from their heads are depicted face to face, probably engaged in a war dance. (In this case, the style comes close to that of the figures engraved on the outer wall of the Cerro Sechín temple in the Valley of Casma, which dates to 1800–800 B.C.E.). Another character is shown in profile, ax in hand and with a trophy-head dangling from his back. Felines, dragon-like serpents, birds, simple or complex mask-shaped faces, eyes with bulging pupils, and rectangular crosses express the religious and symbolic influence of Chavín in the area, which is far from the main temple on the Sierra but close to the Cupisnique Gorge, the main expression of the coastal Chavín style. Many irregular figures, simple and complex anthropomorphs (some reminiscent of Amazonia) engraved with the same technique, lead us to the following question: if, as it seems, they are roughly contemporary with one another, how does one explain their role and meaning? Stone rectangles similar to small pens can be found in this and other sites in Peru. Crossing the Virú Valley, we find at the Queneto site a double structure of this type with monoliths—some of them engraved—which from comparison with the well-known Kalassaya of Tiahuanaco—is judged to be an open-air temple built at some point during the Initial Period. In the vicinity are several petroglyphs carved in some of the rocks found all over the broad San Juan Valley. These petroglyphs are similar to the simpler ones from Alto de la Guitarra, and pose the same problem mentioned earlier. It is almost inevitable to suspect some connection between the rituals held at the ceremonial center and the petroglyphs.

A Chavinoid condor engraved complex can be found farther north at Quebrada de los Boliches, accompanied by serpents and other curvilinear figures. In the same area of the Lambayeque Department we find the large Cerro Mulato complex, not far from Chongoyape, whose rounded rocks also contain loose designs ranging from simple scrawls to well-defined anthropomorphic and zoomorphic figures and symbolic signs. Its possible Chavinoid nature is less evident here than in Alto de la Guitarra, and the same can be said for the other large petroglyph complex at Yonán in the Jequetepeque River Valley, located at the foot and on the slopes of Cerro de los Letreros. Here can be seen more Moche influence, at least in some figures such as a personage with a *tumi* (half-moon-shaped knife) on its head, and a bird on a long staff. There is a little of everything in this extensive site, including symbols shared with the Caribbean and Amazonian areas, such as the concentric circle with a central dot, the spiral, and the cross. There is a depiction which foreshadows others in southern Peru and northern Chile: the square-headed character surrounded by short lines, sometimes wielding a mace or a staff. There are also rocks with deep circular holes surrounded by a jumbled array of petroglyphs.

137. A dancer with certain Chavinoid affinities from Alto de la Guitarra, toward the interior of the Valle de Moche at 2,950 feet (900 meters) above sea level. The four-fingered hands suggest that it is a deity or mythological figure. Height: 30 inches (75 centimeters). Its similarity to the character engraved on Pickman's Strombus has been noted (see fig. 139) (from A. Núñez Jiménez, 1986).

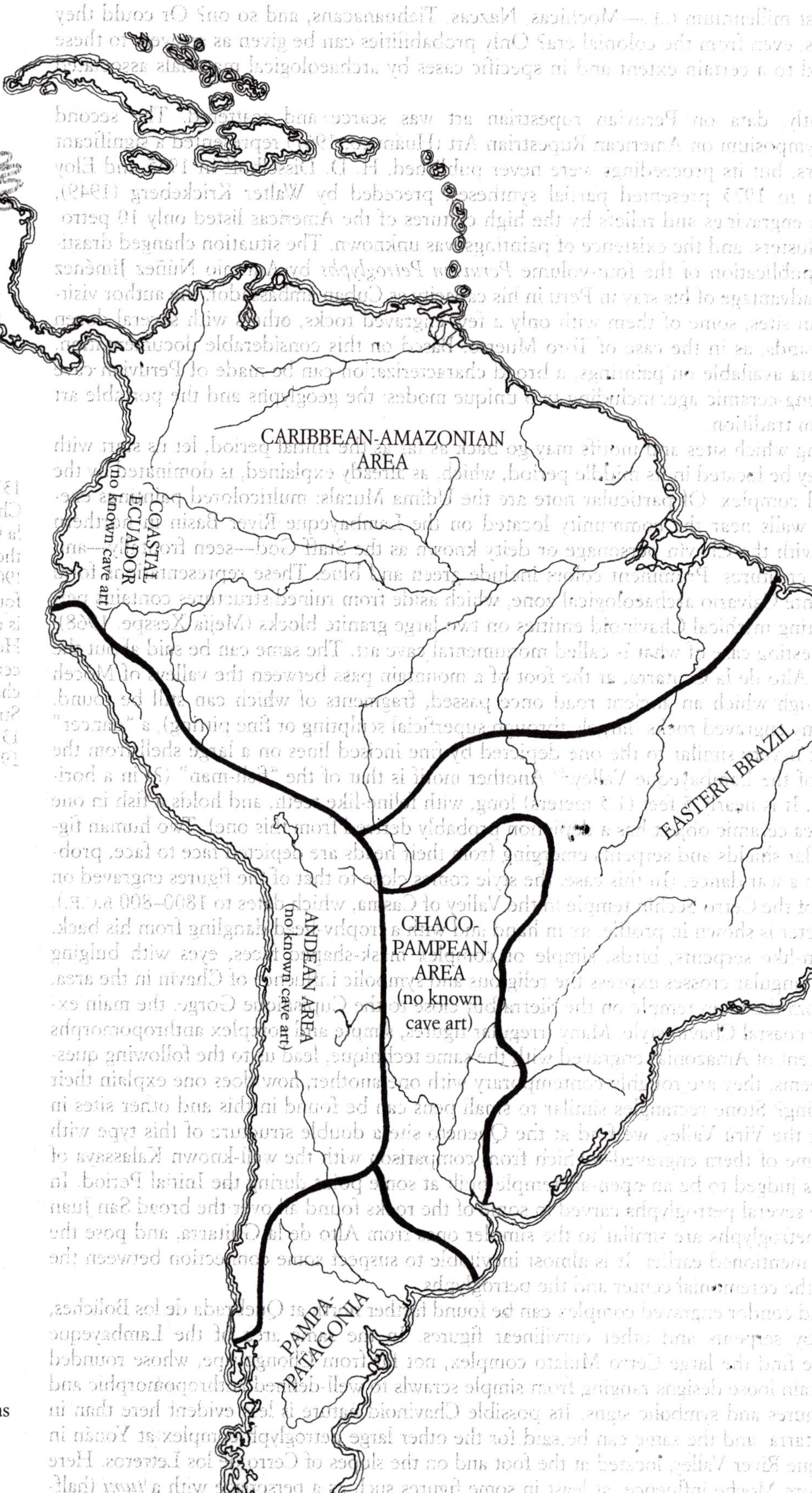

CARIBBEAN-AMAZONIAN
AREA

COASTAL
ECUADOR
(no known cave art)

EASTERN BRAZIL

ANDEAN AREA
(no known cave art)

CHACO-
PAMPEAN
AREA
(no known
cave art)

PAMPA-
PATAGONIA

TIERRA DEL FUEGO
(no known cave art)

138. Map showing the main areas of cave art in South America. Probably due to a lack of systematic research, there is no known cave art in the Andean area and in coastal Ecuador, and the Chaco-Pampean plains lack the necessary rock base for cave art. The Caribbean-Amazonian area is closely linked to Central America.

Victor Pimentel (1986) has surveyed other sites along the lower and middle course of the Jequetepeque, in which the Chavinoid influence appears in many figures, particularly a feline which occupies nearly the entire usable face of a large boulder, and whose form suggests the murals appearing on the walls of some buildings probably used as temples. Another notable figure is that of a single-eyed character with an enormous flower emerging from his chest (a hallucinogenic plant?). Motifs such as this one can also be found on Chavín's Tello Obelisk.

A grotto or rock shelter located on the Zaña River (the El Palmo site) presents petroglyphs of a style different from the others. A number of concentric rectangles with diagonals in their centers, and a schematic feline seen frontally, were executed using very clear lines. These are accompanied by smaller geometric figures, concentric circles, and a spiral. This set forms a wide panel approximately 3 feet (1 meter) tall, and has a certain northern Amazonian or Caribbean flavor, including some rather ghostly faces. An eagle with outstretched wings presides over the upper part of the grotto's entrance. A faded feline figure establishes a connection with the Chavín culture. The stylistic variety suggests that the cave was employed for a long time as a site for ceremonies, possibly initiatory ones.

We cannot leave the northern Peruvian sector without mentioning the natural sanctuary of Cumbemayo. Within a space located at the foot of some towering crags are a complicated cluster of abstract engravings with large crosses, snake-like figures, circles linked by straight lines, and squares with inner parallel lines. There are also irregular incisions on the rocky floor itself. The site is located in the high sierras near the city of Cjamarca, and the famous Cumbemayo aqueduct, 22 inches (55 centimeters) wide and sculpted in stone, passes by at a distance of 650 feet (200 meters). Its walls also hold rather irregular petroglyphs. Some of the superimposed cruciform figures, clearly Christian, show the passage of "eradicators of idolatry" in the sixteenth century.

Heading southward and across the Santa River, another large set of petroglyphs can be found within the city of Timbale. Here are both irregular and simplified figures (such as a three-fingered "lizard-man" or "frog-man"), along with other more culturally defined ones. They include one character with a semicircular, Chimu style headdress, and another which remarkably resembles the Main Chavín Deity, as it is known, with its classic features of snake-like hair, feline fangs, and eyes with bulging pupils (Núñez Jiménez, p. 531).

Pages could be filled with descriptions of petroglyph sites in the central-western and southern parts of Peru, which, despite their enormous variety, bear a certain family resemblance. One worth highlighting, however, is Huaricanga, whose interest lies in both its connection to rocks with circular holes and channels, and its immediate proximity to a small rectangular temple. The center of this temple contains a monument whose surfaces are carved with linear motifs. These petroglyphs form irregular curvilinear sets. A great rocky outcropping in Lachay features abstract engravings, paintings, and an inscribed eagle bearing traces of red paint. In Checta on the Chillón River Valley are a huge set of rocks scattered on a foothill. These feature largely irregular figures, some of them intricate and maze-like, along with simple mask-shaped faces, framed

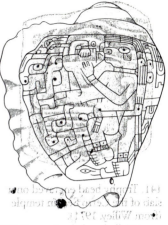

139. Large *Strombus* shell (10 inches, or 25 centimeters, long) depicting a dancer holding a trumpet probably made from the same material as this object. Its style resembles that of Cerro Sechín, but it is surrounded by Chavín-type, snake-like figures (from Willey, 1971).

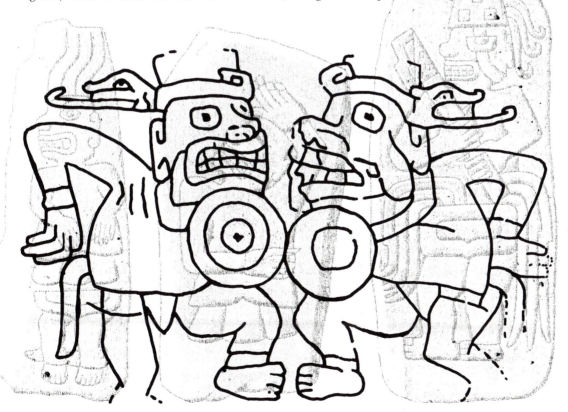

140. Two characters engaged in an energetic war dance. Height: 20 inches (70 centimeters). This group stands out among the numerous petroglyphs located in Alto de la Guitarra for its stylistic details similar to those of Cerro Sechín and Chavín (redrawn after Kauffmann Doig, 1983).

141. Trophy head engraved on a slab of the Cerro Sechín temple (from Willey, 1971).

crosses (which began to appear in Yonán), and suns. These designs are accompanied by small schematic anthropomorphs and zoomorphs, foreshadowing something that will occur with frequency in the Southern Andean Region. Although some schematic felines are visible the Chavinoid influence is no longer present. There is also a rock with a horizontal face covered in small holes.[30]

Akin to the panels over the large rocks of Cohineros, we begin to see farther south the increasing importance of motifs of an Amazonian style, with concentric circles, dotted suns, spirals and serpent shapes, the little three-fingered man, and other small human-like figures arranged in a jumbled fashion. There are *tumis* (half-moon-shaped knives) and a bird that reminds one of the textile motifs of the late Chancay culture, but this could have been of later origin. The southern Andean motif of a man holding or pulling an animal (llama) by a rope also begins to appear. Fantastic and irregular designs appear on the San Miguel de Yangastambo (Cañete Valley) petroglyphs, located around a great rocky outcropping. All engravings appear on the tilted face of a great boulder and may be representations of shamanic experiences. (Similar motifs, possibly inspired by hallucinogenic plants, are engraved at Huari, the great pre-Inca city of the Central Coast.) At Cuchihuayco, in the Department of Ayacucho, a site located at an elevation of some 9,200 feet (2,800 meters) displays the classic Altiplano motif of herds of schematic camelids.

On the San Juan River, parallel to the Chincha River, we find one of the most extensive sets of cave art in the Andean area, appearing in two segments: Huancor to the north, and Caruya Alta to the south. Among the thousands of drawings on the large boulders at both sites are headdress-wearing characters holding trophy heads, others wielding staffs or atlatls (throwing boards), vertical, wave-like serpents, small male figures smoking large pipes,[31] and men with one arm upraised in a probable dancing position. There are also characters wearing complex horseshoe-shaped headdresses in the Paracas style, anthropomorphs and zoomorphs of a probably mythical nature, radial and pointed wheels, suns, crosses, and many other schematic or undefinable figures. A boulder over 13 feet (4 meters) long holds perhaps Huancor's most notable engraved figure: its upper surface consists of a varied cluster of engravings with complex symbolism. One end features a rectangular head with a tiger-like mouth, comparable to the Chavinoid representations of the first phases of Ocucaje (Ica Valley), which gave rise to the cultural tradition known as Paracas (circa 700–100 B.C.E.). The Caruya Alta group, located two-thirds of a mile (1 kilometer) across the San Juan River, is smaller and has relatively simple figures. Upriver are smaller groups depict-

142. Some of the stones with engravings or bas-reliefs that formed part of the outer walls of the Cerro Sechín temple (after Willey, 1971).

ing camelids. Farther south, the Palpa River Valley has tiger-faced characters different from those of the Chavín Style, with Paracas-Nazca affinities. The last important site before reaching the southern edge is La Cabañita, also in the Palpa Valley, featuring anthropomorphs with radiant headdresses, very stylized jaguars, serpents, and more. There is also a lesser group of petroglyphs on the other side of the river.

Beyond lies a desert area crossed by a few rivers. One is the Majes River, in whose vicinity are several groups of petroglyphs. The volcanic rocks of Sarcas feature varied sets which, like those in the nearby Pitis site (where zoomorphs predominate), foreshadow Peru's largest site, known as Toro Muerto. At an elevation of 1,800 feet (550 meters), a wide sandy desert valley opens laterally to the Majes River, filled with medium-sized and large volcanic boulders—nearly all of them featuring engravings by pre-Conquest peoples.[32]

A short characterization of the deposit is provided by its discoverer, Eloy Linares Málaga: "Engraving techniques: pounding, rubbing, scratching, and splintering. Associated remains: Huari Pottery (Expansive Tiahuanacan) in the pre-Columbian cemetery at Toro Grande and fragments of the same style throughout the entire Toro Muerto area; also some fragments of Chiquibamba and Inca pottery. Varied motifs: zoomorphs (birds, mammals, reptiles, fish, frogs); anthropomorphs (dancers, realistic and semirealistic figures, masks); plant-shaped figures (trees, branches, flowers); geometric shapes (dots, lines, circles, zigzags); symbolic figures, mythical figures, and other irregular or incomplete ones. Extension and quantity: surveyor H. Lazo found 0.22 square miles (0.57 square kilometers); maximum length: 12,716 feet (3,876 meters); maximum width: 900 feet (275 meters); approximate total amount of stone engravings: 5,000 individual blocks with figures." (Linares Málaga, 1975, p. 96.) A typical element of Toro Muerto are the dancers with contorted bodies and three lines on the head, surrounded by straight and broken lines (which also appear independently). Other blocks present shamanic dances in states of ecstasy or trance. Symbolic motifs are scarce. We also find here, as well as in Sarcas, some "stoneglyphs," not very large geoglyphs formed by alignments of large, round stones or dark, loose stones.

From Carbon-14 testing, a date of 800 to 1000 C.E. is attributed both to the majority of the Toro Muerto engravings and to those of the neighboring Toro Grande site. This represents a local style, with a rather weak Tiahuanacan influence. It may largely correspond to the Chuquibamba culture (somewhat later than the former), as Antonio Núñez Jiménez believes.

In the next gorge, which corresponds to the Sihuas River, there are several sites featuring petroglyphs located on high cliff walls. There are zoomorphs similar to those at Toro Muerto. Foremost is a deep engraved figure with a radiant headdress, reminiscent of the elaborate anthropomorphs of the Guyanas, but resembling the works of more southerly regions. The Caplina Valley (Tacna area) and its lateral gorges contain petroglyphs of camelids and simple anthropomorphs, often armed, who along with masked figures can be found in a jumbled combination on a boulder of the Challatita site.

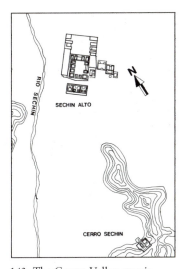

143. The Casma Valley area in which we find two important early ceremonial centers (1800–800 B.C.E.) of Sechín Alto and Cerro Sechín. The more northern structure is 1,000 feet (300 meters) long and rests on an artificial terrace 144 feet (44 meters) tall. Sechín Alto is considered today the oldest temple monument complex in the Americas (predating the great artificial terrace of San Lorenzo, ascribed to Mexico's Olmec Culture, by 150 years). Cerro Sechín contains the oldest works of monumental stone art: the warrior-priests, the trophy heads, and mutilated characters, which were engraved upon the outer walls (redrawn after Kauffmann Doig, 1983).

144. A scene—probably mythical—engraved on an almost vertical rock in Yonán. Panel width: 5 feet (1.5 meters) (redrawn from Núñez Jiménez, 1986).

As noted, a certain link exists between the petroglyph sets and ancient roads along the valleys which later cross the mountains. To the llama caravans that formed part of the exchange networks here and in northern Chile, these sites could have represented a means of contacting the spirits or divinities.

For Peru's upper Andean reaches, the documentation on cave art is much scarcer. It is hard to believe that this practice diminished following the artist-hunter period, so one has to think in terms of unstudied or unreported locations. One of the areas researched is that of Lauricocha, which, as already noted, had two preceramic stylistic phases. Augusto Cardich (1964) distinguishes four other phases: 1) Engravings with naturalized schematic motifs (human figures, felines and serpents, some of them with human-like heads), tentatively placed about 1000 B.C.E.; 2) Similar depictions, painted in red; 3) Painted geometric drawings (laddered and towered, triangular, etc.) and quadrangular human faces; 4) Somewhat crude and irregular drawings obtained by pitting (unlike the first group, which was obtained by scratching), with an abundance of curvilinear motifs. There is no resemblance whatsoever to the petroglyphs of the coastal region, and the presence of this style in a late period of Peru's mountainous interior is mysterious.

Other sites located in the upper Marañón River Valley at 12,470 to 13,450 feet (3,800 to 4,100 meters) of elevation possess red and black paintings on rock walls and shelters with anthropomorphic motifs—including the "praying figure"—and zoomorphs that form clusters or small scenes, alternating with curvilinear and mask-shaped motifs. Despite their proximity to the great religious center of Chavín, there are no evident influences of this artistic style, leading to the possibility that they predate the Chavín culture. Another group of paintings can be found on the cliff walls bordering the Higueras River Valley as it meets the Huallanga, near the city of Huánuco. Here, the anthropomorphs rub shoulders with abstract figures featuring motifs with clearly mythological symbolism, such as an idealized bird surrounded by dots, and a band with internal points almost 28 inches (70 centimeters) in diameter arranged horizontally. There is also a figure with a radiated head at this location, which is known as Quilla-Rumi, situated somewhat farther upstream. It is possible that both sites share a relationship with the nearby temple complex of Kotosh which, as noted in Chapter IV, had several phases of construction. Almost all of the preserved paintings are in red. They have been surveyed by means of tracing by teams directed by Javier Pulgar Vidal (1962), as have a group of paintings on Lomas de Lachay, 56 miles (90 kilometers) northwest of Lima. Simple abstract motifs exist here as well as curiously shaped ones. According to Pulgar Vidal, "it is the only center among the ones we have studied which presents multicolored pictograms in its semi-caverns and rocky places. The colors employed are the following: red, yellow, green, blue, white, and black." (Op. cit., p. 12.)

145. Petroglyph from Cerro Mulato in Peru's northern coastal region near Chongonyape. A curious anthropomorph 35 inches (90 centimeters) long (from A. Núñez Jiménez, 1986).

146. Central component of a wide, petroglyph-bearing panel at the bottom of a rock shelter in El Palmo (Río Zaña Valley, Department of Cajamarca). Circles, spirals, and concentric squares with inner crosses are in abundance (symbolizing the four-part cosmos). The 12-inch-wide (30 centimeters) feline head suggests Chavinoid influences (photo by A. Núñez Jiménez).

In the Apurimac Department (central southern sierra), Rainer Hostnig has revealed the existence of paintings in the *puna* environment, among them Llamayoc (schematic camelids in red and white) and Pintasca (elevation: 12,960 feet, or 3,950 meters), "a cliff wall with a pictorial panel measuring 46 feet (14 meters) long and 6.5 feet (2 meters) tall. Schematic drawings (camel-hunting scenes, dancers) [are] partially superimposed on a naturalist figure of a gigantic camelid entering a semicircle. Red in color, it is a highly aesthetic scene. Sizes range between 4 and 8 inches (10 and 20 centimeters) (schematic drawings) and 7.9 by 4.6 feet (2.4 by 1.4 meters) (naturalistic camelid). These represent the most important cave paintings within the Department." (Hostnig, 1990, pp. 49–50.) The oldest figure could be attributed to Preceramic hunters. Some of the region's sites, such as Pulpitocassa, with its entrapped animals (see Chapter III), could date back 6,000 years or more, while others could be ascribed to preceramic herders, and still others could be more recent. There is no way of differentiating them with any certainty.

In the middle of the Cuzco region at Mantoc, in the valley of Lares, is a similar case: a series of schematic quadrupeds faced by a man, surrounding a subdivided rectangle (Pardo, 1942, pp. 15, 16). We find similar engraved scenes on the wall of a cave in Ichucollo on the plateau surrounding Lake Titicaca. Here, the small figures appear to be driving rows of camelids—probably a caravan, which must have been a frequent sight along the trail linking the lake in question to the Pacific coast—but there are also archers in hunting stances. There is also a schematic feline engraved in superimposition, whose age can be set at some 2,000 years if it is considered a folkloric reflection of the Andean Early Horizon period (Hyslop, 1987).

H. D. Disselhoff has examined some of the portable art of the rupestrian tradition in this region:

> In the archaeological sites of the Arequipa Department, particularly in the basins of the Majes and Sihuas rivers, we often find pebbles with geometric designs eroded by the water. Up to now, the associations of these painted stones had never been described. Large quantities of thick pots that had been painted after firing—and after they were shattered—were found near Chuquibamaba in a cave full of skulls and human skeletons. They apparently belong to the same cultural complex as the stones. In 1965 we had the fortune of finding painted pebbles within a cemetery with 135 mummies outfitted in proto-Nazca style textiles. This cemetery is near Camaná, on the coast. The Institut für Bodenforschung in Hanover, Germany, has supplied Carbon-14 dates for the funeral bundles, which, on average, date back to 135 C.E. The painted stones of Camaná were packed in Achira leaves (*Canna edulis*). The meaning of these packed stones is uncertain. Two bundles of paintbrushes with cane handles, equipped with cotton brushes still preserving traces of red paint, were found beside the stones. The colors used are primarily red, then ocher and

147. Cerro Mulato. A variety of figures, each on a different rock. Various scales. The central petroglyph is 24 inches (60 centimeters) tall and represents a person who has carried out a sacrifice and is holding a trophy head in his hand (from A. Núñez Jiménez, 1986).

148. The engraved Cochineros rocks, with their numerous and varied motifs, are located in the Mala River Valley at 2,300 feet (700 meters) above sea level in the province of Cañete.

white, with green employed very seldom. Geometric designs are predominant. The largest of the Camaná stones (6.7 inches (17 centimeters) long) shows a potentially religious scene with six human beings. (Disselhoff, 1968, p. 80.)

These are reminiscent of some of the figures engraved in Toro Muerto. There is also a cave in Kupará which constitutes a vast repository for this type of piece, particularly paintings on shingles or large fragments of pottery with flattened borders.

Eloy Linares Málaga (1975, 1988) has emphasized the importance of these manifestations, which are largely attributed to the funeral rites of late pre-Incan cultures. They are also attributed to the early Nazca culture, based on the previously noted discovery of the cemetery of "Flattened Heads" (so named for the deliberate cranial deformation witnessed in the mummies). An ancient local antecedent is also indicated among the discoveries of shingles with paintings of camelids in the Toquepala cave (see Chapter III). There also exists a parallel with the engraved stones of Ica, somewhat northwest of the area in question. They appear to have been funeral offerings, with at least three archaeologically documented cases being known: a kind of eight-pointed rosette from a late Paracas tomb from approximately 100 B.C.E., and a schematic llama and bird from the Ica Culture's tombs, circa 1200 C.E. (Pezzia, 1968). Dark-colored pebbles were chosen for this work, and the drawings were done through fine incisions.[33]

As for geoglyphs located on the valleys of the Santa, Pisco, and Cañete in the south, and particularly in the Pampa de Nazca, they represent a monumental variation on the cave art style. The lines of the long rectilinear designs often intersect. Large biomorphic motifs (between 100 and 330 feet (30 and 100 meters) or larger) were formed by removing the dark, oxidized stones which covered the plateau thereby making designs with the lighter, non-oxidized stones beneath. Aside from a variety of birds, Pampa de Nazca features a spider, a fish (similar to the one represented on a ceramic object of this culture, circa 100–800 C.E.) and a monkey with a long tail coiled in a broad spiral. There are also open spirals and other geometric figures. Large human figures on nearby slopes could be dated back to the Paracas culture. Numerous investigators have taken over the surveying and interpretation of these geoglyphs (above all María Reiche, 1968). Some type of celestial or astronomical relationship has been proposed—always in a ritual context—but doubts persist. This is one of the many mysteries of American archaeology. The only thing that is certain appears to be the dating: a careful study of ceramic fragments associated with some of the lines indicates that most date to the Nazca period. Some may date to the earlier Paracas culture, and some appear to have been reworked during the Late Intermediate Period (1100–1450 C.E.) (Silverman and Browne, 1991).

Bolivia

The Andean region of Bolivia (Altiplano and encircling valleys) has a rich and varied store of rupestrian art, which has only been subjected to systematic study in recent years. Unlike Peru, there is a balance between paintings and petroglyphs. In both cases, however, the styles are varied, ranging from schematic naturalism to a geometric approach. Another difference from Peru is the absence of

149. Two plumed dancers (?) with peculiar stylization from the vast petroglyph field of Toro Muerto (Majes River Valley, southern Peru). Height: 16 inches (40 centimeters) (redrawn from A. Núñez-Jiménez, 1986).

150. Deep engraving of a probable deity on the rock walls bordering the Sihuas River. Quillcapampa la Nueva site (Arequipa region) (photograph: A. Núñez Jiménez).

geoglyphs and portable art from a rupestrian tradition, and its persistence into Colonial times and even after Independence.[34]

While we still lack a chronology of Bolivian rupestrian art, there is no doubt that it largely corresponds to the local agricultural and ceramic cultures that emerged from the formative phases of Chiripa and Huancarani cultures (circa 1300 B.C.E.–200 C.E.). Curiously, the culture of classical and expanding Tiahauanco (circa 200–1000 C.E.) has not left any further marks on rupestrian art. On the contrary, the geometric and serpent-like petroglyphs appear on the fallen blocks of the Pumapunku architectural sector of these ruins, and therefore lack any cultural ties to Tiahuanaco's flourishing. Was it a way of celebrating the memory of this civilization, or an effort to avert the possible evil influences of the ruins of a site abandoned by the gods?

From an advanced phase of the Chiripa culture there are several stelae—inscribed stone slabs or pillars—carved in bas-relief. In some cases these were executed on natural blocks, for which reason they can be considered examples of monumental rupestrian art. Interesting examples can be found in those described by Max Portugal Ortíz (1989) involving blocks located in the surroundings of Santiago de Huata, on a peninsula of Lake Titicaca, whose geometric figures in red and white represent a very different style, possibly a late one. Aside from small figures with outstretched arms, a series of cruciform, or cross-shaped, figures with bladed ends draws one's attention.

In the southern area certain sites stand out, such as the rocky Palacios shelter in the Omereque zone in the department of Cochabamba. Here are found geometric red paintings (dotted ones and circles), zoomorphs (deer and winged serpents), rock walls featuring negative-printed images of cruciform figures and zoomorphs (the only occurrence of this technique in Bolivia). Particularly interesting is the case of a piece of a chewed coca leaf stuck to a sector of the paintings. This suggests that the site "continues to be employed as a ceremonial, ritual site, where people walking along nearby make an offering of chewed coca, mud, and stones" (Querejazu, 1984–1985, p. 241, 1987). Chewed coca had also been left on a rock as an offering in Lakatambo—a request for rain?[35] Some 16 feet (5 meters) up a rock wall in a shelter at Aguada-Pasorapa is a large, painted mask with numerous lines radiating from it, as well some partially superimposed quadrupeds.

Other sites deserve mention as well. In El Buey (Saipina), on the Mizque River's boundary with Santa Cruz province, is a large rock shelter with several painted figures in different colors. These mostly show a strong geometric tendency toward lines and pointed forms. There are sectioned human figures and a curious vertical serpent with a segmented body. In the neighboring Santa Cruz area there is El Mataral, a cave painted red and white with remarkable mask-shaped figures, stylized birds, monkeys, felines, and geometric figures. Another important site is Toro Muerto, a cave over a rocky promontory linked to a farmer-potter deposit. The cave has irregular curved lines—some showing vestiges of paint—engraved all over its inner walls. (This site was mentioned in Chapter II when I rejected the notion that it was from the Ice Age.) At the Peña Escrita site at El Túnel (western Santa Cruz) it seems possible to detect an Amazonian influence in the numerous "lizard-men" figures with three digits on both extremities. In Oruro, depictions have been found of engraved and painted camelids at Kalakala and Poopó, where there are also spirals, circles, suns, and human figures. At Potosí, in the Betanzos area, there are two important sites: Inca-Cueva (Inkakaka), with multicolored paintings of simple geometric motifs and human and animal figures; and Lajasmayu, two large rock walls in shelters with a variety of multicolored paintings. Two large human figures (about 20 inches (50 centimeters) tall) stand out among the others, wrapped in tunics with quadrangular decorations. These figures have wide heads with a single eye. Another group includes hunting scenes and small quadrupeds approaching a figure bearing a crisscross pattern. Next to this are depictions of human figures with bodies made of two triangles; they are holding hands. One is very visible, while the other two have had geometric depictions (made up of several rectangular figures) superimposed upon them. At this site were found two and perhaps three stylistic and chronological periods (Strecker, 1986). A little farther north is Tanga-Tanga, which also contains petroglyphs. One of these is a large personage with a round body, and simple mask-like faces or heads endowed with triple antennae. Toward the south is a series of sites containing paintings and engravings around Tupiza, and farther west, near the headwaters of the Grande de Lípez River in the Puna uplands, are some painted sites attributed to the Mallku domain and culture (circa 900–1450 C.E.). "The pictographs appear in caves and shelters and consist of human and animal images with headdresses and facial decorations in different shades of red. Dotted lines and meandering designs form different images and make up scenes that are difficult to interpret; in all probability they are linked to little-known aspects of the Mallku's religious beliefs" (Berberian and Raffino, 1991, p. 145).

Chuquisaca province is rich in cave art. This is where the Huerta-Mayu (Mojocoya) cave is located, with its negative and positive handprints. Several other shelters with geometric, human, and animal figures are found in the surrounding areas. With the evocative name of Supayhuasi ("House of the Devil"), another shelter shows curious stylized animal and human figures in cherry-red with a

151. Red cave painting in the Diablomachay Cave, Lauricocha area, in the central Peruvian region. It represents a schematic feline about 5 inches (12 centimeters) tall (from Cardich, 1964).

152. Red cave painting from the Quilla Rumi rock shelter (Huánuco area, central Peruvian Sierra). A bird (parrot or raptor) appears within a 28-inch (70-centimeter) circle surrounded by dots. A cosmic bird? (after Ravines).

153. Archer with headdress, kneeling. Height: 8 inches (20 centimeters). One of the motifs of the Ichucollo petroglyphs (redrawn from J. Hyslop).

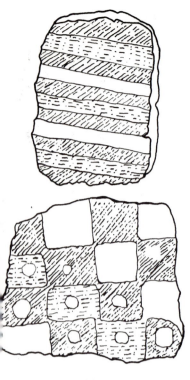

154. Pieces of flat stone, painted red and yellow in a style similar to others found in southern Peru from the late pre-Incan period (approximately 1000–1450 C.E.). From the Toquepala Cave (after Linares Malaga, 1988).

white outline. In some sites, like Kakapintaska, one finds figures outlined within a patterned border. This is known as the "bordered style." In other sites, like Patatoloyo, there is a preponderance of stylized human figures in a praying or dancing position, next to cartouches with straight-lined decorations, in red and white. In Tarija are a series of sites along the eastern border of the Altiplano. Some of these contain petroglyphs on large blocks, while others have paintings in different colors, like the shelter at Cabildo in Padcaya. This shelter contains mask-shaped human figures, geometric designs (circles, triangles, wavy lines with dots) and animals dubiously identified as foxes and lizards. The petroglyphs at Rinconada de la Victoria stand out, with their curiously stylized animals and irregular geometric figures, including the double S-shaped spiral. In certain other places is a motif typical of the Puna—the llama caravan, a stylized depiction of six llamas used as beasts of burden, led by a man.

Two other important sites containing petroglyphs in southern Bolivia have recently been examined. One is Angostura de Sococha, northeast of Villazón, an impressive multicolored rock wall presided over by a large circular figure of probable cosmic symbolism (A. Fernández Distel, 1994). The other is in the valley of Cinti near Camargo, where colorful, mainly abstract designs cover the rocks that have fallen away from a high sandstone outcropping (Rivera and Michel López, 1995).

In contrast to these two Bolivian writers, I do not include as cave art the large, geometrically engraved groups on rocky surfaces, such as the so-called Fuerte de Samaipata in Santa Cruz, or Intikala in Copacabana. (The latter are from the Inca period, and their prototype may be found at ceremonial sites at Kenko in the Cuzco complex.) There are very few data referring to channels and pits in the rock that are linked to petroglyphs, but some do exist at Lakatambo, and are used in modern times to hold offerings. Achocalla is a special site in the valley next to the city of La Paz, at an altitude of 12,100 feet (3,700 meters). The group was discovered by Matthias Strecker in 1983 and was later studied by Maria Heredia and Claudia Rivera (1991). On one of the rocks scattered over one section of the valley is a double-faced petroglyph 6.5 feet (2 meters) long. The rest consist of large- or medium-sized pits spaced in isolation or in rows (this occurs on the vertical faces of the

155. *Top:* "The Engraved Stones of Ica"—the only three which can be considered genuine (reduced to approximately half their actual size). *Top left:* A finely outlined rosette, found in association with a funeral bundle of the Paracas culture (circa 500 B.C.E.–0) at Hacienda Ocucaje in the valley of Ica. *Top center:* A stone with an engraved fish, associated with a skeleton found together with ceramics classified as Ica-Epigonal (circa 1300–1450 C.E.) at Hacienda Toma Luz, valley of Ica. *Top right:* A stone with a stylized llama found in an Ica Culture tomb with the remains of two individuals and pottery (redrawn from Pezzia Assereto, 1967). *Middle and bottom:* Some of the better-known motifs of the great geoglyphs of Pampa de Nazca (circa 100–700 C.E.) (from Maria Reiche).

53. Samanga (Peru). Site with
Chavín-style cave engravings
discovered by an Italian
archaeological mission from the
Centro Studi Ligabue
(photograph: M. Polia).

Following pages:
54. Samanga. Abstract
engravings on a rock from a
large cave group (photograph:
M. Polia).
55. Chongoyape (Peru).
Petroglyphs possibly
representing vulvas
(photograph: G. Orefici).

56. *Callapuma (Peru). Paintings of human figures (photograph: G. Orefici).*
57. *Facing page: El Faical (Peru). Abstract paintings in red (photograph: V. Domenici).*

58. *Following page: Yonán (Peru). Large rock with abstract petroglyphs (photograph: G. Orefici).*

59. Above: *La Pitaya (Peru). Faces,
arrows, and other engraved motifs*
(photograph: G. Orefici).
60. Right: *Quilla Rumi, Huánuco*
(Peru). Bird within a circular motif
(photograph: G. Orefici).

61., 62. Chungal, Quebrada del Felino (Peru). General view of the area and feline engraved on a rock (photograph: G. Orefici).

*63. Checta (Peru). Mask-
shaped petroglyph with
headdress (photograph: G.
Orefici).*

64. Above: *Checta (Peru).*
Intensely carved abstract
petroglyph (photograph: G.
Orefici).

Following pages:
65., 66. *Chichitara (Peru).*
Large double-headed serpent
and a quadruped (a fox?)
(photograph: G. Orefici).

67. Chichitara (Peru). Rock with engraved anthropomorphic figures (photograph: G. Orefici).
Facing page:
68., 69. Toro Muerto (Peru). Rocks engraved with a large group of cave art. Note the characteristic dancers (photographs: D. Domenici).

70. Above: *Toro Muerto (Peru).
Superimposition of a human figure (?)
over older animal figures
(photograph: D. Domenici).*

71. Right: *Abstract engravings on a
large rock face (Bolivia)
(photograph: V. Domenici.)*

72. *Jukumari (Bolivia). Abstract multicolored paintings discovered by an archaeological mission from the Centro Studi Ligabue (photograph: V. Domenici).*

73. *Toro Muerto (Bolivia).*
Jumbled group of abstract
engravings (photograph: J.
Schobinger).

First page following:
74., 75. *Atacama Desert (Chile).*
Engravings of human figures,
camelids, and other animals
(photographs: V. Domenici).
Second page following:
76., 77. *Santa Barbara (Chile).*
Petroglyphs with animal and
abstract motifs (photographs: V.
Domenici).

Second previous page:
78. Tucumán Province (Argentina). A monolith from the Tafí culture (300 B.C.E.–800 C.E.). This is one of the oldest monoliths from the farming-ceramic period of northwest Argentina (photograph: J. Schobinger).
Previous page:
79. Famatina, La Rioja province (Argentina). Top part of an anthropomorphic monolith. This monolith was found near two others (photograph: J. Schobinger).

80. Above: Quebrada de Aguas Blancas (Argentina). Rock with human figures (photograph: J. Schobinger).

81. *La Tunita (Argentina). One of
the characteristic dancers attributed
to the La Aguada culture. This one
is holding darts and an atlatl
(photograph: J. Schobinger).*

82. Above: *Tunduqueral
(Argentina). Mask-shaped head
(photograph: J. Schobinger).*

83. Top right: *Quebrada del
Leoncito, San Juan (Argentina).
Rock wall covered in engravings
depicting variations of the mask-
shaped head (photograph: J.
Schobinger).*

84. Bottom right: *Valle Hermoso,
Mendoza (Argentina). Large rock
formation covered in abstract
petroglyphs (photograph: J.
Schobinger).*

85. Above: *Agua Botada, Mendoza (Argentina). Group of abstract petroglyphs (photograph: J. Schobinger).*

86. Right: *Rincón Amarillo, Mendoza (Argentina). Multicolored panel with a cross-shaped and stepped group (photograph: J. Schobinger).*

87., 88. Pedra de Ingá (Brazil). Detail and general view of the engravings. These petroglyphs, known as itacoatiaras, are usually found near water (photographs: J. Schobinger).

*89. Paraiba (Brazil). Abstract
petroglyph near an old carnivorous
dinosaur print (photograph: V.
Domenici).*

two rocks) distributed in five groups somewhat distanced between each other. There are also channels that sometimes run from the pits toward the earth, which suggests that they were used for libations—such as a drinking ceremony or the pouring of a liquid as a sacrifice to a deity. Although they were sometimes reused for other purposes, these sites probably had ritual functions in farming cultures. During the period of conquest, missionaries engraved Christian crosses on some of these rocks.

Northern and Central Chile

Along the valleys that descend from the Andean Cordillera toward the Pacific are several rocks, rock walls, and shelters with engravings and cave paintings. These extend from the Lluta River in Arica to the Aconcagua River in central Chile. Also, from the extreme north to Quillagua in the lower reaches of the Loa River are several groups of geoglyphs which form a continuation of those in southern Peru, although they posses somewhat different characteristics. The group constitutes an excellent and varied sample of Andean art, attributable to local farming-ceramic cultures ranging from 1000 B.C.E. in Arica through 200 B.C.E. in the Central region to the Spanish conquest in the fifteenth century. However, cave art motifs seldom coincide here with those of portable art or ceramics.[36]

Going from north to south, one comes across a first subarea of cave art between the Peruvian border and the San Pedro de Atacama region, at the level of the Tropic of Capricorn. As well as petroglyphs with more or less schematic life forms there are cup-like forms that encompass the whole horizontal or inclined face of some blocks, like the group associated with the prehistoric cemetery at Sobraya in the Azapa Valley. In Ausípar—the middle-upper region of this valley—is an exceptional scenic group engraved on the inclined face of a large rock: a series of archers facing each other, surrounded by camelids. This scene has been interpreted as a battle between two groups to settle a conflict over the possession of the camelids (Mostny and Niemeyer, 1983, p. 25).

The Camarones gorge, investigated by Niemeyer and Schiappacasse (1981), presents two great conglomerations of petroglyphs: Huancarane in the middle part of the valley near archaeological deposits from the late local period, and Taltape in the easternmost part. A hammering technique has been used in the majority of cases, and the motifs are disorganized, with snaking, irregular lines next to suns, and anthropomorphic figures with bows and arrows linked to groups of stylized camelids. There are also several sites containing petroglyphs along the Camiña and Aroma gorges, and another extensive and important site at the Tarapacá gorge. This has two principal concentrations: Tarapacá 47, at an elevation of 4,760 feet (1,450 meters), and Parcollo at 8,200 feet (2,500 meters), in the foothills of the Altiplano area. Following a detailed comparative study, Lautaro Núñez (1965) concludes that both sites represent different functions. At Tarapacá 47, ceremonies must have been represented among the engravings in which shamans or other prestigious individuals participated along with the agricultural communities. These ceremonies are believed to have focused on the worship of animals, shamanic practices, sacrifices, ritual dances, and events connected to war and to commerce. In Parcollo, engravings of worship by humans duly attired are infrequent, as there was no participation here by a stable community. On the contrary, it would seem that the groups of isolated herders at Parcollo (an important site owing to the existence of an old river) engraved scenes related to their magical and religious beliefs resulting from the domestication, breeding, and protection of their flocks of camelids. For example, they may have sought magical stimuli to increase and protect the flocks, and other scenes with hunting motifs may have served to secure the success of these tasks. (Op. cit., p. 115.)

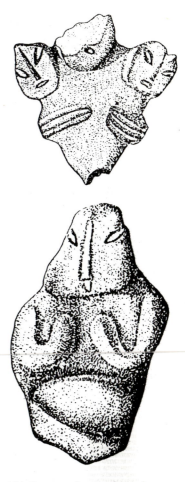

156. Stone sculptures from the Initial period of the central Bolivian region (Cochabamba area) (by Alcina Franch, 1965).

157. Elongated stone block showing motifs engraved in bas-relief, similar to those of the old religious center of Chiripa, Guerra Pata, in the Santiago de Huata region south of Lake Titicaca in Bolivia (by M. Portugal Ortíz, 1989).

158. Abstract, symbolic petroglyphs at Peña Colorada, San Pedro (near Camargo, Chuquisaca province, Bolivia) (photograph: R. Querejazu Lewis).

On the rock walls of one high area of the Aroma gorge is an extensive and remarkable group of petroglyphs at Ariquilda, displaying striking figures of individuals seen from the front bearing weapons and insignia. In the adjacent Pampas or plateaus is an interesting group of geoglyphs that includes large geometric figures. (Both sites are being studied by the Azapa Archaeological Museum in Arica.)

Even more interesting is the Guatacondo gorge, in one of whose great rocky outcroppings near the Tamentica oasis is a large group of lively, carefully wrought, stylistic engravings. Within the scope of its symbolism, which probably derives from shamanic practices, there are also images taken from daily life. The most frequently repeated theme is the condor motif, and for this reason the site is believed to have been a sanctuary dedicated to this majestic Andean bird. It is presented in isolation in a great variety of styles that range from the greatest naturalism to the abstract. A "condor-man" appears, and very frequently one finds depictions in which only the wing of the bird is seen. This is quite frequent among the petroglyphs of the Tarapacá region.

"The most interesting themes at Tamenica, in which men and animals are seen interacting closely together," Grete Mostny and Hans Niemeyer write, "include rafts made from sealskins, crews maneuvering the rafts with poles, and men fishing from rafts, with the fish caught on a hook; men driving camelid herds; men carrying harnessed llamas; rows of musicians; rows of hunchbacks; a pair of dancers; and rows of linked men. The isolated depictions include masked faces; men wearing tunics; lizards; isolated fish; a llama with an elongated neck; a condor wing; a pair of pumas; and figures enclosed in quadrangular forms. A large group of llamas organized in rows could be interpreted as a counting of the flock. The most frequent abstract signs are continuous geometric shapes, spirals, suns, star-shaped forms, zigzagging lines, broken or wavy parallel lines, and crosses." (Mostny and Niemeyer, 1983, pp. 43–45.) What is striking here—so far from the Pacific coast—are the depictions of men fishing from rafts made of inflated seal skins, which continued to be in use in northern Chile until the end of the eighteenth century.

A more direct relationship with the sea is offered by the scenes painted in red on the rock walls in the Médano gorge, which descends from the Cordillera de la Costa to south of the city of Antofagasta. Mostny and Niemeyer have described this site as "an immense sanctuary of art devoted to the protection of good fishing and especially to the hunting of large marine animals and guanacos. Located beyond the reach of both the *camanchaca* (coastal mist) and vegetation, it contains scenes showing the harpooning and hauling away of marine animals (seen in profile with their tails in a vertical plane) from sealskin rafts with one, two, and occasionally three individuals as crew. The species that can be made out include aquatic mammals, especially black dolphins, sperm whales, gray whales, and seals. Swordfish, hammerfish, and tortoises are also distinguishable. The raft and its crew are extraordinarily small compared to the animals. This phenomenon is also observed in other examples from the Médano site, such as the hunting scenes. An archer faces a herd of guanacos descending the sides of the gorge. The man is barely visible next to the large animals. Some of these are shown with arrows piercing their chests." (Mostny and Niemeyer, 1983, pp. 47–48.) These paintings have not been dated, and could be from any period. They are, without doubt, one of the most original groups of cave art in the Americas.

North of Caldera, in a rocky outcropping very close to the sea (Las Lizas site on the Obispo Inlet), is another extensive set of fish-shaped depictions, in this case engraved and showing no links to human beings or fishing scenes. There are also cracks or rubbed linear grooves (Niemeyer, 1985).

Returning to the inland region, one comes to the Atacama Desert and its most important area for cave art: the high reaches of the Loa River. It has already been noted (Chapter III) that the area's first painting and engraving style (Taira-Calina) could be attributed to Preceramic hunters and early farmers. According to research by José Berenguer, C. Aldunate, and V. Castro, they fall under three other stylistic phases: the La Isla phase; petroglyphs showing a high degree of technical control; and a phase of surprisingly conventional symbolism. On rock walls facing east, where the San Pedro volcano looms, the main motif is "a personage in a headdress with appendages sticking out and with crossed canine teeth, holding two pointed objects similar to the ones on his head. At waist level to this figure is a large, double-headed camelid looking in the opposite direction, which stands out clearly through the depth of its engraving." (Berenguer et al., 1985, p. 93.) Smaller camelids surround the figure, variants of which are also found in the La Angostura site, about 2 miles (3 kilometers) north in La Isla. They are somewhat less elaborately drawn here and are accompanied by "demon-like" shapes interpretable as dancing shamans and, at least in two cases, as highly schematic felines (Mostny, 1964). There is a similarity between the double-headed camelid and the deity depicted at the famous Puerta del Sol de Tiahuanaco. This similarity probably stems from a common central Andean root. The double-headed llama (also found in the Argentine Puna) constitutes an invention of the Altiplano-southern Andean area. Parallels have been pointed out with figures painted on wooden tablets in the San Pedro de Atacama region, although here the double-headed animal found at the base is a feline. The ritual

159. Cave paintings in red and white, with anthropomorphic and geometric figures. Patataloyo (Inca Machay, Chuquisaca province, Bolivia) (by M. Strecker, 1987).

nature of this style is confirmed by the existence of stone blocks used as altars. The one at La Angostura "has its upper face covered by a large number of circular grooves, the largest of which are no more than 1.2 inches (3 centimeters) in diameter. They form rows and irregular groups, some of which are interconnected via grooves; two camelid figures are also distinguishable" (Mostny, 1964, p. 59).

At a later period there was another petroglyph style known as the Santa Bárbara style, characterized by rather schematic group scenes, with man and llama as their main theme. These are rectangular-bodied personages with lines and dots inside, which may represent tunics, mantles, or leather overalls, like examples that were uncovered archaeologically. The heads are represented by semicircles with simple plumes. Rows of camelids tethered to each other suggest the caravans that regularly traversed the Andean area to barter all kinds of products since the heyday of Tiahuanaco in the first millennium C.E. Crosses and what may be vulvas sometimes occasionally appear together, as does a hunter carrying an ax and a head. A parallel to this has been pointed out on fire-engraved gourds found in the area (Berenguer, et al., 1985, pp. 97–101). Some shield-shaped forms associated with this style suggest a connection to the Argentine northeast in the Late farming-pottery period (900–1470 C.E.). In general, the high Loa River Valley—a very old commercial, migratory, and pilgrimage route—constitutes one of the most important concentrations of cave art in South America.

A series of three-fingered individuals with a certain supernatural air (associated with faces that as a group are reminiscent of the Amazonian-Venezuelan sites) are engraved on the rock walls of the Salado River, near San Pedro de Atacama. On other blocks there are also some rather irregular circular and animal figures (Niemeyer, 1968). Geometric figures (circles, zigzags, and spirals) have been observed at different points in the area, as well as human footprints and rhea tracks (a rhea is a bird resembling an ostrich), sometimes on horizontal rocks and at other times on shelter walls (Spahni, 1976). As far as we know, these are the northernmost Andean depictions of items in the so-called footprint style. The same author has explored two grottoes located in high areas: at Tulán, decorated with different engravings, and at San Lorenzo, east of Toconao, with its naturalistic multi-colored paintings that include plumed individuals holding hands and apparently dancing, archers, two individuals fighting, and more.

A complement in monument form to the petroglyphs, the geoglyphs that border the Lluta, Azapa, and Tana valleys in the north follow the Cordillera de la Costa south of Iquique (at an altitude of between 1,640 and 4,600 feet, or 500 and 1,400 meters) to the edge of the Pampa de Tamarugal (where these geoglyphs are called *Pintados*, or paintings), and finally come to an end at the southern border of the Guatacondo gorge and the lower Loa River in the Quillagua region. Both techniques (the extraction and accumulation of stones) are found, sometimes in combination. These depictions, generally between 13 and 33 feet (4 and 10 meters), are predominantly found on mountain slopes. They are usually found in grottoes with human and animal figures juxtaposed with llamas (sometimes in rows), stepped rhomboidal shapes, cross-shaped or honeycombed figures, and arrow shapes. According to one detailed description, albeit a very preliminary one referring just to the province of Iquique, there are about 70 sites there, some with only one figure but the majority with numerous ones, such as the Cerro Pintados, which has 420. The Cerro Maní has 346, the Cerro Plomo del Salar de Soronal 628, and the pampas that border the Tarapacá gorge have the exceptional number of 1,021, although some of these are not identifiable.

The authors of this inventory remark that "the people who engraved the petroglyphs were familiar with the climatic and wind conditions of the area in which they lived, and generally took advantage of rocky, high contrast terrain for scraped or extracted figures, and low-contrast, rock-free terrain for figures executed by accumulation or addition. When comparing figures seen from the air with those seen from the ground, intentional deformations are observed showing a familiarity with and mastery of the notion of perspective." (Cerda, Fernández, and Estay, 1985, p. 347.)

From the motifs depicted and the way in which they are represented, the north Chilean geoglyphs are considered to have been executed mostly during the Late Horizon (circa 1000–1450 C.E.). There is at least one site, however, that should be placed before then, as a product of fairly direct Peruvian influence. This is Cerro Unita (or Unitas) at the exit from the Tarapacá gorge, which features an enormous human figure 282 feet (86 meters) long. It has a square head with straight lines radiating from it—a motif also found in one of the Tamentica petroglyphs. The figure holds a long tube, which is likely a pipe, in one hand. Farther up are some straight bands that bring to mind others from southern Peru, but with the addition of animal figures, particularly a schematic feline with pointed spots. This interesting group clearly shows a shamanic underpinning.

Lautaro Núñez (1976) has convincingly described a relationship between the geoglyphs and the caravan traffic in which the llama was employed as a beast of burden—the traditional means for the exchange of products between the Altiplano and the outlying valleys, and the Pacific Coast region. "There was an intense redistribution of surplus goods between the coast and the

160. Scene engraved on a rock wall at Ausípar, in the middle-high reaches of the Azapa valley in northern Chile. It has been interpreted as a confrontation between archers over the possession of the herd of llamas or alpacas (from Mostny and Niemeyer, 1983).

161. This rock showing probable religious symbolism comes from Tamentica, an important region for cave art in the northern Chilean valley of Gatacondo. Also visible are two small fishers in their sealskin rafts. The large anthropomorphic figure probably represents a deity, and it is similar to the Cerro Unitas geoglyph farther north (from Mostny and Niemeyer, 1983).

162. Set of cave art depictions in red from the El Médano gorge in the Taltal region on the northern coast of Chile. It represents the capture and dragging away of marine fauna from sealskin rafts (traditionally used until the nineteenth century). (Drawing by F. Maldonado.)

244

farming and pastoral centers of the uplands. The geoglyphs of northern Chile are part of that culturally dynamic context. Men and herds of llamas managed to successfully transform in their favor their apparent ecological limitations through a long process of specialization in the transportation of materials and spread of ideas. The groups bartered and colonized, but they had to control an extensive universe through old contact routes that even traversed one of the most rigorous deserts in the world. . . . [Although difficult to identify,] there is undoubtedly a symbolic, religious aspect to the pre-Conquest Andean commercial traffic. The ethnological documentation for the region shows that present-day caravans of llamas and human beings hold traditional ceremonies aimed at nurturing the best conditions between the Altiplano groups and those of the lower oases. Until now, journeys between the high valleys and the Altiplano included ritual practices in the *apachetas*, where rocks and coca leaves are deposited. Because of this, we believe that the geoglyphs were sacred places (*pascanas*) where the caravans stopped to spend the night after long trips between different ecosystems. It is likely that through these journeys certain traders responsible for mythical and religious beliefs carved the geoglyphs by traditional routes." (Op. cit., pp. 173–75, 180.)

163. On the walls of the Angostura site (upper Loa River, not far from Taira) is a large group of stylized figurative engravings, of which this is one section. A mythical feline is associated with an individual sitting on a double-headed llama, and beings with rayed heads. It has been interpreted as a shamanic initiation rite, possibly invoking the *Coquena*, the Andean Lord of the Camelids (by Mostny and Niemeyer, 1983).

Passing through an extensive region on which no data are available, cave art resumes south of the river Salado de Atacama, in the Quebrada de las Pinturas, on whose walls some schematic human figures approximately 31 inches (80 centimeters) tall stand out. They show triangular or zigzagging lines on the torsos, lines which must represent symbols of some sort rather than garments. One of them shows both painting and engraving. Continuing onto the high basin of the Copiapó River, there is a striking multicolored figure of a bird with an extended body and long neck. It measures 11.5 feet (3.5 meters) from one end to the other, and gives its name to the site: El Pájaro Verde—the Green Bird. The cultural attribution of both these sites remains unknown.

Beyond the Huasco River is an area with many petroglyphs and very few paintings, which extends to the Aconcagua River Basin. This region is usually known as Norte Chico as far as the Choapa River. Three pre-Inca pottery cultures have been identified here: El Molle, Las Animas, and Coquimbo or Diaguita Chileno. The majority of the most typical examples of cave art, comprise the Limarí style and belong mainly to the first of these three archaeological cultures (circa 0–700 C.E.). The engravings are found on different-sized rocks that usually show a desert patina which, when hammered, allows the light color of the lines to stand out. The fundamental element of this style is the mask-shaped head, whose prototypes are the figures engraved with deep strokes in the Valle El Encanto located southwest of Ovalle, a place with large rocks penetrated by an arroyo. There are also geometric paintings and several rocks with deep pits or channels. In one case at least, because of its position facing a rock with five heads engraved on it, one might be led to believe that its 17 channels were designed as places on which to deposit offerings, and that the rock had once been a kind of altar. The headdress on the figure is semicircular with wavy lines or rays inside it, although simplified or incomplete variations of this do exist. The surrounding area indicates that this is a sanctuary, and some interesting studies have been done on it (Klein, 1972; Gordon, 1985). In the thirty or so sites where this motif appears there are wide variations and simplifications. One of the more remarkable of these shows spiral extensions toward the ribcage and farther up. Others are markedly geometric, like the 10 figures engraved on the cliffs facing the Pacific at Puerto Manso, 22 miles (36 kilometers) north of Los Vilos. There are also small, schematic human figures, sometimes dancing, that show these head extensions or headdresses. Other motifs in the region include herds of camelids, either by themselves or associated with small, simple human figures in scenes possibly showing the domestication process. An abundance of irregular, wavy, or snake-like designs is also present.

There are some differences between the petroglyphs in the north of the Elqui Valley and those to the south. The first group shows a greater richness in the scenes depicted, and there are fewer mask-like forms and more suns and crosses, while the opposite is true to the south. This has led Gastón Castillo (1985) to subdivide the El Molle cave art into two categories: La Silla (an extensive group of engraved rocks on the slopes of La Silla peak, also studied by Dominique Ballereau, 1981), and Limarí.[37]

The precursors of some of these motifs—particularly the human figures wearing large headdresses—come from Peru and the Chilean Norte Grande, while other motifs—such as the mask-like heads, which are sometimes given small, schematic bodies and sometimes the suggestion of a feline mouth, or depicted showing their teeth—constitute an original element. It has also passed into the regions east of the Cordillera, that is, the territory of present-day Argentina. When I studied this motif I stated, with particular reference to the Valle El Encanto site, that "this quasi-monumental cave art, linked to numerous rocks with pits and cups, is an artistic and symbolic expression of a religious shamanic-visionary development, in which the vitality of the forces within the human head played a predominant role. We can imagine their influence on the region's populations and their duration, although gradually the theme of the mask-shaped head may have become simplified or deformed." (Schobinger, 1985, p. 198.) The Sierra de Santa Marta group of petroglyphs in northern Colombia may be considered an interesting example of convergence, and

164. Geoglyph from northern Chile formed by an accumulation of stones, after cleaning and restoration by technicians of the Arica Regional Museum. About 26 feet (8 meters) in diameter, it seems to represent a monkey (after Briones).

so also, to a certain degree, may the elaborate anthropomorphs of the Guyanas region mentioned earlier.

In the Aconcagua River Basin the pitted technique of the Norte Chico is the same, but the art is much more abstract. The human figure is infrequently seen and schematic, sometimes to the point of being unrecognizable. The most frequent motif is the oval or rectangular "shield sign," whose symbolism remains unknown. Farther south, and except for one pre-Cordilleran site (Cerro Los Ratones), petroglyphs are practically unknown. There are, however, two important sites located in valleys of the Cordillera: one is Cajón de los Cipreses (high basin of the Cachapoal River), which has irregular, abstract figures. This site foreshadows the second group, which is in the interior at Linares. Hans Niemeyer and Lotte Weisner (1972–73) documented several large groups of petroglyphs at this site. These had been engraved on plank-like rocks that were horizontal, tilted, or—more rarely—vertical. They were found in the Guayquivilo River basin and at the headwaters of the Achibueno, at between 4,900 and 6,600 feet (1,500 and 2,000 meters). In spite of the almost total absence of human and animal figures, this art is remarkably rich and varied, featuring parallel lines, motifs with a longitudinal axis and wavy outlines, ladders and rakes, different kinds of circles, series of triangles, pleated figures, forms with networks and continuous patterns, and groups of pointed designs, as well as (and undoubtedly influenced by northern Patagonia) human footprints, handprints, and feline or rhea tracks. The feet are sometimes geometric, and may even take on a mask-like shape. The unknown creators of these petroglyphs must have belonged to nomadic groups, because these regions are totally snow-covered during the winter.

These Chilean sites and those on the Argentine side in the basin of the upper Neuquén River (easily accessible from the west) basically form a single ecological and stylistic group. The Argentine sites were studied by Juan Schobinger (1956, 1965) and by Jorge Fernández (1979), and constitute a somewhat impoverished version of the Chilean sites owing to their lack of human and animal footprints. Nevertheless, both sections are included in one large group of southern Andean cave art called the Guayquivilo-Colomichicó style, which is without a doubt one of the most interesting and enigmatic of South America.

In the Mapuche region (south of the Bío-Bío basin) cave art is almost nonexistent, but its two principal works are significant. One is the Llaima rock near Curacautín, which is covered with vulvar signs similar to those on the rocks on the Pachene River in Bolivia. The other is a large rock at Chan-Chan on the Bueno River southeast of the city of Valdivia. Here are parallel curved grooves that remind one of owl faces. The meaning of neither of these is known, nor is their cultural attribution or the date at which they were made.[38]

If the "rocks with cups" constitute a particular variation of their own in cave art, they are frequent both in the Norte Chico and in central Chile, although they are rarely associated with petroglyphs. A remarkable site, located in the Talca province a little north of the Cordilleran group of the Guayquivilo, is the site at Alto de Vilches, with 19 granite rocks located—as at the Llaima site—in a forested region. They are associated with a late hunter-gatherer deposit. The largest rock has 47 oval-shaped cavities, that is to say, instead of cups they are dishes (Medina et al., 1964). In central Chile (Las Cenizas site, not far from Valparaíso), rocks with large cups are associated with burials from the later preceramic period.

Northwestern Argentina

This region forms a wide inverted triangle with its base along the present border between Bolivia and Argentina whose apex is in the north of Mendoza province. It encompasses three basic regions: the Puna (a prolongation of the Bolivian Altiplano), the valleys and ranges east and south,

165. Reconstruction of a frequent scene in some northern Chilean valleys around 1000–1200 C.E.: a caravan of llamas passing by a peak whose slopes are covered with geoglyphs. (Plate from the Chilean Museum of Pre-Columbian Art, Santiago, redrawn by J. O. Ferrari.) Modeled on the Cerro Sagrado at Alto Ramírez, Azapa Valley.

and the forested fringe on its southeastern slopes. It also includes part of the flat regions of the western Chaco.

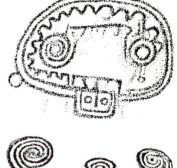

The only Preceramic paintings in the region, located in the Puna area, have already been mentioned. The most characteristic motif of Pictorial group B of Inca-Cueva, associated with the oldest pottery of the region and dated at between 1000 and 800 B.C.E., is an elongated human figure without limbs, or with arms that are barely outlined over the chest. There are short lines on the upper part of the figure that suggest a headdress, forming rows of two or more forms. Apart from the site mentioned, manifestations of this group also appear on the rock walls of the Doncellas River in Quichagua and in the Cueva de Cristóbal, where the dates mentioned above were obtained (Fernández, 1988–1989).

Except for this still little-known group, the cave art of northwestern Argentina belongs to the archaeological culture known from about 600 B.C.E. in valleys of the extreme north and from 300 B.C.E. in other regions. They are usually included under the early farming-ceramic period, which lasted about a thousand years and which had a Neolithic cultural level although there was occasional use of gold and copper for ornamental objects. Then followed a middle period best represented by the La Aguada culture (circa 600–900 C.E.), in which influences coming indirectly from the Altiplano (Expansive Tiahuanaco) have been detected, including the use of bronze. Between the tenth and sixteenth centuries the Late or Regional Developmental period evolved, when incipient urbanization grew. This was established by groups known through ethnohistory as the Humahuacas or the Diaguitas. Between 1475 and 1535 the Inca expansion took place. Despite its brevity, it left interesting signs (although none are connected with cave art).

Outside of the Andean area is another mountainous region centered on the provinces of Córdoba and San Luis, generically known as the Sierras Centrales, which is also the home of small farming-ceramic groups that did not appear much before 500 C.E. There are numerous sites here containing art, particularly in the form of cave paintings.

166. Mask-shaped heads from the Coquimbo region. The technique used is pitting with strongly marked lines. *Top:* Estancia Zorrilla, Ovalle (now in the La Serena Archaeological Museum), about 3 feet (1 meter) wide. *Bottom:* Mincha Sur, in the Choapa River Valley (by Mostny and Niemeyer, 1983).

Generally speaking, the early period of the farming-ceramic phase is expressed through petroglyphs. Cultural correlations are extremely rare. Only in the Tafí culture—which flourished at the beginning of the Common Era—can a specific correlation be made between two types of petroglyphs. One is formed by a simple round face with a prolonged body on the lower part and also on the upper part of the figure by way of long horns or straight antennae. The other type shows figures engraved on some of the monoliths that constitute a typical element of this culture. These have been found in certain sites in the high Tafí valley (Tucumán province), in one case associated with a ceremonial platform and in others with the interior of circular courtyards that formed the heart of some dwelling areas. (This simple face motif reappears, surprisingly, south of Mendoza, at the very gateway to Patagonia, although how the motif appeared remains a mystery.)

167. Large mask-shaped head with deep lines, from a rock in the Valle El Encanto, Ovalle area in the Coquimbo region of the Chilean Norte Chico. Approximately 20 inches (50 centimeters) wide (redrawn from a photo by the author). This type—of undoubtedly symbolic expression—is from an early period of the El Molle culture (circa 0–700 C.E.).

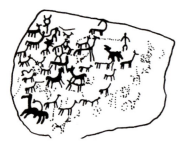

168. Two of the numerous rocks showing petroglyphs in the Cerro La Silla (north of the Valle de Elqui, Coquimbo region in Chile). Note the schematic camelids (from Ballereau, 1981).

There is another site in Tucumán province that shows a technical and stylistic relationship that probably corresponds to this time period: the engraved stone at La Ovejería in San Pedro de Colalao. This is a block located in the eastern foothills of the Sierra de Aconquija, within the area of influence of the Candelaria culture, which had early contacts with Tafí. Remarkable here are the human-like figures with a certain larva-like appearance; in some, the head shows rays that suggest a solar symbolism; in others, the face is schematic and reduced to one single point (an eye?) surrounded by two circumferences. Other figures are more irregular and abstract, to the point of being composed of a circumference with a central dot. There are also snake-like forms and a depiction of a quadruped, perhaps dating from an earlier time. The Guyanan-Amazonian flavor of this site is very curious.

Figures wearing crowns or with rays proceeding from their heads are occasionally found, but their lines are thinner and their bodies more geometric. They occur in some of the sites in the south of Salta province. They also show concentric circumferences and other signs, and in one case (El Lajar), a circular rayed mask with two short lines emanating from each eye. This is the figure that has been mistakenly called "the weeping deity," which appears frequently on ceramic pieces. This example and the previous ones represent the beginning of a cycle of cave art lasting a millennium and a half, with one of the principal symbolic motifs carved in the rocks and the shelters of the southern Andean region: the mask-shaped head (whose importance in Chile has already been noted).

Apart from these cases, there exists a certain number of petroglyphs in northeastern Argentina whose link to the cultural phases of the first half of the first millennium C.E. can be determined by comparing them with some decorative motifs used in pottery. These petroglyphs are located at Ciénaga II and Condorhuasi, and among them are schematic felines seen in profile; camelids with feline teeth, hooves, and tails; and double-headed camelids, to which may be added the human face with simple lines on the head in triangular, quadrangular, or quasi-circular shapes, sometimes with earmuffs. There are also feline (?) pawprints and the schematic depiction of human feet and hands. Some of these motifs are associated with very large quadrupeds, forming rows although sometimes isolated, like those that appear on rock walls at Antofagasta de la Sierra in the southern Puna. (This rich zone, recently studied by Mercedes Podestá in 1987, contains works from several periods.) Others are found in the valley of the Hualfín and its tributaries, and in the pre-Punan basin of Laguna Blanca, where elements from the cultures mentioned above have been found. It should be pointed out that as well as the principal elements there are very often different drawings, such as geometric, symbolic figures, schematic camelids, and irregular lines, that are not connected with portable art and which could belong to any period. There is also a framed cross with arms of equal length, which is found almost without interruption from Peru to northern Patagonia.

Going south of the area, which belongs to the Cuyo region (San Juan province and the northern half of Mendoza province), are an early group of paintings in shelters or grottoes located in the Cordilleran area of southwest San Juan, which belong to small farming groups included under the Ansilta culture. At the entrance and inside one of them, as well as in others within the same area, abstract cave paintings have been documented, in black, red, and a combination of both. The most striking motif is rectangular and maze-like, with volutes on either side. There is a puzzling group of three highly schematic, curved-lined beings, located on the ceiling of a passage between the two grottoes. "The largest figure located below is wearing a crown of feathers outlined in red and with black spots," Mariano Gambier observes. "The left

169. *Left:* Engraved rock from the great field of petroglyphs of Colo Michi Co (at an altitude of 6,560 feet (2000 meters) in the Cordillera del Viento, Neuquén). Example of the "parallel lines style" (photograph: the author). *Right:* Remarkable petroglyph showing the eye motif in deep engraving. Chan-Chan site, near Cachillahue on the Bueno River in the heart of the Chilean Araucana region (photograph: E. Jensen).

hand is holding a short dart by the middle (as in the Aguada-type figures) and in the right he is holding a large scepter which is resting on the ground. The scepter's top forms a kind of club, and six black, vertical lines ending in hooks pointing to the right of the figure emanating from it. Some of the lines are outlined in red. This individual has classical attributes of command characteristic of the most ancient cultures of Peru, which were preserved until the Inca tradition: rods or scepters in both hands or a rod in one and a shield in the other, or another symbolic object." (Gambier, 1980, p. 46.) Gambier assumes that the figure represents a sun god, and that the group represents personifications of stars. In one of the grottoes at Los Morrillos are also rocks with circular holes, like the paintings associated with the funeral rites practiced there and dating from the early years of the Common Era. Along with these abstract figures, some stylized animals that appear in two other of the region's sites are attributed to this culture—perhaps to its late phases.

170. A monolith from the Tafí culture, with a deep mask-shaped engraving similar to some petroglyphs. Height: 3 feet (1 meter) (photograph by the author).

The rest of the cave art of the Cuyo area consists of petroglyphs, which are probably from between the second and fifteenth century C.E. Their technique (deep pitting) and other aspects show their connection to Chile (Norte Chico) and the Argentine northwest. There are about 80 known sites of Cuyo petroglyphs, including some that border on La Rioja province.[39] Twenty of these sites stand out as especially important, owing to their quantity and the symbolic meaning of the figures depicted, many of them near the Cordilleran area. The engravings are found on walls, gorges, groups of rounded rocks, the sides of hills, and on old debris cones. These are usually inhospitable places, almost never associated with residential areas. In only two cases were they connected to burial sites—in Los Colorados de Barreal and Villa Dominguito, the latter in the Pie de Palo Sierra, eastern San Juan—both of which had already been plundered by the time this study had been carried out.

The main connection with Chile is represented by the haloed, mask-shaped heads, whose prototypes are found in Valle El Encanto. These prototypes are considered a peculiar variation of something central in many South American cultures: the attention given to the human head as an energy center. In some areas, this gave rise to a "head cult" and the manipulation of the trophy-head, while in others it inspired this kind of cave art. Earlier variations included the addition of a body, or sometimes just the limbs. As in many other cases, this kind of petroglyph is connected to shamanic ideas and practices, which have been revealed by different archaeological findings. These findings include dishes and circular holes for the preparation of hallucinogenic plant substances, and sometimes decorated pipes for smoking, a practice that was proved by the "shaman" buried about 1400 B.C.E. in the Huachichocana cave. The arrival of the La Aguada culture north of San Juan doubtless meant an enrichment of cave art, exemplified in the engraved rock of Palque de Pachaco (currently in the Archaeological Museum of San Juan) and in sites north of this province such as Colangüil and in western La Rioja like the spectacular Cañón de Talampaya. Some sites with petroglyphs are found at quite high elevations, like those located near ancient paths that crossed into Chile (Aguas Blancas, Guardia Vieja, the Carnecería River, Las Casitas, in San Juan, between 7,500 and 9,800 feet (2,300 and 3,000 meters); Quebrada Colorada in Mendoza at 7,900 feet (2,400 meters).

Returning to the central region of the Northwest, the paintings in caves on the eastern slopes of the Sierra de Ancasti in Catamarca province deserve special mention. The region is wooded, and one of the trees that grows there is the *cebil* (*Anadenanthera*). The background, theme, and placement of the paintings, which are done in several colors, suggest that at this very spot initiatory-shamanic practices took place, including the inhaling of hallucinogenic substances prepared from the leaves of that tree. The most important site is La Tunita, discovered by N. de la Fuente (1979). On its rocky dome are dancers, men with feline heads and a weapon in one hand (a deity or shaman in a trance?), spotted felines (jaguars) in pure form or slightly dragon-like, and an exceptional human figure with profiles of two feline heads and with other heads in the place of hands. This shows a direct correlation with other elements of a well-defined culture, like the decoration on many ceramic pieces at La Aguada (circa 600–900 C.E.), which are recognized as being of the highest technical and aesthetic quality in the entire Argentine northwest. In other sites in the Ancasti area are large serpents with dragon-like heads, masked anthropomorphic figures with ears, birds and camelids, geometric figures, and other motifs less characteristic of that culture.

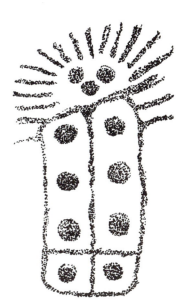

171. One of the motifs engraved on la Ovejería rock (San Pedro de Colalao, Tucumán). These are human figures that have been depicted as individuals and whose heads apparently have a solar symbolism. Height: 10 inches (25 centimeters) (redrawn from a photograph by the author).

There is no doubt that many of the area's petroglyphs also belong to La Aguada, but the association is less clear in such places as Talampaya (where there are also rocks with deep, circular holes), Ampajango in the Santa María Valley, and Campanas in La Rioja. Many figures seem to have become fragmented and irregular, and are sometimes combined with symbols such as the framed cross, the simple or double circumference with a central point, the three-toed sign, the puma track, and the human footprint. Something similar occurs farther north (Cachaquíes and Quebrada del Toro valleys), where there are numerous petroglyphs on rocks that are difficult to classify culturally. On some of them there are animal and mask-like forms that suggest early origins. Ercilia Navamuel has interpreted a depiction at El Duraznito (near the important develop-

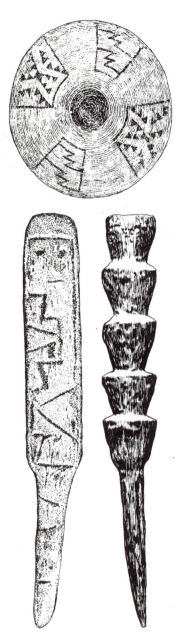

ing urban center of Tastil) of a sort of star framed in three circles with subdivisions as a calendar counter (Navamuel, 1986).

The feline symbolism practically disappears during the Late archaeological period. Art in general becomes more descriptive and to a certain extent superficial. Group C from the Inca-Cueva paintings at Jujuy should be mentioned here. There is a schematic camelid (sometimes in rows like a caravan) that plays an important part, as do the little human figures in different poses. The rock shelter paintings that surround the Quebrada de Humahuaca—where the llamas or plumed warriors are associated with circumferences or complex geometric compositions in white, black, and red—were probably inspired by textile art (Hernández Llosas, 1992). Another important group is at Carahuasi at Salta, with its characteristic shield-men (or men wearing long tunics), bearing weapons or insignia, that also appear in infants' burial urns of the Santamarina culture.

The artistic tradition extends in part until the time of the conquest of South America. In Inca-Cueva and other sites around Quebrada de Humahuaca, and in the Cerro Colorado de las Sierras de Córdoba, Spaniards appear brandishing lances, on foot or horseback, during their first incursions in the sixteenth century. (Something similar has been observed in cave sites of Lago Nahuel Huapi, in northern Patagonia.)

There is a curious group of undated petroglyphs located in the Cueva del Toro, 13,600 feet (4,150 meters) from the western Puna. In both its technique—scraped—and theme of the human figure, treated in a highly original way, this site shows an innovative style for which no immediate parallels are known. The "praying" position of the frontally presented figures dressed in long tunics and with pointed heads suggest a priestly dance. The long, geometric snake-like forms that frame them suggest once again the religious underpinnings of cave art. There is a remarkable small scene of two smokers, each with a tubular pipe, located at either side of a central figure (Fernández, 1976).

Outside the sub-Andean areas and belonging to groups of small farmers that continued to hunt intensively, are three regions with cave art in central Argentina. It is not clear when these cultures began. The high point of their development could be placed at the thousand years before the arrival of the Spaniards. The chief region is the Sierras de Córdoba and extreme south of Santiago del Estero. Here there are three special sites with very diverse engravings: Para-Yacu in the north, presenting a remarkable set of circular figures—partly rayed and also dotted—on the wall of a shallow cave; Ampiza, in the west of Córdoba, with circular and wavy designs with strange symbolism (probably late Preceramic according to unpublished excavations), obtained, as in the previous case, by deep engraving; and San Buenaventura, near Cosquín in the same province, featuring a large rock located beside an arroyo and on whose horizontal surface motifs characteristic of the footprint style (animal and human prints) and a snake have been engraved. The principal focal point of this style is in Patagonia, but it is also expressed in other sites in Argentina as well as in Brazil. Among the sites with paintings, Cerro Colorado in the extreme northeast of the Sierras de Córdoba is outstanding, with numerous rock shelters and small caves covered in naturalistic depictions of different animals, birds like the condor with outstretched wings, and masked personages with an Amazonian air.

172. *Above:* Plate-shaped basketwork piece, 17 inches (43 centimeters) in diameter, with geometric painted motifs. These pieces were used to cover the head of the funeral bundles found in Grotto Number 1 at Los Morrillos, belonging to the early farming-ceramic culture of Ansilta (circa 4500 B.C.E.–500 C.E.) (redrawn from Gambier, 1980). *Below: Tupus* or pins in bone and wood from the Ansilta culture of southwest San Juan (by Gambier, 1980).

173. Symbolic figure painted in black and red, with part of the drawing in the negative, 26 inches (67 centimeters) wide. Los Morrillos grotto at Ansilta (southwestern San Juan), associated with burials dated at the early years of the Common Era (by Gambier, 1980).

There are also other profiled figures in rows holding both hands out toward a small bow, with a head decoration in the form of small dots and a wide dorsal band from which radiate short and long appendages, which may be plumage. This gives them a certain dynamism, and at certain moments the appearance of wafting in the wind and even flying through the air. We believe that, as in other cases, the visual reproduction of a form of clothing, probably ceremonial, points to the depiction of mythological or supernatural beings. Other sections of this great deposit display more abstract paintings of shield forms, zigzags, different circles, and suns with feet.[40]

Additional sites in southern and western Santiago del Estero province feature some paintings, but mostly abstract engravings. There are circles, some with a central dot, rectangular sets, point-like forms, rhea and feline tracks, and the occasional schematized owl (a frequent motif in the pottery from the Chaco-Santiago area). In several cases they are associated with circular holes or cups.

The other two sections are less important: the Sierra de San Luis and south of the Comechingones. These have painted rock walls and shelters with groups of large and small guanacos and rheas, different circular figures, an occasional feline and mask, and in certain sites like the great shelter at Angostura, geometric, multicolored motifs that probably represent a penetration of the fret style of the late hunters of Patagonia. There are also circular holes dug into the rock here. A partly cylindrical rock in the shape of a hand forms a circular hole; excavated in the upper levels of the famous Intihuasi grotto, it features straight-lined geometric paintings of the same kind.

The third area mentioned is the Sierras de los Llanos in the south of La Rioja province, which forms a kind of island between the sub-Andean region and the Sierras Centrales. The petroglyphs constitute a poor reflection of those of the Northwest and the Cuyo region. Most frequent are irregular, wavy-lined, geometric forms, concentric circles with a central dot, schematic animal and human figures, and in particular some geometric shield- and mask-like shapes.[41]

Except for two isolated cases, there are no known geoglyphs in Argentina. One is the so-

174. *Left:* Map of central-western Argentina and central-northern Chile, showing the main sites or concentrations of cave art. The circles correspond to paintings, and the dots to cave engravings or petroglyphs. (Also shown are some of the principal cities of the area, which are also provincial capitals.) *Right:* Ritual dancers, camelids, and spiral figures, on an engraved rock at Aguas Blancas (San Juan province).

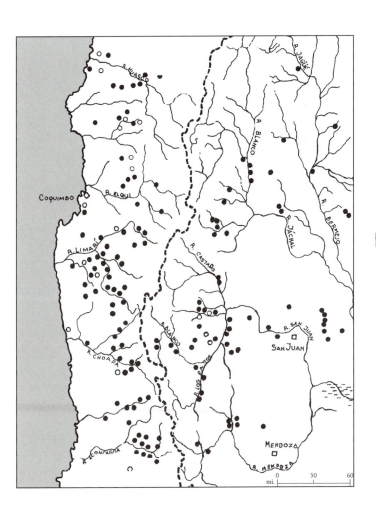

251

called Estrella e Vinchina, located at a site near Vinchina in La Rioja province. It is a circular figure about 50 feet (15 meters) in diameter with pebbles in three colors lined up in the shape of a star. From the pottery associated with it, it likely belongs to the La Aguaga culture. The other example was recently discovered by Ricardo Prieto (1992) on terraces of the Jáchal River north of San Juan. It consists of three groups of highly stylized anthropomorphic figures within a frame, placed in an oval shape about 40 feet (12 meters) in diameter. Medium-sized red and white pebbles were transported here in order to create it. There are no indications of its age.

In conclusion, the cave art of the Andean area shows a "family resemblance" and numerous common elements. However, there are many variations and the art comes from very diverse time periods. We will now return to hunter-gathering communities, particularly those groups that survived in the marginal areas of the continent until the arrival of Europeans in the sixteenth century.

175. On a rock at Puerta de la Talampaya is an engraved scene of a large human in front of a row of llamas. The large feet, the phallus, and the three-fingered hand suggest that this represents a mythological being (redrawn from a photo by the author).

176. *Left:* Large rock at the foot of the rock walls of Puerta de Talampaya (La Rioja province). At the top are human figures with wings on their heads, and other symbolic figures (photograph: J. Schobinger). *Right:* Associated with the cave art group of the Puerta de Talampaya are two rocks on whose horizontal face are rows of large, circular holes (photograph: J. Schobinger).

Northeastern and Eastern Brazil

While the whole central part of the Americas was transforming itself from a hunter-gathering way of life to a sedentary, food-producing lifestyle (a process which occurred between the fourth and second century B.C.E.), the enormous area on its periphery preserved a hunter-gathering way of life much longer, in some cases into the post-Conquest era. This area runs along the Atlantic coast from the extreme northeast of Brazil (Piauí, Ceará, and Río Grande do Norte) to Patagonia and Tierra del Fuego. Because there are great geographical and climatic disparities within this area, as well as biological and cultural differences, the following subdivisions must be made: the Eastern Brazil area, and the Pampean-Patagonian area, with El Chaco and Uruguay as an intermediate zone, although this region is much more closely related to the Pampean-Patagonian area. These same divisions can also be applied to cave art. Studies by Brazilian researchers over the past 20 years—already mentioned in part in Chapter II—have raised Brazilian territory from a virtually unknown area to one of the richest and oldest regions of prehistoric art in the world.

Moving toward the northeast, it should be remembered that the great Northeastern Tradition possesses different variations, some of them very old (the Baixão de Perna I) and others as recent as 4000 B.C.E. Before this date, the Agreste Tradition existed, centering on Pernambuco, Río Grande do Norte, and the neighboring areas. The word *Agreste*, which means rugged, comes from the name given to the region between the humid coast and the semi-arid *sertão* more toward the interior. This cave art group, possibly derived from some assemblages of the Northeastern Tradition, has been studied by Alice Aguiar (1986). Gabriela Martín has also studied it and gives the following description:

The Agreste Tradition is distributed all over northeastern Brazil, but systematic research has only been done on it in Pernambuco, Paraíba, and Piauí. Because of its wide dispersion, the subtraditions and styles are numerous and still being studied. In Pernambuco State, where we have documented about 100 deposits in this tradition, the dates obtained are from around 2000 B.C.E., so it extends to the beginning of the era.

The main characteristics of cave art from the Agreste Tradition are very large drawings, generally isolated and without forming narratives. Where they do, the scenes are always composed of very few individuals or animals. Pure drawings—that is, drawings that are identifiable by their geometric form—both simple and highly elaborate, accompany the animal or human figures. They are about equal in number, with perhaps a slight majority of human forms. Typical of the Agreste Tradition is a human figure, sometimes very large and

177. Personage painted in creamy white, with some parts in red, as a dancing warrior, holding an atlatl and an arrow. One of the remarkable motifs on the walls and ceiling of the granite grottoes of La Tunita (Ancasti region, Catamarca province). Height: 4 feet (1.2 meters) (redrawn after N. de la Fuente, 1979).

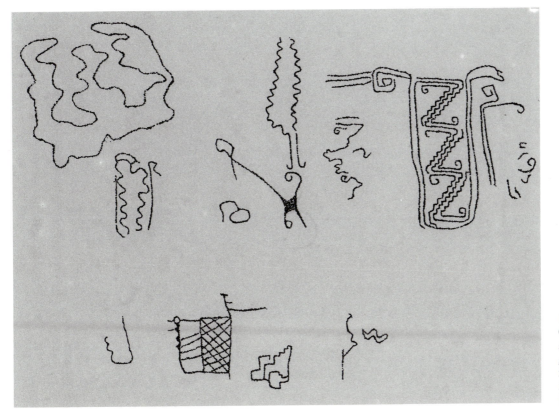

178. On a rocky wall at Los Colorados (La Rioja Province) is an engraving showing a varied group of symbolic geometric figures. The one on the upper left is 26 inches (65 centimeters) high (survey by the author).

179. Curvilinear petroglyph, approximately 24 inches (60 centimeters) high, near others in the Ampiza cave (western Cordoba province). The lower figure is probably a mask-shaped head (redrawn from Romero, 1978).

grotesque-looking, and presented in isolation and in static poses like a totemic figure. This is found infrequently throughout the northeast. In contrast to the paintings in the Northeastern Tradition, in which it is often possibly to recognize different species among the animal figures, the Agreste animals can rarely be classified in greater detail than by bird or quadruped, except for large tortoises, iguanas, and lizards. It is also common to find depictions of birds with wings, long outstreched feathers which, at times, show a tendency toward anthropomorphism, as if intending to represent a "bird-man." Handprints and sometimes footprints are also common.

These deposits are usually located at the bottom of valleys or *brejos*—small humid, tropical enclaves in the semi-arid areas. In Pernambuco the paintings are supported by great granite monoliths, which emerge from the valleys due to the effect of erosion on the softer rocks. They are not usually far from water, and cave paintings from this tradition rarely appear in the shelters high up in the sierras. The color red predominates, but there are also less frequent multicolored paintings in yellow and white. From the latest results obtained in recent excavations at Venturosa (Pernambuco), which are still incomplete, one can state that certain Agreste Tradition styles, with their very elaborate geometric tendency, may belong to farming and ceramic groups. (Martín, 1992, pp. 9–10.)

André Prous believes that Agreste is not a distinct tradition, but rather represents "a mix, within individual sites, of elements from the Northeastern and the San Francisco Tradition, probably from different periods" (1989, p. 20).

In other sites within the area are paintings that have been grouped together in the Northern Geometric Tradition, whose dates have not been calculated. The most important concentration is at the Parque Natural de Sete Cidades (north of Piauí). The other group of cave art has been called the *Itacoatiara* Tradition, and includes all the cave engravings of northeastern Brazil. There are no dates calculated here either, and these engravings belong to different periods, even to ceramic groups. (The Ceramic period begins in 880 B.C.E. with the Peri-Peri phase on the Bahía coast.) There are exceptions, but in general the petroglyphs of eastern Brazil are abstract, or pure drawings.[42] The *itacoatiaras* represent a very enigmatic element, and "because they are almost always in watercourses and therefore often in contact with water," Martín continues "it is very difficult to connect them to any human group because it is impossible to find remains of material culture nearby. However, there are some exceptions in which it has been possible to connect the *itacoatiaras* to hunting cultures. This has occurred in shelters near rivers or in *caldeirões*, which are round cavities formed in the rocky faults of the northeastern sierras. These natural deposits that fill with water during the rainy season sometimes have walls covered in petroglyphs, and in some cases it has been possible to carry out excavations in the surrounding areas. One example is the Letreiro do Sobrado shelter in the San Francisco River Valley (Pernambuco), located about 2,300 feet (700 meters) from the great river and whose walls are covered with schematic engravings. At this site stratigraphic dates have been obtained going back between 1,200 and 6,000 years. Evidence also exists of stone industries with single-faced

180. One of the curious masked groups engraved in the Cueva del Toro, in the Puna de Jujuy at an elevation of 13,600 feet (4,150 meters). The figures seem to be praying, some naked and others dressed in tunics. The technique is scraping, which is relatively rare in the Argentine Andes (redrawn from Fernández, 1976).

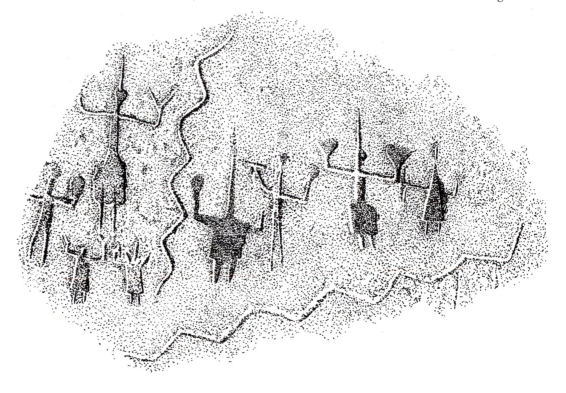

implements of silex, quartz, and chalcedony. In addition, there are remains of the bones of rodents, birds, and fish, campfires, and fragments of engraved rocks, which have fallen from the shelter walls. This site was used by prehistoric hunters and fishers from the San Francisco Valley, who engraved the shelter walls repeatedly, reusing them in several superimpositions. When a piece of sandstone support fell away, the remaining part of the wall was engraved. Dates obtained for the levels where engraved fragments appeared went back 1,680, 1,630, and 1,639 years." (Martín, 1992, pp. 11–12). Another example of a site with engravings is Cachoeira do Riacho Santana, 50 miles (80 kilometers) east of São Raimundo Nonato. This site contains geometric figures on its walls, as well as highly schematic human figures, lizards, hands, feet, and vulvas. These elements point to the arrival in the north of something that is usually called the Footprint style in other regions.

"Most of the petroglyphs of northeastern Brazil were likely related to the worship of water," Martín writes, "and also, many of these engravings bring to mind groups who worship of the forces of nature and of the heavens. Depictions of what appear to be stars are frequent, as are wavy lines that seem to imitate the movement of water. These are merely guesses, however, and in 99 percent of the cases little more can be said about these mysterious engravings that, discovered in the immense solitude of the *sertões,* have lent themselves to the most diverse and fantastic interpretations." (Martín, op. cit., pp. 12–13.)[43] In the northeast there is also a consistent variety of "painted petroglyphs," in which the schematic engravings have been filled in with red paint (as in Boi Branco in Pernambuco, and Grossos in Río Grande do Norte). The doubt remains as to whether the people who painted them were the same as those who made the initial engravings.

One famous site is Pedra de Ingá, a large granite rock 82 feet (25 meters) long and 10 feet (3 meters) high located 62 miles (100 kilometers) from the Atlantic coast, on the edge of a sierra between the villages of Ingá and Campina Grande. Its vertical wall faces northeast and is totally covered in carefully executed engravings with deep, broad lines and a polished finish. Except for one lizard, there are no observable depictions of living beings, although some of the signs could be very schematic anthropomorphic figures, as in the case of what may be two plumes whose body is suggested by a series of vertical holes. Some ovals and arched signs could be female sexual symbols. Throughout the central section and for several yards the petroglyphs are framed at the top by a a row of 117 holes, and by another row—somewhat smaller—underneath. Pavía Alemany (1986) believes the upper row is a solar astronomical record, but despite his ingenious mathematical calculations, this remains extremely doubtful. Near the far right is a spiral, which lends support to the idea that this group of cave engravings—in which can detected a certain Amazonian air—harbors a profound symbolism, but one yet to be deciphered. Farther north, in Ceará, sites have been surveyed with engravings assignable to the Footprint style, owing to the frequency of the three-toed sign and its variations. The largest of these sites, Pedra do Letreiro in Quixeramobim, consists of a long wall that borders a lake (Parnes and de Souza, 1971).

Finally, let us remember the supposedly astronomical or stellar paintings discovered by V. Calderón on the Diamantina plateau in western Bahía. Maria da Beltrão et al. (1990) later studied these, but their dates remain extremely unclear (Chapter II).

Central-Southern Brazil and Neighboring Regions

No strict dividing line exists between this area and the previous one. The division employed is mainly for geographical reasons. The chief stylistic group here is the San Francisco Tradition, which partly coincides with the Planalto Tradition but extends farther west and north. André Prous provides a summary of its characteristics:

> Based in the San Francisco River Valley, the tradition is found in Minas Gerais, Bahía, and Sergipe, as well as in the states of Goiás and Matto Grosso. We define it as a tradition in which there is an overwhelming majority of abstract marks (geometric drawings) compared to animal and human figures, and in some cases make up all the drawings. Except in the oldest style, there is an intense use of two colors in the paintings. The rare animal figures almost exclusively depict fish, birds, snakes, lizards, and sometimes tortoises. There is a notable absence of deer, and no scenes are depicted.
> Regional and chronological varieties are clearly marked in the extreme north of Minas Gerais, where we documented almost 80 sites with works belonging to the San Francisco Tradition, and one should probably define other varieties both downriver and upriver. The northern region is characterized by representations of human feet (sometimes with four toes), weapons (lances, atlatls), instruments (baskets, pots, maracas, tipití for treating manioc, etc.), but there are no scenes that show these being used. Near Montalvania, in the heart of the assemblage of the same name, there are few themes, and depictions are characterized by the pitted-engraving

181. Mask figure: cave painting from the Sierra de San Luis (by Ochoa de Masramób, 1980).

technique on a horizontal or slightly tilted rock base. The engravings are generally covered in a natural veneer, a vestige from a time when the climate was extremely dry. The result is a well-defined contrast between the parts that have been worked—which are light in color—and the dark, shiny background. Simple, linear figures like those at Montalvina (where there are many footprints with between three and six toes) and figures from the older levels of other regions are also found painted in the Sete Cidades area (Piauí), where they have been assigned to a Geometric Tradition from the east. Near Januaria the technique is much more varied, and only paintings are found. In the region of the headwaters of the San Francisco River there is an increase in the percentage of animals, perhaps owing to influence from the Planalto Tradition. The characteristic two-colored Planalto style is present here, consisting of a yellow principal figure on a red background. In the mining area to the north, black and white were also used, particularly in depictions from later periods. The creators of all these works have frequently shown a feel for effect in the interplay of bright colors and the internal organization of the more complex geometrical figures (Montalvina and Caboclo assemblages at the Sol de Curral de Pedra site in Jequitaí). This makes the sites extraordinarily spectacular. (Prous, 1989, p. 20.)

The area covered by the San Francisco Tradition roughly coincides with that of the Gé ethnographic group, formed by simple hunter-farmer groups. These basically sedentary groups had settled before the arrival of other groups from the Amazon (Tupí-Guaraní) in eastern and southern Brazil. Analogies have also been observed between some of the cave art motifs and the body painting of some Gé groups, as well as between some circular or rayed figures and how they are arranged (Gruhn, 1983). For this hypothesis to be feasible one would have to prove that the prehistoric age of the Gé group is the same as that of the San Francisco Tradition and that there is continuity between this stylistic cave art group and the ethnographic period. There is no such continuity, at least not in the north of Minas Gerais (Januaria-Montalvania area). Here Prous has determined a succession of pictorial periods that begins with linear designs similar to those of the Geometric Tradition of Piauí, continues with the multicolored flowering of the Caboclo and Rezar phases, generally in regions of high altitude, and then changes theme as it moves into naturalism. In this recent (but yet to be accurately dated) phase are plant motifs (apparently maize and palm trees), and animal forms with deer, anteaters, birds, and jaguars. These figures appeal in orange, yellow, and white. There are also pitted engravings, sometimes on a red background (Desenhos style).[44] The latest phase is due to a surprising appearance of the Northeastern Tradition, manifested in several sites by the superimposition of small scenes further to the south at the Lapa do Ballet site. This is seen again in eastern Bolivia. How does one explain how something farther north goes back to the end of the Ice Age and yet here is from a time not much before the arrival of the Europeans? This question remains unsolved, one of the many facing archaeologists in the Americas.

The Planalto Tradition, which flourished around Belo Horizonte, continued through various phases until late periods. Recent explorations have shown that in some of the sites in the center of Minas Gerais there are groups of fine incisions forming lines or networks, as well as rubbed incisions forming grooves or slots (which also exist in the Amazon area). There are also circular depressions like pans or cups, which are sometimes found with the petroglyphs. Their connection to the paintings is unknown.

182. *Facing page:* Abstract and human figures, examples of paintings in the Agreste Tradition of northeastern Brazil (Pedra Redonda site, Pernambuco). Height of the large human figure with "knee-pads": 4 feet (1.2 meters) (from Aguiar, 1986).

183. One of the engraved rocks in northeastern Brazil, included within the *Itacoatiara* Tradition (from the Guaraní name for this type of rock). Most belong to farming-ceramic groups; their motifs are symbolic, abstract, and tend to be curvilinear (redrawn from a photograph by G. Martín).

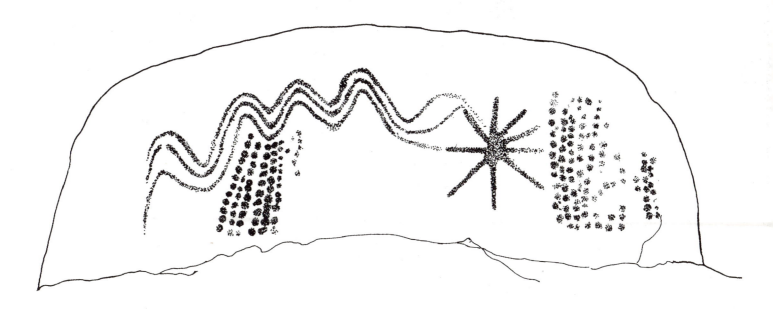

Farther west there is another great cave art province in the south of Goiás that combines elements of the Planalto and San Francisco traditions. There are rock walls and shelters in the Serranópolis municipality, from which this style took its name. Now that we seem to be dealing with art by hunters, it should be pointed out that up to now it has been impossible to attribute this to any time period. There are also engravings—at the sites themselves or in isolation—with abstract motifs in which there is a preponderance of three-fingered signs and human footprints, sometimes with four toes, sometimes with six. Another important group of examples of cave art is 125 miles (200 kilometers) north in Caiaponia, on the high Araguay River. Here the Planalto Tradition predominates, with an interesting northeastern influence observable in the dynamic human figures—not to mention the handprints that also probably came from farther north—and numerous geometric motifs. The framed crosses are no doubt later superimpositions, elements that originated in agricultural societies (the Andes?). In both areas vertical walls in large rock shelters are used as supports, and in both the color red predominates.[45]

In the central-eastern area of this large state, not far from Brasilia, is the archaeological region of Formosa. Its cave art has also been studied by a team from the Universidad Católica de Goiás led by P. I. Schmitz. From its characteristics it has been considered an assemblage from the Geometric Tradition, although there also appears depictions of the human foot and some strange reptile or bird. These red paintings have not been dated. In the limestone rock shelters of the nearby municipality of Niquelandia, some primarily abstract (geometric and point-shaped) figures have been found. There are without doubt more sites along the southeastern edge of the ranges that divide the Amazon Basin from that of the Río de la Plata. This is suggested by data about the existence of rock walls with symbolic, geometric paintings on the Sucuriú River, not very far from Serranópolis in the neighboring area of Mato Grosso do Sul.

In recent years, varied paintings and engravings have been discovered farther west in the state of Mato Grosso. Several dozen sites were located between Cuiabá and Rondonópolis, the most important being Ferraz Egregia, with numerous red geometric and circular signs that suggest the existence of some kind of symbolic code. Some stylistically different engravings have been superimposed onto the paintings. Stratigraphic probes revealed Preceramic as well as Ceramic cultural levels, the preceramic ones being dated at up to 2600 B.C.E. (Vialou and Vialou, 1984). Another important site is the extensive Santa Elina rock shelter, 75 miles (120 kilometers) northwest of Cuiabá, a stone with extensive limestone and sandstone folds in the Serra das Araras. Along a 200-foot (60-meter) stretch, a large rock wall tilted to the northeast

184. Panel Number 3 of the Lapa do Caboclo, in Januaria, in the upper San Francisco River Valley (Minas Gerais). This is a notable example of the San Francisco Tradition, characterized by multicolored geometric motifs, often enclosed in cartouches, or ornamental frames, and accompanied by some schematic animal figures. The black lines are red; the dotted areas are yellow; and the slashed lines are white. This group is attributed to hunter-gathers that came after those of the Planalto Tradition (from A. Prous, 1986).

presents about 700 animal figures. These include tapirs, deer, monkeys, felines, nude men and figures wearing headdresses, earmuffs, or bracelets. There are also geometric signs, elemental signs like points and parallel lines, and figures with crisscross patterns. The violet-colored human and animal figures are older and located at a greater height. They are large—more than a yard in some cases—and spectacular. The others, like the signs, are red, orange, yellow, brown, or black, and often very small (less than 4 inches, or 10 centimeters). Analysis of the arrangement of the depictions has shown that certain types of figures are grouped together, such as rows of one or two male deer followed by several females, or abstract themes such as sets of pointed or arrow signs (Vialou, 1989, p. 92). Excavations done on this site identified six levels of Preceramic occupation dated between 4000 and 400 B.C.E., as well as a later one with rough pottery. The oldest level included vestiges of painting in red ocher on limestone blocks, which prehistoric people selected in order to make a kind of paved area, in front of the central concentration of violet paintings of large animals and monstrous anthropomorphic figures. If both artistic expressions came from the same period, this would probably be a ritual site 6,000 years old. At all levels there are numerous fireplaces surrounded by stones, which together with the stone implements (mainly chips) are indicators of intense domestic activity among groups of gatherers.[46]

In Mato Grosso there are also sites containing engravings in the Southern Geometric Tradition. Its most typical element is the triple-toed sign and its triangular variants. These are generally interpreted as female sexual symbols. The technique usually employed here is rubbing. One example is the Letreiro dos Bugres, near Cuiabá; another very notable one is Morro da Rapadura (Coronel Ponce), 62 miles (100 kilometers) east of Cuiabá. Here, along with some signs repeated vertically on one wall, are large oval figures with cross designs on the inside—an unusual symbol (Passos, 1980). Sometimes these are combined to look like plants; sometimes puma and deer tracks are found near them, as well as cup-like depressions of different sizes. This style, by analogy with that of Patagonia, is called the Footprint style. Examples of this in other northern areas of Brazil have already been noted, but its main center is in the states of São Paulo, Santa Catarina (for example at Morro do Avencal), and especially Río Grande do Sul. At the eastern extreme of Mato Grosso, not far from the Guaporé River that forms the border with Bolivia, is the Abrigo do Sol. Excavation of this site produced Ice Age levels with rough industries, and other later levels with very old ceramics. Petroglyphs made by the rubbing technique were found on partially buried blocks, including several depictions of human feet, which were also part of this style.[47] Other sites were found in southeastern Bolivia and southern Mato Grosso; in the latter site are sandstone walls in the Antonio José area near the Paraguayan border. These are no doubt related to a more extensive group located in the Sierra de Amambay of the Paraguayan side (Cerro Guazú). As well as the motifs already mentioned, there are alignments of vertical grooves; sometimes framed, geometric signs; very schematic anthropomorphs, and rather well-defined vulvar signs placed in a rectangular format. The cultural context for these works, located in shadowy rock shelters, remains unknown.[48]

Within the large group of abstract petroglyphs it is necessary to distinguish a variation in which curvilinear trends prevail. In the lower Mato Grosso is a rocky outcropping near Corumbá (Laje Moutinho), whose horizontal surface shows engraved circles in various combinations. Farther south in the Argentine province of Misiones we find a similar rocky outcropping east of the city of Posadas, with numerous large circles.

The main center of the Pisadas style is represented by an east-west strip nearly 250 miles (400 kilometers) long and about 30 miles (50 kilometers) wide, located on the southern edge of the Río Grande do Sul. It consists of a total of 11 isolated rocky blocks, four rock walls, and six rock shelters or caves, some of them very wide, like the ones at Virador. We owe what is known of them to P. A. Mentz Ribeiro (1969–1970, 1973, 1978); and to J. P. Brochado and P. I. Schmitz (1972–1973, 1982). By pitting or rubbing, it was possible to produce on these sand-

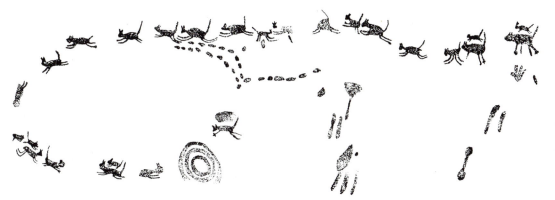

185. Long row of running quadrupeds—probably monkeys—and abstract figures on one of the numerous rock walls with cave art in Caiaponia, southwest of Goiás State (by P. Schmitz et al., 1984).

259

stone surfaces classic signs associated with this style in a variety of sizes. These signs are sometimes accompanied by small holes. At some sites, like the Canhemborá rock shelter, are circles and ovals with a short central line, a variation of the female sign. Excavations at this site yielded a hunting cultural level lacking projectile points, dated around 1000 B.C.E. In other cases, the association can be made with a late period of the Umbú Tradition (hunters using stemmed points). Certain stylistic differences between Phases A (Canhemborá) and B (which predominates in eastern areas) can be observed, featuring a greater level of abstraction and crisscross work, with parallel lines sometimes divided by one or more horizontal grooves, or else assuming the shape of a fishbone. The three-toed image does not appear to represent a real bird, and at times becomes a rubbed design with only two angular lines. Sometimes there are four or five angular lines, and the distribution is largely disordered. At two of the sites the petroglyphs have been filled in with color.

It has already been noted that elements of this style appear even in the Brazilian northeast, as well as in Argentina. In the northwest are more complex motifs, while in Patagonia it is the style of the late hunters (see below). The meaning and date of this type of engraving is unknown.

Joao Alfredo Rohr (1969) has surveyed a special group of petroglyphs on the coast of Santa Catarina Island and other islands nearby. "The petroglyphs," he writes, "are located on the vertical black rock walls of those beaches most exposed to the fury of the ocean waves. Only on the island of Porto Belo do we find petroglyphs located away from the beaches. The engravings are superficial, reaching a minimum width of 0.1 inches (3 millimeters) and a maximum width of 1.2 inches (30 millimeters). The inner surface of these designs is pitted and rough to the touch, although it is occasionally polished and smooth. Among the most frequent design motifs are concentric circles, sets of parallel straight lines, others with wavy parallel lines, and sets of broken or zigzagging parallel lines. There are also sets of oval or triangular figures combined with squares, rows of dots or small holes, and finally, stylized human or animal figures. These same motifs are repeated in a variety of combinations on several islands, a sign that the petroglyphs appearing on these islands are the product of a single cultural group." (Rohr, 1969, pp. 2–3.) In some cases, such as that of the Praia do Santinho site (which draws its name—The Beach of the Little Saint—from an anthropomorphic petroglyph venerated by fishers), there are also associations with rubbed surfaces shaped like grooves (grinders) or circles (plates). The circles are also found next to some of the remains of beach installations in the *Sambaquí* style. Their shape and polish cast doubt on their purely utilitarian function—the sharpening or pol-

186. Cave engravings from Serranópolis (southern Goiás), attributed to late hunters. Because of the human footprints (some with an unnatural number of toes) and the three-toed signs that look like rhea tracks, these engravings have been included in the Footprint style of southern Brazil and Patagonia (from Schmitz et al., 1984).

ishing of stone tools, or grinding of vegetables. (The Santa Catarina coast has yielded very well-polished stone plates.)

This set of island petroglyphs represents one of the few cases worldwide of cave art directly linked to the ocean. Their creators would have been members of the populations which, from about 4000 B.C.E. to the first centuries of the Common Era, lived off the sea's bounty, leaving behind large heaps of shells known as *sambaquí*, which are frequent on the coasts of São Paulo, Paraná, and Santa Catarina. The relatively good state of preservation of these engravings suggests a later date—the middle of the first millennium C.E.—and possible contact with the first Tupí-Guaraní contingents to reach the coast.[49] This is a rather restricted stylistic group which was created locally, although a certain Amazonian flavor can be detected in some of the Santa Catarina complexes.

Proof that the occupants of these *sambaquis* engaged in artistic activities can be found in their remarkable zooliths, or stone sculptures of animals, carved on offering trays. These were more or less flattened, polished objects with a fish or bird shape or—much less frequently—another animal. They generally have a rather shallow circular indentation in the center, which is why they are thought to be trays for the holding of offerings or of some liquid. The birds have a peculiar cross-shaped style.

It was believed that the models for this art could be found in the Andean area, but the chronology of certain pieces, which goes back to 2000 B.C.E., suggests that the Brazilian zooliths are a local invention. They are an example of how societies with a simple economy and technology may be endowed with deep symbolism relating to ideas and rituals concerning life and death. (Many of these pieces originally formed part of their simple burial collections.) Some of these objects were found in sites located at the interior of Río Grande do Sul as well as in certain areas of Uruguay, most likely as the result of a late diffusion.[50]

Another element of portable art—albeit a rather different one—is represented by the engraved stones, which are largely rectangular pieces of sandstone featuring crisscross, geometric motifs. These designs are finely incised or executed through aligned holes. One was found in Río Grande do Sul and many others in the Salto Grande (Uruguay, on the river of the same name). These have been described by Jorge Femenías (1985–1987), as have the ones excavated at the Bañadero deposit, at a hunting culture dated at 2700 B.C.E. Its function is unknown. Given that these are non-utilitarian elements, one comes to the inevitable conclusion that as in the case of the Patagonian en-

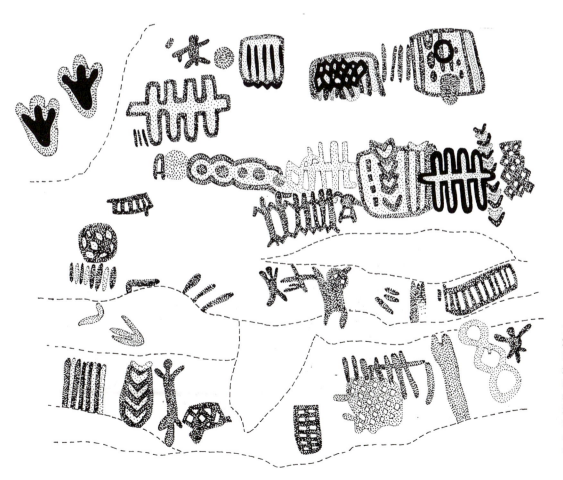

187. In a great rock shelter of the Sierra de Ramalho in Coribe (western Bahía) are numerous multicolored, geometric representations and highly stylized human and animal figures. The full design is black; the dense dots are brown or red; and the open dots are yellow or orange (from Schmitz et al., 1984).

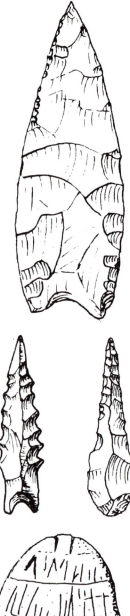

graved stones or the Australian *churingas*, these are ceremonial items. A similar piece has also been found on the Argentine side.

Returning to the interior of Santa Catarina and to the north of Río Grande do Sul, we find one of the oddities of Brazilian archaeology: underground galleries of mainly circular or oval design which penetrate 30, 130, or more feet (10, 40, or more meters) into sandstone hillsides. Natives attributed these to seventeenth-century Jesuits who concealed their treasures in them. The discovery of pottery shards on the ground and petroglyphs on the walls of two of them (and the fact that skeletons were extracted from them at some point) leads to the belief that they are pre-Conquest. I agree with Pedro Mentz Ribeiro's opinion (1985) that they are natural formations produced at some point by river erosion and subsequently adapted or retouched by the unknown inhabitants who employed them for ritual purposes. The petroglyphs are linear, abstract designs that could be ascribed to the Pisadas style. These galleries have not yet been systematically studied.

Finally, mention should be made of the remarkable extension of Brazilian-type cave paintings to the Bolivian Oriente. This vast tropical plain drains largely to the north, forming part of the Amazon Basin; some of its petroglyph-bearing sites have been noted earlier. At the southeastern end, the terrain slopes gradually downward toward the Pantanal of the upper Paraguay River and toward the Gran Chaco, forming part of the La Plata Basin. Here are two vegetation-covered ranges that rise up 2,950 feet (900 meters) above sea level: the Chiquitos and Santiago ranges, the latter farther east. There are also smaller rocky outcroppings, on whose surfaces are Pisadas style petroglyphs, accompanied by the dotted circle and more complex variations of it, as well as holes of various sizes (at the Capinsal, El Carmen, and Mutún sites). The Pope Sántosch site (Saint's Foot) has two well-outlined human feet bordered by a groove. These are accompanied by three circular cup-marks also joined by a narrow groove that almost certainly collected the liquid for libations (Riester, 1981, pp. 159–62). Some anthropomorphs such as the San Pedro "Devil" are reminiscent of the ghostly figures from the center of the state of Goiás.[51]

More interesting than the engravings are the cave paintings discovered and studied in recent years by Gabriella Erica Pia in the Chiquitos and Santiago mountains.[52] In the Urasiviquía arroyo in the Roboré-Santiago area, Pia managed to locate several painted shelters, three of which are particularly interesting. The one known as Ur I, over 330 feet (100 meters) wide, features numerous superimpositions. Beginning with the oldest ones, the most important phases are characterized by the following motifs: large crisscross symbols, straight white lines, rows of rheas and little men holding hands. The "rhea-man" also puts in a few appearances, and there are large white birds seen in profile (probably rheas); human figures in white and red; rows of monkeys and hunting scenes; handprints in the upper reaches of the shelter; and rows of stylized men holding hands. The "frog-man" is also present but belongs to a later period. There are also irregularly drawn lines over all the other motifs. These paintings have not been dated, and some of the superimpositions may belong to the same cultural

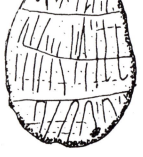

188. *Above:* Elements of the Umbú Tradition of the late hunters of southern Brazil: a hole-boring tool, a pair of two-faced points, and a stone with geometric designs (similar to some from Salto Grande in Uruguay). Different scales (from A. Prous, 1986).

189. *Right:* Abstract and crisscross petroglyphs achieved through rubbing on a horizontal rock. Morro do Sobrado site in Montenegro (Río Grande do Sul) (redrawn after a photograph by P. Mentz Ribeiro).

period. As happens in some of Europe's Paleolithic caves, "these ancient peoples had their own special reasons for continuing to paint the same section of wall and superimposing figures, almost as if the remaining rock lacked the same magical and religious significance." (Pia, 1987a, p. 31.)

Pia notes that the Ur III site—one of the numerous sandstone walls bordering the arroyo in question—has a notable characteristic: "There is a very intense, loud sound, like that of a waterfall. One tries to find the water but to no avail. The noise emanates from within the wall, but not a single drop of water issues from it. One can well imagine how amazed and enchanted the ancient inhabitants must have been at this particular phenomenon." (Ibid., p. 54.)

From his analysis, Pia concludes that it is possible to speak "of two important pictorial periods: the first is characterized by the depiction of the 'rhea-man' in multiple variations and transformations; the second is characterized by the 'frog-man' drawn in his particular frontal position with his arms and legs stretched straight out. The two styles are totally different, not only because of the type of pictorial representation displayed but also because of the pictorial technique employed." (Ibid., p. 57.) There are many dynamic representations, including two men facing off with axes (the only chronological and cultural indication, since stone axes of this type began to be used around 1000 B.C.E.). There are also schematic sexual scenes, hunters with lances, and rows of potbellied men. In many cases there is a remarkable resemblance to figures from distant Piauí, to the extent that it can be said that the Northeastern Tradition reached the Bolivian southeast, although probably at some late period. This can also be seen on other painted rock walls, such as the one at Saba. (These influences may be further observed at Goiás and in northern Minas Gerais.)[53]

The anthropomorphic figure with ambiguous traits between "frog-man" and the "praying" figure is largely found in the San José de Chiquitos area, sometimes associated with a sun and ladder, which suggests a shamanic scene. Geometric motifs are abundant in this area, which Pia suggests are derived from other naturalist ones. A site rich in such motifs, reminiscent of Brazil's San Francisco Tradition, is the María Chica rock wall. Aside from solar symbols, there are framed crosses similar to those of Caiaponia (Pia, 1987a, pp. 116–18). For his part, Jurgen Riester (1981) discovered another great rock shelter to the west of Santiago de Chiquitos, ascribed to the second stylistic group, using large rhomboidal crisscross patterns as a base and numerous schematic geometric and anthropomorphic figures, including the frog-man. Some of these paintings appear to have been repainted by local people.

In order to understand the "rhea-man" figure, Pia resorts to ethnography, which shows that certain tribes of the Chaco spoke of "the Great Ñandú (rhea, or American ostrich) that protects its species." This would then be an ancient mythological figure, originating among the people who shared the land with this terrestrial bird, which also exists in southern and eastern Brazil under the name *ema*. We now wonder: are the recent inhabitants of this area descended from the creators of the paintings of the first stylistic group of the Urasquivía arroyo?

The Southern Region (Pampa-Patagonia)

The great plains of the Chaco do not possess any cave art sites due to the absence of rocky backdrops. The same is the case in the coastal provinces of Argentina and on the plains of the Pampa. In Uruguay a dozen sites with geometric paintings are known, and because of their probable relationship to those of Patagonia—which is rich in both cave art and portable art—they will be discussed

190. *Left:* A bird zoolith seen in profile. From the *sambaquis,* or shell heaps, of the state of Paraná (photograph: A. Prous). *Right:* Large fish-shaped stone piece (approximately 16 inches (40 centimeters) long), from the Paraná State *sambaquis* (photograph: A. Prous).

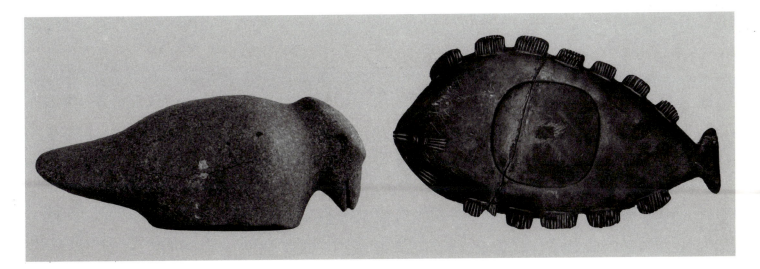

191. Three engraved stones from the Salta Grande region (on the Uruguay River) belonging to a Late Preceramic phase (circa 2600 B.C.E. at the Bañadero site). The top one measures 4 inches (102 millimeters), the middle one 4.3 inches (110 millimeters), and the bottom one 4.6 inches (117 millimeters) (photograph: J. Fermenías).

later. The same can be said for certain sites located in the hills of Buenos Aires and La Pampa provinces.[54]

We have already seen that the Pinturas River has a stylistic sequence through which—after the A and B groups or phases (of late hunters)—we arrive at C (circa 1000 B.C.E.). This is characterized by very schematic human figures and linear treatments colored an intense red. Other late elements are zigzags, triangles with their points aiming at each other, and the schematic drawing of hands. No motifs are found here of the late paintings, with frets and ladders, although they can be found in other sites of the area (i.e., the Cárdenas shelter).

The second great technical and stylistic form of Patagonia after that of the ancient hunters is what Osvaldo Menghin (1957) named the Pisadas style, which almost without exception manifests itself in engravings. Their origin and initial chronology remain an unsolved problem. Scholars initially put their origin in the Andean region and later in Brazil, where we have seen the sites associated with the Umbú Hunter Tradition. The rock shelters of the Pinturas River, particularly the art of phase B-1, provide several painted negative prints of real rhea legs. These would then be, at least for southern Patagonia, the models for what is known as the three-toed motif. The same can be said about the rosettes (circles with surrounding dots) from which puma tracks could have evolved. In this case the circle is surrounded by four, five, or six dots. A hand engraved in the rock of Cerro Morado de Norquín, Neuquén Province, along with three-toed figures, serpent shapes, and circular holes and channels, suggest that they derive from the negative handprint images farther south (there is one in the Los Toldos cave). The guanaco trail is also relatively uncommon (two thick, short parallel lines), appearing in Cerro Nonial, La Media Luna, northern Neuquén, and Angostura de Gaimán, which borders the Chubut River Valley (Gradin, 1979). These can be likened to the Pisadas style. This style sometimes includes circles, diverse abstract signs, and animal-shaped figures of lizards and serpents. The Pisadas style emerged among the inhabitants of central and northern Patagonia as a reflection of their hunting beliefs: the sign symbolizes life and the animal's properties in a quasi-magical relationship. In a study of the cave art of Patagonia, Rodolfo Casamiquela (1981) concludes that the so-called Pisadas style is associated with puberty rituals, as also occurred with the negative handprint paintings. It is also related to the existence of symbolic ancestors. This does not rule out the presence of external stimuli that may have played a role in these cave ceremonies and traditions. (It has already been noted that some of their signs are also related to other motifs in the Argentine northwest, and also constitute the Huayquivilo style of the Linares Cordillera in Chile.) The method of execution is generally by hammering or deep pitting, but also includes rubbing and linear incision. The backgrounds employed can be rock walls and shelters as well as loose rocks.

Although less frequent, some circular motifs with two or three internal radial designs were interpreted in the past as horse tracks. Later, Menghin (1977) interpreted them as simplified forms of curvilinear mazes, based mainly on the existence of a figure known as the "Museum Stone," which is of this type and which exists in a cave in northeastern Santa Cruz.[55] Other variants could be derived from vulvar signs (appearing at Llano Blanco, a site in northern Neuquén), although the subject of fertility does not appear to have been an important notion to the late Patagonian hunters. There is an association with numerous groups of *morterillos* (pits and grooves) at other sites, such as the Chocón Chico rock shelter on the Limay River in Neuquén. On the Norquín rock are found to this day coins and other small offerings left by the people who inhabit the area. Other examples of sites with engravings include Cerro Yanquenao and Angostura de Gaiman in Chubut, and Punta del Lago Viedma in western Santa Cruz—one of the southernmost sites to feature animal-shaped representations. There are also scattered sites on the plateaus of the Strobel lakes in Buenos Aires and Las Plumas in the central valley of the Chubut River, where curvilinear complexes are in abundance. Las Plumas features irregular engravings on sandstone rock along a mountain slope (Menghin and Gradin, 1972). The shelter consisting of a large boulder located in southern Neuquén (Malavaca) has a series of engraved feet which were repainted in red, probably during a second phase of execution, which also included late geometric paintings. In southern Mendoza—also the realm of hunters—are sites with an abundance of three-toed symbols beside motifs such as the simple faces, which are of Andean origin.

Gradin believes that the beginning of the stylistic group under discussion coincides with the beginning of the Patagonian cultural phase, which corresponds to the most direct ancestors of the ethnographic Tehuelches. This process began toward the middle of the first millennium B.C.E., and therefore coincided with the settlement of the first agricultural and ceramic cultures in the Argentine northwest. Since these cultures possessed the technique of stone engraving, one hypothesis suggests that these techniques spread from here to Patagonia. Recently, however, traces of older techniques have also appeared in Patagonia.[56]

The blossoming of the Pisadas style lasted about 2,000 years. Around the middle of this period, it began to be displaced by the third great Patagonian stylistic set known as the "geometric paintings of the late hunters" and more commonly *Estilo de Grecas* (Fret style). It has been intensely studied in recent years by Gradin as well as by Carlos Aschero, Maria Onetto and Jorge Fernández, not to mention the pioneering work of Osvaldo Menghin and Rodolfo Casamiquela. Gradin provides the following description of this style.

It is largely composed of motifs of an abstract nature, and its diffusion mostly occurred in the southern region. As a stylistic device the frets—including ladders, cruciforms, zigzags, etc.—are particularly well-distributed in the provinces of Río Negro and the neighboring areas of Neuquén and Chubut. Here this third major Patagonian stylistic set achieved its greatest splendor, not only because of its quantity but also due to the complexity of its motifs and multiple colors. The frets, named for their staggered or step-like shapes, originated in northwestern Argentine pottery. Its links to the ceremonial axes shaped like figure 8's and to the engraved slabs of northern Patagonia are obvious (although the slabs sometimes present the same finely engraved decorative motifs). Their age, therefore, cannot go much beyond the fifth century of the Common Era. The most important sites featuring this type of paintings can be seen at Mamuel Choique, Cerro Carbón, Estancia Los Sauces, in the province of Río Negro, and at Paso del Sapo, Cerro Shequén, and Estancia Los Libres in the province of Chubut. In this last instance, the fret paintings are covered by a large quantity of very fine engravings, which are randomly superimposed. They appear to have been done with a shaky hand, even when they depict small painted motifs.

These miniatures cannot be entirely separated from the fret group by virtue of their small size. They are linked by the similarity of their designs—laddered lines, combinations of triangles, and very simple borders—and may have evolved from the frets, which flourished in the last phases of their development. The miniatures' motifs appear frequently on Chilean and Incan pottery, and could be dated to somewhere between the eleventh and fifteenth centuries. Examples of these miniatures are the paintings at Estancia San Ramón (Río Negro) and those in the Cañadón de las Manos Pintadas (Chubut).

Patagonia's final stylistic group covers a series of painted motifs and engravings showing a preference for the use of curved or bowed designs which are often surprisingly ornamental. The human figures included within this group are small and schematic. In fact, these various motifs do not constitute a style. They are more like an eclectic assortment, very probably resulting from the mutual influence of several coexisting modes which in some cases fused during the final years of Patagonia's artistic development. This occurred with the paintings at Estancia San Ramón, the engravings of the Piedra Calada at Las Plumas, and the pictograms of Sierra Paileman. Silhouettes of the first European horsemen, who arrived in the early seventeenth century, are found at Nahuel Huapí lake.

In the last century, natives no longer recognized this cave art, and its meaning fell into the realm of lost traditions. The renowned explorer Francisco P. Moreno only managed to recover—as would other researchers later on—the name of Elengásem, the mythical hero of the Guénnaken or southern Tehuelches, to whom they attributed the authorship of paintings in general." (Gradin, 1984, pp. 48–50.)[57]

192. The rock walls of the Angostura de Gaiman (Chubut) feature Pisadas style cave engravings. The section photographed shows holes and rosettes as well as rhea and guanaco prints. This style has been estimated as beginning between 1000 B.C.E. and 1000 C.E. (photograph: Carlos J. Gradin).

193. A special stylistic group of Patagonian cave engravings carved into blocks is at the Piedra Calada site (Las Plumas, central Chubut). As can be seen in the photo, curvilinear motifs—probably bearing a religious significance—are predominant here (photograph: Carlos J. Gradin).

Coinciding with the very limited introduction of ceramics toward the eighth century in northern Patagonia, cave art becomes notably diversified. Painting and engraving exist side by side, but painting acquires renewed importance with the development of the simple geometric paintings, which already occasionally formed part of the ancient hunter's repertoire. This type of geometric painting—dots, crisscross and curvilinear designs, broken or zigzagging lines, positive handprints—is widely distributed, extending from the far south (Cerro Benítez, Palli Aike, in Chilean Patagonia) to the provinces of the Pampa (Chicalcó, Lihuel-Calel) and Buenos Aires (Coto de Caza Mayor and other sites along Sierra de la Ventana). Moreover, it appears in the Sierra de San Luis and crosses the Río de la Plata and its tributaries to Uruguay, whose late hunters known as *Charrúa* present cultural affinities with the Tehuelches. In these last two regions are further depictions of the geometric-ornamental type, such as the rock shelter of La Angostura in the Sierra de San Luis and in the painted blocks of the Maestre de Campo and Chamangá arroyos in central-southern Uruguay. Two positive hand prints are also found here.[58]

Other important sites showing the Fret style and its variations include the Cardenas rock shelter and Cerro de los Indios above Lake Posadas in northwestern Santa Cruz (these are the most southern ones); the vicinity of Lake Puelo and the El Bolsón Valley, Piedra Parada, and other areas along the middle Chubut River; and Norquincó, Comallo (with remarkable variety and multiple colors), and others in Río Negro. In southern Neuquén is the Abra Grande rock wall (on the Huemul Peninsula in Lake Nahuel Huapí), featuring a maze-like complex ending in concentric circles. This is similar to the engraved motifs of the Ciénaga pottery of northwestern Argentina (circa 200–650 C.E.). Another remarkable multicolored complex can be found on a rock wall at Estancia Chacabuco. Farther north we have the Cerro Huemul Cave, with its unique cross-shaped paintings. Crossing the Río Colorado on the border with Mendoza are the Pincheyra Caves and Rincón Amarillo in the Department of Malargüe, and finally, Cueva del Indio and two other sites near the Río Atuel.

Several studies have been conducted on this broad cave art mode discussing their magical and symbolic nature.[59] This research goes from the formulation of genealogical models for one of the motifs (the staggered X anthropomorph), to a recent analysis of the staggered cross-shaped motifs as representing imaginary figures taken from broader geometric sets where the positive-negative arrangement plays a basic role. Jorge Fernández suggests that this mechanism contributed to the psychological aspects of the rituals without the need to resort to hallucinogenic substances: "Consequently, in cave art, images that are depicted in an individual

194. Engraved stone slabs from northern Patagonia, whose motifs are related to the cave paintings of late hunters. The one on the left comes from Villa La Angostura, and the one on the right from the Río Limay Valley in southern Neuquén province. Size somewhat smaller than life-size (Patagonia Museum, Bariloche; drawing by author).

or dismembered way are generated by a model that consists of complicated and essentially repetitive—or endless—compositions from a more complex form of art." (Fernández, 1988–89, p. 385.) Their origins are probably related to those of basket weaving techniques and leather tooling.

All of these approaches, while interesting, fail to capture the deeper sense of the late forms of Pampean-Patagonian cave art—the manner in which it carried out its social function, the causes for site selection, and the causes for its appearance and disappearance. One should also consider the role the art played in contact with the Araucans who began to penetrate the area in the sixteenth century but with whom the local inhabitants had already had prior contact. Nor do we know anything about the functional or social relationship between cave art and the objects engraved with the same geometric motifs, except for their widespread explanation as sacred artifacts.

In regard to the above, it is worth noting that "archaic" forms also exist for the carved stone plates featuring simple and sometimes irregular geometric decorations. There are also elaborate rectangular or slightly trapezoidal-shaped pieces with rounded angles, sometimes rather large in size. While there may well be cases of "secondary primitivism," the first group of plates are considered the oldest, related to the simple geometric motifs of cave art. (Curiously, the majority of these plates have been discovered on the Atlantic coast.) Although there are no dated finds, they are probably more than 4,000 years old. I make this statement bearing in mind that Bird found a polished bone tube with a simple geometric engraving (two longitudinal zigzags), corresponding to Period IV of Fell Cave in southern Patagonia. Another indication—an indirect one, since it comes from another cultural area—can be found in the small engraved plates excavated by Alberto Rex González at the Intihuasi Grotto in the Sierra de San Luis. These can be attributed to the Ayampitín Culture (circa 6000–3000 B.C.E.). More elaborate engraved plates have decorations comparable to the Fret style, made by finely incised lines. Their web-like nature suggests that they were influenced by cultures with a high degree of textile development, such as Chile or the Andean region. There are also some rather well-defined comparisons with the Paracas, Tiahauanaco, Condorhuasi, and other cultures.[60]

Incised decoration (largely zigzag) sometimes appears on arrow shafts made of *coligüe* (*Chusquea*) cane in certain caves of northern Patagonia. Small flat pebbles with staggered line paintings have also been found at these sites.

As another sample of prehistoric Patagonian art, mention must be made of two strange objects sculpted in stone. These have not been precisely dated but are probably of late origin. One is from the Gaiman (Chubut) area, measures 14 inches (35 centimeters) in length, and probably represents a peccary, a wild boar extinct in the area. The other consists of a stylized depiction of a sea lion's head in relief on a large flattened pebble, measuring 12 inches (30 centimeters) in diameter. Somewhat resembling the Brazilian zooliths, it was found a few years ago among the remains of a

195. Maze-like drawing in red, one of the motifs of late cave art (approximately 700–1500 C.E.) in central and northern Patagonia. Campo Cosmen site, Languiñeo, western Chubut (survey by N. Giménez and M. Martínez).

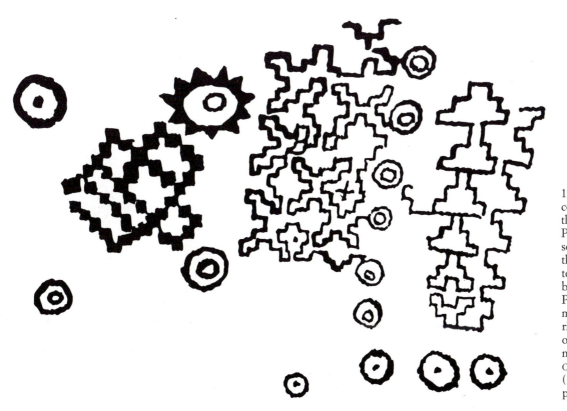

196. A remarkable abstract complex in red paint on a rock in the Abra Grande site (Huemul Peninsula on Lake Nahuel Huapí, southern Neuquén). This is one of the models which gave rise to the term Fret style for the paintings by the late hunters of southern Patagonia. The central figure is maze-like, and the one on the right resembles the incised motifs of the Ciénaga culture of northwestern Argentina (200–650 C.E.). Width of the panel: 4.8 feet (1.47 meters) (redrawn from a photograph by M. Vignati).

mound-shaped burial beside a shallow, seaside archaeological site at Punta Médanos north of Santa Cruz.[61]

A singular example of this archaic art are the harpoons excavated by Luis Orquera and his assistants at the El Túnel site on the Beagle Channel in Tierra del Fuego. Elegant curvilinear ornamental incisions have been made on a double-pointed bone harpoon with a cross-shaped base, a typical element of the Phase II period (4000–3000 B.C.E.). Similar finds by Annette Laming and J. Emperaire on the Chilean island of Englefield present a crisscross decoration.[62] This shows that the Canoe, or Fuegian, Indians (shellfish gatherers, fishers, and seal hunters) were not as primitive as once was thought. What is still unknown is whether these designs were purely ornamental or whether they had some specific purpose. Given the lack of cave art on the island of Tierra del Fuego and in the other islands of the Magellanic region, these are the only works of art known in the remote southern tip of South America.

During our journey across two continents and thousands of years we have covered a vast amount of territory. The purpose of this book has been basically descriptive, to let the material speak for itself. The book also has one overarching goal: to fully integrate 50,000 years of the Americas into universal prehistory. Growing research into its processes, adaptations, and rich creations as varied as its geography has enabled us to develop an outline of the continents' cultural history. Its art is less ancient—and is at first sight poorer—than that of the broad artistic provinces of Europe. However, when seen from the perspective of naturalism or figurative expression, the art of the Americas has nothing to envy Europe if we consider it as an expression of powerful psychic experiences which translate into an artform generally marked by abstraction and symbolism. The art of the High Cultures represents the development of a long tradition based on magic and religion in which shamanic practices appear to have played a basic role. When it comes to cave art—the most outstanding aspect of prehistoric American art—much still remains to be discovered. Much also remains to be interpreted and published. Nevertheless, one can state that as a whole it marks one of the highest expressions of the human spirit's quest for contact with what is termed the higher, mythical, or divine world.

197. Piece of cane with incised geometric decorations, natural size and enlarged drawing. From a cave in Cerro Leones near Bariloche, northwest of the Río Negro (drawing by A. Schimmel).

198. Decorative art of the most ancient Canoe, or Fuegian, Indians (fishers, shell-gatherers, and seal hunters) of southernmost South America. Among the artifacts excavated at Englefield Island (Chile) are three long, patterned bones, two cross-shaped harpoons with incised linear decoration, and one harpoon with multiple teeth. This phase also appears in the Straits of Magellan and the Beagle Channel, and is dated between 4500 and 2000 B.C.E. (after Schobinger, 1988, based on drawings by Emperaire and Laming). The bone harpoon (on the far right) with the cross-shaped base is similar to those of Englefield Island, and shows curvilinear engravings. Its length is 5 inches (13 centimeters). Excavated at the El Túnel site on the southern coast of the Tierra del Fuego, on the Beagle Channel, and dated at about 4000 B.C.E. (redrawn from a photograph by L. Orquera).

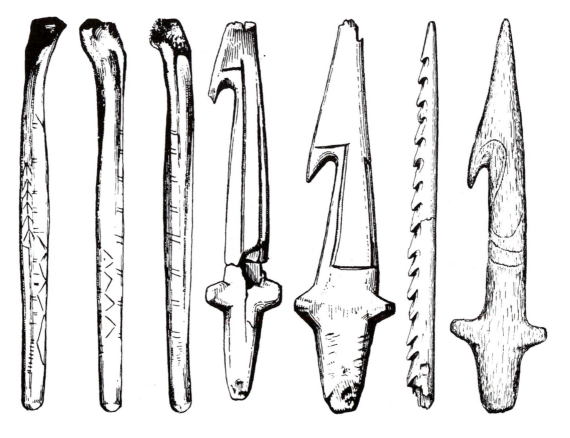

268

1 At the Xothe site, white handprints "are arranged in pairs and can be perceived as appearing just prior to being imprinted; the people involved had folded their forearms, because the thumbprints point outward." (Hernández, Reyes, 1973, p. 78.) At Cerro de Tres Peñas (Tepeapulco area), the numerous red handprints appear to belong to eight-to-ten-year-old children, and are displayed in a fan-shaped arrangement around simple geometric figures (Ibid., p. 82).

2 The doubtlessly ceremonial complex of Chalcatzingo has been studied by a number of authors, particularly Piña Chan (1955) and Gay (1971). A number of excavations have been undertaken in recent times (Grove, 1984). A summary of this and other sites with reliefs can be found in Soustelle, 1984. The most recent and best illustrated work on the Olmec culture is found in Piña Chan, 1989.

3 This work, associated with petroglyphs, is reminiscent of the shamanic ladder carved in wood employed in Chile by the Araucan *machi*. For an overall view of the Mexican works see Krickeberg, 1968. In his 1949 book, Krickeberg also discussed Texcotzingo and Malinalco—two great "rupestrian temples," by which he meant temples carved out of bare rock; he also mentioned the Xochicalco underground site. These three sites imitate natural caverns with ritual and funeral purposes. They were previously used by the Maya and Olmec.

4 To the right—looking from the entrance—there is another, simpler panel with suns and other figures attributed to the early days of the Spanish Conquest, and farther to the right we find modern paintings which include a bicycle. The set is completed by an altar which is still used to pray for rain and good harvests (Chac-Chac). The cave has thus preserved its character as a sacred place throughout ages and cultural changes.

5 Stone, 1987, p. 106. Aside from this article, a useful and updated summary of Yucatan cave art is provided by María Casado López, 1988. Annotated bibliography up to 1982: Strecker, 1982.

6 Lunardi, 1943. All of the bibliography available for Central America is collected in Strecker, 1982, together with useful comments.

7 Matilló Vila, 1965, 1973. (The author sometimes signs his works with his religious pseudonym Hildeberto María.) For Ometepe, there is also a study by Haberland, 1968.

8 Ibid., 1973, p. 52. In the Chontales region to the north of Lake Nicaragua are significant anthropomorphic stone statues (more reminiscent of Andean rather than Mesoamerican influences) whose dates are not certain. This poses the possibility that a ceremonial center of sorts could have existed, and that there could have been a relationship between these statues and the petroglyphs.

9 Harte (1961) attributes the Panamanian petroglyphs to the Caribs arriving from South America. Many authors follow this ethnographic trend because of their ignorance of the corresponding cultural context. In the words of Matthias Strecker (1982, p. 6), "Future investigation will probably disclose the existence of strong ties between Central America and the Caribbean on the one hand, and with South America on the other." In order to reach valid conclusions, many more analytical and comparative studies will be needed.

10 A large group resembling megalithic structures and associated with an artificial mound can be found at Capá, Puerto Rico (Willey, 1971, pp. 387–92). Simpler structures appear to have existed during the Ostionoid phase (circa 600–1200 C.E.). The scheme presented here, highly simplified, is the one generally accepted by specialists on the peopling of the Antilles. (See, for example, Núñez Jiménez, 1975, 1986, *La Cultura Taína*, 1983). More recently Chanlatte (1986) has refined this model, giving more importance to local developments than to migrations. According to his data, the main peopling of the Antilles by ceramic cultures took place between 200 B.C.E. and 450 C.E. From this date to the year 1000—according to a series of Carbon-14 datings— we find the Ostionoid culture in Puerto Rico, which also extends to the island of Santo Domingo and from which a number of subgroups have emerged.

11 A number of skeletons were unearthed in nearby Cave Number 4 at Punta del Este, were there is only one red cross-shaped sign formed by four opposing angles. One of the skeletons was Carbon-14 dated to the year 850, but this date does not necessarily have to apply to the paintings and material from Cave Number 1. The caves on the Isle of Pines produced a rather extensive bibliography collected by Socarrás Matos (1985), who undertook a numerical study of Cave Number 1's circular figures. According to Socarrás Matos, this suggests that there could have been some type of time measurement system, as Herrera Fritot suggested in 1943.

12 A. Núñez Jimenez, 1986, pp. 14–15, plate 67. Both are from Banes, in the island's far south. These are museum pieces lacking any certain archaeological context. Still, they are interesting pieces, particularly the second one, which shows certain analogies with the Australian *churingas*.

13 In fact, comparisons between the incised fragments and excavated models with those of the Ostiones phase published by Chanlatte (1986) show great similarity. If this could be generalized, we would have a basis for the contextualization and chronology of a large part of the Antillean petroglyphs. Excavations at the Duey Bajo site, corresponding to a late Ostiones phase, yielded a stone ax fragment with a somewhat crudely incised face similar to that of the petroglyphs (op. cit., fig. 40).

14 This is the subdivision given in Willey's classic book, 1971, Chapters 5 and 6. Other authors include the uplands of Ecuador and Colombia in the northern Andean Region.

15 Pérez de Barrados collected numerous drawings made by others whose documentary value is not very trustworthy. In the past decade, Guillermo Muñoz and collaborators of the Grupo de Investigaciones de Pintura Rupestre (GIPRI) have undertaken a systematic review of the area's rupestrian paintings. To date, there has been little official interest in the protection of these sites and research into this aspect of archaeology. In Colombia "it is not known if cave art should be treated simply as Art, or as a strange object, or as a capricious

199. Large ceremonial ax from northern Patagonia, from El Cuy (province of Río Negro). Height: 13 inches (33 centimeters). It shows maze-like engravings (after a photograph published by O. Menghin).

manifestation which has not been connected to what little is known of the archaeological areas that have been studied." (Muñoz, 1991, p. 12.)

[16] Or also, cercado del Zipa, given the existence of a tradition claiming that the last Chibcha chieftain hid in this gorge, bordered by picturesque sandstone crags, before being defeated by the forces of Gonzalo Jiménez de Quesada in 1536. Aside from Triana, L. Zerda and Pérez de Barradas, this site was also discussed in A. Núñez Jimenez's monograph (1959), where it is described as the Frog Sanctuary.

[17] The cup-shaped holes (which Granda supposes to be related to water worship) probably exist in many South American sites, alone or accompanied by petroglyphs, although reports do not always mention them. There is also information on their presence in Ecuador's mountainous region.

[18] Published in his 1941 book, pp. 47–49, plates 98–105.

[19] There is preliminary documentation on these sites: *Centro Arqueológico Kuayu*, 1981, pp. 49–91.

[20] Like many others, these sites deserve to be described with more detail and precision. There are at least four opposing drawings on Cerro Pitnado de Atures (Sujo-Volsky, 1975, fig. 90). An ancient author estimates the serpent's length at 400 feet (120 meters). Tavera Acosta (1956, p. 43) says that the figures are painted and "appear white"; Koch-Grünberg (1907, p. 6) says that they are engraved, and Delgado (1976, p. 106) classifies them as "glyphs." No one thought to climb the rock wall and make a direct, well-documented study!

[21] Dubelaar (1986b), the main scholar of the region's petroglyphs, ventures no interpretations at all for this figure. Some believe it depicts a funeral bundle (!); others "an Egyptian priest in full regalia" (!) (Tavera Acosta, 1956, p. 72).

[22] To obtain his documentation, Dubelaar had to resort to such fantasy writers as Bernardo Da Silva Ramos and Marcel Homet (whose book *The Children of the Sun* claimed that Pedra Pintada was a colossal monument), but the area's cave art has been systematically studied by Pedro A. Mentz Ribeiro and his team (1987, 1989).

[23] For Indian legends regarding the South American petroglyphs, see Dubelaar, 1986a, pp. 58–69.

[24] Willey, 1971, pp. 399–416; Simões, 1981–1982. The pottery of the island of Marajó shows characters in a frog-form posture with three fingers on each extremity, as shown in many petroglyphs.

[25] Koch-Grünberg, 1907, plates 8, 21. There are also masked depictions similar to certain ethnographic garments (Tipiaka-*cachoeira*, Caiari-Uaupés River, plate 22 and figs. 24–27), which probably belong to relatively modern times. See another sampler of area petroglyphs in Rouse, 1949, figs. 163–64; Pérez de Barradas, 1941, plates 119–23 (according to older surveys). P. Jackson (1982) provides some photographic documentation for the Uaupés River petroglyphs, without contributing almost anything new regarding the studies made by Koch-Grünberg (whose important 1907 publication he ignores!).

[26] Baer et al., 1983; Fernández Distel, 1972–1973; Pardo, 1957.

[27] The Cassiquiare Channel, as it is known, links the Orinoco and Amazon basins and could also be considered the link between both rupestrian areas. Numerous engraved faces along the Urubú River (a northern tributary of the Amazon) are similar to the ones of northern Venezuela. Sites such as Los Tamarindos, with its combinations of concentric and spiraled circles, or Campo Elías (Caura) with its series of shells surrounding a face (Delgado, 1976, figures 25–26, 27–29), have an undeniable Amazonian flavor shared by the more complex ones on the central rock of Aishalton and other sites in Guyana (Dubelaar, 1986b, pp. 189–90, 195–96; Núñez Jiménez, 1986, plate 61).

[28] While this book was being printed we received word on the results of the excavations directed by Anna Roosevelt at Caverna de Pedra Pintada, one of the caves in the Monte Alegre region. Its rich, well-defined geological composition begins with the provisional occupation of hunter-gatherers during the last millennium of the Pleistocene period (9200–8000 B.C.E.), revealing an adaptation to a forested region which was then in the process of expansion. The stone industry includes triangular points with short bases, similar to some found earlier in the vicinity of the Tapajós River which in turn resemble some found in Ecuador and in Peru's Paiján Complex. This confirms the existence of already diverging traditions and adaptations during the Ice Age, unrelated to the large-animal hunters represented, among others, by Clovis, El Jobo, or Los Toldos/Fell. The paintings in this cave—which have yet to be described in detail—include curious curvilinear anthropomorphic figures and adult and infant handprints. They probably go back to the stage in question, but this still awaits confirmation. Following an interruption toward 5500 B.C.E., the cave was reoccupied by a population that favored fishing, along with gathering activities in rivers and on land. These are the same people who left behind the Taperinha refuse pile, which has yielded the oldest pottery known. Fragments of it were also excavated in this important site. See A. Roosevelt et al., "Paleoindian Cave-Dwellers in the Amazon: The Peopling of the Americas," *Science* 272 (April 19, 1996), pp. 373–84.

[29] Núñez Jiménez, 1986, I, pp. 366–67; Willey, 1971, p. 114. The Pickman Strombus, 10 inches (25 centimeters) in length, probably served as a trumpet, and the character represented is playing precisely this instrument. In the petroglyph, whose height is 31.5 inches (80 centimeters), the four-fingered hands do not hold any objects.

[30] The Checta petroglyphs, located a mere 37 miles (60 kilometers) from Lima, were first studied around 1929. They were also analyzed by J. Guffroy (1980).

[31] Núñez Jiménez (1986c, pp. 142 and following) says that they are "blowing *pincullos* or large trumpets," but it seems more correct to interpret the instruments as pipes.

[32] This deposit was discovered in 1951 by Eloy Linares Málaga, who made only brief descriptions (1973). They were also mentioned by Disselhoff (1955) and other researchers. The fact that Antonio Núñez Jiménez

has devoted almost the entirety of the fourth volume of his work on Peruvian petroglyphs to them (1986) and included 536 figures (also published as a separate book), indicates their size and the importance of the Toro Muerto site. Taken as a whole, the sub-Peruvian department of Arequipa is rich in rupestrian sites. In 1990, Linares Malaga accounted for a total of 20 sites with paintings (many of them from the hunters' phase), 65 of them with engravings, six with geoglyphs, and 30 sites where the "portable art of the rupestrian tradition" had been discovered.

[33] There are also hundreds of these stones in museums and collections, but they are considered to be forgeries or made by locals for the tourist trade.

[34] The important contributions of the Sociedad de Investigación del Arte Rupestre Boliviano (SIARB) must be noted. Since its foundation in 1987 it has dealt with surveys, conservation, and education through its publications, as well as organizing international symposiums. An overview of Bolivian cave art can be found in the work of Roy Querejazu Lewis (1984–1985) and Matthias Strecker (1987). More recently, an important volume on Colonial and Post-Independence Rupestrian Art (1992) has appeared. As a result of SIARB's activities, Strecker was able to compile a total of 311 rupestrian art sites in Bolivia as of late 1994.

[35] One of the cup-marks or pits and grooves contained small stones impregnated with *jach'us* (chewed coca residue). A significant amount of chewed coca was also found within a triangular crack in a ceremonial rock, as well as a piece of flat white quartz about 4 inches (10 centimeters) long, deposited as an offering (SIARB Bulletin, Noticias, p. 16).

[36] Along with numerous other publications there is an excellent book summmarizing Chilean cave art by Grete Mostny and Hans Niemeyer, 1983. We should also note a number of articles appearing in the book *Studios de Arte Rupestre* (1985).

[37] This important rupestrian area was unknown until the pioneering work of León Strube Erdmann in the 1920s, continued in the 1950s by Jorge Iribarren, and later by Hans Niemeyer, Dominique Ballereau, and others.

[38] See photographs in Mostny and Niemeyer, 1983, pp. 78–79. In Cueva de los Catalanes, some 25 miles (40 kilometers) southwest of Los Angeles, there are fine engravings with Mapuche or Araucan motifs (including the shamanic drum known as the *cultrun*) as well as some deeper ones with vulvar signs, which are possibly older. Other similar ones shaped like a U with a central vertical line, are found beside footprints in Llano Blanco cave, north of the neighboring Argentine province of Neuquén. This motif appears on the rocky coast of the Pacific near the port of Huasco, at an intermediate location between the Pachene River and the engraved rock of Llaima. Menghin (1964) believed in a cultural link between the three sites, a manifestation of an ancient fertility cult and an indication of an Amazonian paleoagricultural trend which would have constituted one of the bases of the Araucan culture. On the other hand, Americo Gordon (1980) reinterprets the Llaima figures as guanaco fertility symbols, and their authors as hunters who met at the site for related festivities. This hypothesis seems less probable.

[39] They have largely been surveyed by the author, who has a joint publication under way. (See Schobinger, 1982b, 1988b, also 1962, on the mask-shaped motif, among others.)

[40] The complex of sites gathered under the name Cerro Colorado (known today as Parque Arqueológico Provincial) was the first to merit a luxury book on South American cave art (although it was published in England: Gardner, 1931). Subsequently, Asbjorn Pedersen undertook an exhaustive survey aided by infrared illumination which allowed for the completion of numerous friezes in the area and the addition of new ones. His numerous tracings remain unpublished.

[41] For this area there is an old work by Cáceres Freyre (1957); for Santiago del Estero there is a recent one by Amalia Gramajo de Martínez Moreno (1988); and for San Luis we have a detailed survey by Mario Consens (1986).

[42] Summarizing all petroglyphs within one single tradition is questionable, not only because of their geographical, chronological, technical, and aesthetic variety, but also because of their very name: *itacoatiara* means "marked, engraved or painted rock" in the Tupí-Guaraní language. In other words, it is tantamount to saying rupestrian engravings—a much too generic designation to apply to a group or stylistic tradition. (Gabriela Martín, 1992, p. 11, acknowledges that it would be best to refer to several *itacoatiara* traditions.)

[43] Beginning with the alleged presence of Phoenicians, Hebrews, Greeks, or Vikings and ending with vanished civilizations and extraterrestrials. At the end of the last century there was talk of a "Piedra de Paraíba" (never found) which bore Phoenician inscriptions, considered apocryphal by specialists in spite of its modern reappraisal by Cyrus Gordon. For all these subjects see Schobinger, 1982. For the special case of the Pedra de Ingá: Martín, 1975.

[44] The richest example of these superimpositions is Lapa dos Desenhos, a large rock wall located in the rainforest. Other more important sites are Lapa do Boquete and Lapa do Caboclo (Prous, 1986, 1989). Good illustrations appear in the book *Herança,* pp. 62–66, whose author has recently published a clear synthesis on cave art throughout Brazil (Prous, 1994).

[45] Schmitz et al., 1984, 1986 (very detailed on the Caiaponia area).

[46] Vilenha Vialou and Vialou, 1988–1989, 1989 (et al.). On March 18, 1992, Vialou advised me of an interesting development: the most recent excavations reached an Ice Age level 10,120 years old, with fossil fauna (*Lestodon*).

[47] From this important site there is only the preliminary data provided by excavator E. Miller.

[48] Aside from a photograph published by Passos (1980, p. 3), the available documentation for this complex

comes from fantasy writers who have interpreted them as runic inscriptions (Jacques de Mahieu) or Celtic ones (Jim Woodman) within the framework of untenable theories on the arrival of medieval Europeans to South America (see Schobinger, 1982).

[49] Some scholars have attributed these rupestrian complexes to the Guaraní. But with the exception of some geometric motifs, it cannot be said that there is a similarity to the decoration appearing on typical painted urns by the Guaraní (nor do we know of any of their petroglyphs in the Brazilian interior).

[50] Good photographs of a variety of zooliths can be seen in the book *Herança*, pp. 80–90. There are also birds sculpted on the thicker ends of whalebone pieces. A typical object of eastern Brazilian archaeology is the anchor-shaped ax, as well as common axes with lateral grooves or notches, presenting a perfect shape and polish (op. cit., pp. 92–93). On zooliths in general, see Prous, 1977.

[51] Pia, 1987a, p. 130; Schmitz et al., 1984, p. 68. The yard-high Bolivian figure has been redrawn several times, and rubbed with stones "on one occasion during the Macumba rituals which are held at the site at certain times of the year"(!). In other words, a probable ethnographic survival has been absorbed or substituted by an African ritual from Brazil.

[52] Pia, 1987a, 1987b, 1988. Summary for the Santa Cruz department: Querejazu Lewis, 1991.

[53] There are many examples of parallelism with Brazil: the rows of running monkeys, some of them carrying offspring on their backs, at Caiaponia and Ur I (Schmitz et al., 1984, p. 51; Pia, 1987a, p. 39); the two human figures carrying a smaller one (child?) between them (Pia, 1987a, p. 69); the "little headless men" (ibid., p. 87); and the long-legged characters with swollen knees (ibid., p. 63).

[54] Schobinger and Gradin, 1985, published in another series by the Jaca Book Publishers and Ediciones Encuentro. See further bibliographic references here. Patagonian cave art bibliography: Gradin, 1988.

[55] A site recently restudied and excavated by Laura Miotti, 1991. Miotti has identified "Paleoindian" levels (Toldensian culture) and therefore accepts the possibility (very remote, in my opinion) that the depictions reproduce the tracks of the extinct American horse.

[56] Schobinger and Gradin, 1985, pp. 35, 37: "To chronologically place the south-central Patagonian engravings we have a valuable piece of information supplied by the excavations conducted in the Manos Pintadas de las Pulgas rock shelter (Chubut), which allowed us to date the collapse of an enormous block from the rock shelter at between 660 and 490 B.C.E. Subsequently, a series of typical engravings in the Pisadas style was executed there: puma tracks, three-toed symbols, and curvilinear motifs shaped like the number 6 upon which fine incised lines were superimposed, including small crisscross patterns. The engraving technique would therefore go back to the end of the first millennium C.E. and would have flourished during the Patagonian era proper, for which we have radiocarbon data of 40 C.E. at the deposit in question." (Ibid., p. 39.) The rocky floor of the Epullán Grande cave (near the Limay River in southern Neuquén), excavated by Crivelli et al., 1991, has numerous irregular linear engravings resembling small to medium-size slashes. Their doubtful function and antiquity (a campfire 9,900 to 10,040 years old located on the rock) indicate that there is no relationship whatsoever to the Pisadas art. On the other hand, engravings in this style can be found on the walls of the cave itself, partly covered by archaeological sediment. The same occurs at two nearby sites from which archaeological sediment 2,500 to 2,700 years old was obtained. These engravings in northern Patagonia date to before 500 B.C.E., with their point of origin therefore being somewhat older than was supposed. The Visconti Cave in northwest Río Negro provides similar indications, where the engravings of footsteps were covered by sediments dating to around 600 B.C.E.

[57] Elengasém is a complex, apparently androgynous, and sometimes terrifying entity. The strong Patagonian winds are the product of his breath, and "all of the petrified bones found in the region come from his body (a relationship surely construed from his giant stature). According to native beliefs, these bones have certain therapeutic powers. It can be inferred that in the ceremonies of the Gününa Kena, the spirit of Elengasém was also closely linked to engraved slabs, ceremonial axes, and other objects with magical and religious properties." (Casamiquela, 1960, pp. 12, 19.) We are reminded of Amilvaca in the Venezuelan-Caribbean region, who is the legendary creator of the cave drawings found there.

[58] Massone, 1982; Gradin, 1975; Consens, 1986; Consens and Bespali, 1981. (Corresponding to the four sections discussed.)

[59] Casamiquela, 1960, 1981. In his valuable archaeological investigations, this author reached the conclusion that there is a basic relationship between maze-like and staggered pyramidal constructions: "both are—universally—representations of the path of the spirits of the dead" (1981, p. 135).

[60] Evidence for the latter is provided by Jorge Fernández in an unpublished work (and also in 1988–1989b). For complete documentation on the engraved Patagonian slabs, see Losada Gómez, 1980.

[61] For the first piece: Schobinger and Gradin, 1985, p. 37, fig. 82; for the second: Menghin and Gradin, 1972, pp. 57–58.

[62] Orquera y Piana, 1986–1987. Harpoons from Englefield can be seen in Schobinger, 1988, p. 351.

Bibliography

ABRAMOVA, ZOYA
  1990   L'art mobilier paléolithique en Sibérie. *Bollettino del Centro Camuno di Studi Preistorici,* vol. 25–26: 81–98.

ADAMS, RICHARD E.
  1977   *Prehistoric Mesoamerica.* New York: Little, Brown.

ADOVASIO, J. M., BOLDURIAN, A. T., and CARLISLE CARKUSKEM, R. C.
  1988   Who Are Those Guys?: Some Biased Thoughts on the Initial Peopling of the New World. In *American before Columbus: Ice-Age Origins,* pp. 45–61. Ethnology Monographs 12, Department of Anthropology, University of Pittsburgh.

AGUERRE, ANA, FERNÁNDEZ DISTEL, ALICIA, and ASCHERO, CARLOS
  1973   Hallazgo de un sitio acerámico en la quebrada de Inca-Cueva (Jujuy). *Relaciones de la Sociedad Argentina de Antropología,* vol. VII: 197–235.

AGUIAR, ALICE
  1986   A tradição Agreste: estudo sobre arte rupestre em Pernambuco. *Clio,* no. 8 (Serie Arqueológica, 3), 7–98. Universidade Federal de Pernambuco.

ALLISON, MARVIN
  1986   Las momias más antiguas del mundo. *Mundo Científico* (Madrid), vol. 55: 232–234.

ALLISON, NANCY
  1989   Anzick Collection Reunited. *Mammoth Trumpet,* vol. 5: 1–6. University of Maine, Orono.

ALMAGRO, MARTIN
  1969   *Las pinturas rupestres de la cueva de Maltravieso, en Cáceres. Guía del visitante.* Madrid, Ministerio de Educación y Ciencia.

ANATI, EMMANUEL (Editor)
  1983   International Seminar and Consultation of Specialists on the Study, Documentation and Conservation of Rock Art. A Summary of the Debates (1981). In *Preservation and Presentation of Rock Art, 1981–1983:* 5–98. (Studies and Documents on the Cultural Heritage, 1 UNESCO).

ANATI, EMMANUEL
  1984   The State of Research in Rock Art. A World Report Presented to UNESCO. *Bollettino CCSP,* vol. 21: 13–56.
  1988   *Origini dell'arte e della concettualità.* Milano, Jaca Book.

ANATI, E., FRADKIN, A., and SIMÕES DE ABREU, M.
  1984   Rock Art of Baja California Sur: Preliminary Report of the 1981 Research Expedition. *Bollettino CCSP,* vol. 21: 107–112.
  1983   *Ancient Images on Stone. Rock Art of the Californians.* (Compiled and edited by Jo Anne Van Tilburg.) Los Angeles, University of California.

ANTHONIOZ, S., COLOMBEL, P., and MONZON, S.
  1978   *Les peintures rupestres de Cerca Grande, Minas Gerais, Brésil.* Cahiers d'Archéologie d'Amérique du Sud, 6, Paris.

APARICIO, FRANCISCO DE
  1935   Viaje preliminar de exploración en el territorio de Santa Cruz. *Publicaciones del Museo Antropológico y Etnográfico* (Buenos Aires), Serie A, vol. III: 71–92.

ASCHERO, CARLOS
  1981–1982   Datos sobre la arqueología del Cerro Casa de Piedra, Sitio CCP 5, Santa Cruz. *Relaciones SAA,* vol. XIV, no. 2: 267–284.
  1979   Aportes al estudio del arte rupestre de Inca-Cueva 1 (Depto. Humahuaca, Hujuy). *Primeras Jornadas de Arqueología del Noroeste Argentino* (Universidad del Salvador, Buenos Aires).

ASCHERO, CARLOS, and PODESTÁ, MERCEDES
  1986   El arte rupestre en asentamientos precerámicos de la Runa argentina. *Runa* (Buenos Aires), vol. XVI: 29–57.

AVELEYRA ARROYO DE ANDA, LUIS
  1964   *El sacro de Tequixquiac.* México, Museo Nacional de Antropología. (Cuadernos del Museo, 2).

BAER, G., FERSTL, E., and DUBELAAR, C. N.
  1983   Petroglyphs from the Urubamba and Pantiacolla Rivers, Eastern Peru. *Verhandlungen der Naturforschenden Gesellschaft* Basel, vol. 94: 287–306, Basel.

BALLEREAU, DOMINIQUE
  1981   *Trois sites à pétroglyphes du Norte Chico,* Paris, Societé des Antiquités Nationales.
  1988   Les représentations anthropomorphes du Cerro Calera (Sonora, Mexique). *L'Anthropologie* (Paris), vol. 92, no. 1: 317–360.
  1989   Découverte d'un panneau rupestre dans la vallée de la Sierra El Alamo (Sonora, Mexique). *L'Anthropologie* (Paris), vol. 93, no. 2: 605–614.

BATE, LUIS FELIPE
  1970–1971   Primeras investigaciones sobre el arte rupestre de la Patagonia Chilena. *Anales del Instituto de la Patagonia* (Punta Arenas, Chile), vol. I: 15–25. Segundo informe, id., vol. II.
  1983   *Comunidades primitivas de cazadores recolectores en Sudamérica,* vols. I and II. (*Historia General de América,* 2). Caracas: Academia Nacional de la Historia de Venezuela.

BEDNARIK, ROBERT G.
  1989   On the Pleistocene Settlement of South America. *Antiquity,* vol. 63, no. 238: 101–108.
  1994   *The Pleistocene Art of Asia.* Journal of World Prehistory, vol. 8, no. 4: 351–375, New York, Plenum Press.

BELTRAÕ, MARÍA DA C. M. C., DANON, J., NADER, R., SOUSA MESQUITA, S., and MACHADO PORTELLA BOMMFIN, M. T.
  1990   Les représentations pictographiques de la Serra da Pedra Calcaria: les Tocas de Buzios et d'Esperança. *L'Anthropologie,* vol. 94, no. 1: 139–154, Paris.

BERBERIAN, EDUARDO E., and RODOLFO, A. RAFFINO
  1991   *Culturas indígenas de los Andes Meridionales,* Madrid, Alhambra.

BERDICHEWSKY, BERNARDO
  1972   *En torno a los orígenes del hombre americano,* Santiago de Chile, Editorial Universitaria.

BERENGUER, JOSÉ, CASTRO, V., ALDUNATE, C., SINCLAIRE, C., and CORNEJO, L.
  1985   Secuencia del arte rupestre en el Alto Loa: una hipótesis de trabajo. En *Estudios de Arte Rupestre,* 87–108, Santiago, Museo Chileno de Arte Precolumbino.

BERENGUER, JOSÉ, and MARTÍNEZ, JOSÉ LUIS
  1989   Camelids in the Andes: Rock Art Environment and Myths. In *Animals into Art,* 390–416, London, Unwin Hyman.

BERNAL, IGNACIO
  1973   Petroglifos en Dainzu. *III Simposio Internacional Americano de Arte Rupestre,* 1970, 59–61. México. (Resúmenes editados por Carlos Hernández Reyes).

BIGARELLA, JOÃO, BELTRÃO M. C., and TÖTH, E. REGO
  1984   Registro de fauna na arte rupestre: possíveis implicações geológicas. *Revista de Arqueología* (Belém, Brasil), vol. 2, no. 1: 31–37.

BITTMANN, BENTE, LE PAIGE, GUSTAVO, S.J., and NUÑEZ, LAUTARO
  1978   *Cultura Atacameña.* Santiago, Ministerio de Educación. (Serie Patrimonio Cultural Chileno).

BONINI, WILLIAM E. (Editor)
  1984   *The Caribbean-South America Plate Boundary and Regional Tectonics.* Boulder, CO: Geological Society of America.

BOSCH GIMPERA, PEDRO
1964   El arte rupestre en América. *Anales de Antropología* (México), vol. I: 29–45.
1967   *L'Amérique avant Christophe Colomb. Préhistoire et Hautes Civilisations,* Paris, Payot.
1975   *La América Pre-Hispana,* Barcelona, Ariel.

BOSINSKI, GERHARD
1984   The Mammoth Engravings of the Magdalenian Site Gönnersdorf (Rhineland, Germany). In *La contribution de la zoologie et de l'ethologie à l'interpretation de l'art des peuples chasseurs préhistoriques,* 295–322. (3rd Colloque de la Societé Suisse des Sciences Humaines, 1979), Fribourg, Editions Universitaires.

BOYRIE MOYA, EMILE DE
1955   *Monumento megalítico y petroglifos de Chacuey, República Dominicana,* Ciudad Trujillo, Publicaciones de la Universidad de Santo Domingo.

BREUIL, HENRI
1979   *Four Hundred Centuries of Cave Art.* New York: Hacker Art Books.

BROCHADO, JOSÉ P., and SCHMITZ, PEDRO I.
1972–1973 Aleros y cuevas con petroglifos e industria lítica de la escarpa del planalto meridional, en Río Grande do Sul, Brasil. *Anales de Arqueología* (Mendoza), vol. 27–28: 39–66.
1982   Petroglifos do estilo Pisadas no centro do Rio Grande do Sul. *Pesquisas* (São Leopoldo, Brasil), Antropologia no. 34: 3–47.

BRYAN, ALAN L.
1983   South America. In *Early Man in the New World,* 137–146. Sage Publications (Beverly Hills-London-New Delhi).

BRYAN, ALAN L. (Editor)
1978   *Early Man in America, from a Circum-Pacific Perspective.* (Edmonton (Canada), University of Alberta, Occasional Papers of the Department of Anthropology, no. 1).
1986   *New Evidence for the Pleistocene Peopling of the Americas,* Orono (Maine), Center for the Study of Early Man.

BRYAN, ALAN, and GRUHN, RUTH
1964   Problems Relating to the Neothermal Climatic Sequence. *American Antiquity,* vol. 29, no. 3: 307–315.

BURROWS, RUSSELL E.
1992   *Rock Art Pieces from Burrows Cave; In Southern Illinois; Vol. I.* Marquette: Superior Heartland.

CÁCERES FREYRE, JULIÁN
1957   Arte rupestre en la provincia de La Rioja, *Runa,* vol. VIII, Parte 1.

CAIN, THOMAS
1950   *Petroglyphs of Central Washington* Seattle: University of Washington Press.

CARDICH, AUGUSTO
1964   *Lauricocha. Fundamentos para una prehistoria de los Andes Centrales.* Studia Praehistorica, II, Buenos Aires, Centro Argentino de Estudios Prehistóricos.
1979   A propósito de un motivo sobresaliente en las pinturas rupestres de "El Ceibo". (Prov. Santa Cruz, Argentina). *Relaciones SAA,* vol. XIII: 163–182.

CARPENTER, JOHN (Editor)
1997   *Prehistory of the Borderlands: Recent Research in the Archaeology of Northern Mexico and the Southern Southwest.* Tucson: Arizona State Museum.

CASADO LÓPEZ, MARÍA DEL PILAR
1987   *Proyecto Atlas de Pictografías y Petrograbados, México,* México, Instituto Nacional de Antropología e Historia.
1988   Subproyecto de pictografías y petrograbados. In *Zonas Arqueológicas: Yucatán,* 91–98; México, Instituto Nac. De Antropología e Historia.

CASAMIQUELA, RODOLFO
1960   *Sobre la significación mágica del arte rupestre nordpatagónico,* Cuaderno del Sur, Bahía Blanca, Universidad Nacional del Sur.
1981   *El arte rupestre de la Patagonia,* Neuquén, Siringa Libros.

CERDA, PABLO, FERNANDEZ, S., and ESTAY, J.
1985   Prospección de geoglifos de la provincia de Iquique, Primera Región Tarapacá, norte de Chile, informe preliminar. In *Estudios de Arte Rupestre,* 311–348, Santiago, Museo Chileno de Arte Precolombino.

CLEGG, JOHN
1983   Australian Rock Art and Archaeology, *Bollettino CCSP,* vol. XX: 55–80.

CLOTTES, JEAN
1998   *The Shamans of Prehistory: Trance and Magic in the Painted Caves.* New York: Harry N. Abrams.

COLLINS, MICHAEL B., HESTER, T., OLMSTEAD, D., and HEADRICK, P.
1991   Engraved Cobbles from Early Archaeological Contexts in Central Texas. *Current Research in the Pleistocene,* vol. 8: 13–15. Center for the Study of the First Americans, Corvallia (Oregon), Oregon State University.

CONSENS, MARIO
1986   *San Luis: el arte rupestre de sus sierras,* 2 vols., San Luis: Dirección Provincial de Cultura.
1988   First Rock Paintings in Amazon Basin. *Rock Art Research,* vol. 5, no. 1: 69–72. Melbourne, Australian Rock Art Research Association.

CONSENS, MARIO, and BESPALI DE CONSENS, Y.
1981   La localidad rupestre de Chamangá. (Dpto. Flores, Uruguay), *Comunicaciones Antropológicas del Museo de Historia Natural de Montevideo,* vol. I, no. 9:1–24, Montevideo.

COSGROVE, R., and JONES, R.
1989   Judds Cavern: A Subterranean Aboriginal Painting Site, Southern Tasmania. *Rock Art Research,* vol. 6, no. 2: 96–104, Melbourne, Australian Rock Art Research Association.

CRESSMAN, L.S.
1937   *Petroglyphs of Oregon,* Eugene, University of Oregon.

CRIVELLI, EDUARDO, M., FERNÁNDEZ, and PARDIÑAS, U.
1991   Diversidad estilística, cronología y contexto en sitios de arte rupestre del área de Piedra del Aguila (Provs. Río Negro y Neuquén). In *El arte rupestre en la arqueología contemporánea,* 113–122, Buenos Aires, M. M. Podestá.

CHANLATTE BAIK, LUIS A.
1986   *Cultura Ostionoide: un desarrollo agroalfarero antillano,* 40 pp., San Juan de Puerto Rico. (Tirada aparte de *Homines,* vol. 10, no. 1).

DAHLGREN, BARBARA, and ROMERO, J.
1951   La prehistoria bajacaliforniana. Redescubrimiento de pintura rupestre. *Cuadernos Americanos,* vol. 58: 153–178, México.

DAVIS, EMILY CLEVELAND
1931   *Ancient Americans: The Archaeological Story of Two Continents.* New York: H. Holt & Co.

DELGADO, RAFAEL
1976   *Los petroglifos venezolanos,* Caracas, Monte Ávila.

DEWDNEY, S., and KIDD, K. E.
1967   *Indian Rock Paintings of the Great Lakes,* 2nd edition, Toronto, University of Toronto Press.

DISSELHOFF, H. D.
1955   Neue Fundplätze peruanischer Felsbilder. *Baessler-Archiv,* Neue Folge, vol. III: 55–73, Berlin, Dietrich Reimer.

DUBELAAR, C. N.
1986 a   *South American and Caribbean Petroglyphs,* Koninklijk Instituut voor Taal-, Land- en Volkenkunde, Caribbean Series, 3, Dorderecht-Holland, Foris Publications.
1986 b   *The Petroglyphs of the Guianas and Adjacent Areas of Brazil and Venezuela: An Inventory,* Monumenta Archeologica, 12. The Institute of Archaeology, Los Angeles, University of California.
1988   Petroglyphs in St. Lucia: Introduction, *Latin American Indian Literatures Journal,* vol. 4, no. 1, 72–83. Beaver Falls, PA, Geneva College.
1992   Lesser Antilles Petroglyphs Problems. Idem, vol. 8, no. 1: 95–101.

DURÁN, VICTOR A.
1983–1985   Arte rupestre de los cazadores patagónicos en "El Verano", área de La Martita, Depto. Magallanes, Prov. Santa Cruz, *Anales de Arqueología y Etnología,* vol. 38–40: 43–75, Mendoza, Universidad Nacional de Cuyo.

ENGEL, FREDERIC
1963   *Preceramic Settlement on the Central Coast of Peru; Asia; Unit I.* Philadelphia: American Philosophical Society. Series: Transactions Ser.; Vol. 53, Pt. 3.

ERICSON, J. E.
1992   *The American Southwest and Mesoamerica: Systems of Prehistoric Exchange.* Cambridge: Perseus Books. Series: Interdisciplinary Contributions to Archaeology.

EUBANKS, MARY W.
1999   *Corn in Clay: Maize Paleoethnobotany in Pre-Columbian Art.* Gainesville: University Press of Florida.

FAULKNER, CHARLES H. (Editor)
1986   *The Prehistoric Native American Art of Mud Glyph Cave.* Knoxville: University of Tennessee Press.

FEMENÍAS, JORGE
1985–1987   La piedras grabadas de la región de Salto Grande (Uruguay y Argentina). Partes I y II. Comunicaciones Antropológicas del Museo de Historia Natural de Montevideo, vol. II, nos. 11 and 12, Montevideo.

FERDON, EDWIN N.
1951   The Granite Ruin of Tonalá. *Archaeology,* vol. 4, no. 2: 83–88, Cambridge (Mass.), The Archaeological Institute of America.

FERNÁNDEZ, JORGE
1976   Arqueología de la cueva de El Toro (Susques, Jujuy). *Relaciones SAA,* vol. X: 43–65.
1979   Petroglifos del Departamento Minas, Neuquén. In *Miscelánea de Arte Rupestre de la República Argentina,* 83–149. Monografías de Arte Rupestre, Arte Americano, no. 1, Barcelona, Diputación Provincial de Barcelona.
1982   *Historia de la Arqueología Argentina,* Mendoza, Asociación Cuyana de Antropología. (Separata especial del vol. 34–35 de los Anales de Arqueología y Etnología.)
1984–1985   Reemplazo del caballo americano por camélidos en estratos del límite pleistocénico-holocénico de Barro Negro, Puna de Jujuy. *Relaciones SAA, XVI:* 137–152.
1988–1989   Ocupaciones alfareras (2.860±160 a.p.) en la Cueva de Cristóbal, Puna de Jujuy, Argentina. *Relaciones SAA,* vol. XVII, no. 2: 139–178.
1988–1989b   Caracterización de los motivos geométrico-ornamentales del estilo rupestre de Grecas del Noroeste de la Patagonia. *Ars Praehistorica,* vol. VII–VIII: 375–386, Sabadell (Barcelona), Editorial AUSA.
1990   *La Cueva de Haichol. Arqueología de los pinares cordilleranos del Neuquén,* Mendoza, Instituto de Arqueología y Etnología, Universidad Nacional de Cuyo. (Anales de Arqueología y Etnología, vols. 43–45.)

FERNANDEZ DISTEL, ALICIA
1972–1973   Petroglifos del río Keros (Dep. Cuzco, Perú). *Anales de Arqueología y Etnología,* vol. 17–18: 67–80, Mendoza, Universidad Nacional de Cuyo.
1986   Las cuevas de Huachichocana, su posición dentro del precerámico con agricultura incipiente del Noroeste Argentino. *Beiträge zur allgemeinen und vergleichenden Archäologie,* vol. 8: 353–430, Mainz, Philipp von Zabern.
1994   *Tres complejos con arte rupestre en la Provincia Modesto Omiste, Departamento de Potosí,* Bolivia. SIARB, Boletín no. 8: 55–89. La Paz.

FORD, JAMES A.
1969   A Comparison of Formative Cultures in the Americas. *Smithsonian Contributions to Anthropology,* vol. XI, Washington D.C., Smithsonian Institution.

FOSTER, MICHAEL (Editor)
n.d.   *Greater Mesoamerica: The Archaeology of West and Northwest Mexico.* Salt Lake City: University of Utah Press.

FRISON, GEORGE C.
1988   Paleoindian subsistence and settlement during post-Clovis times on the northwestern plains, the adjacent mountain ranges, and intermontane basins. In *Americans before Columbus: Ice-Age Origins:* 83–106. Ethnology Monographs, 12, University of Pittsburgh.

FULLOLA, J.M., CASTILLO, V. del, PETIT, M.A., and RUBIO, A.
1994   *Premières datations de l'art rupestre de Basse Californie (México).* I.N.O.R.A. (International Newsletter on Rock Art), no. 9: 1–4, Foix (Francia).

GAMBIER, MARIANO
1980   *La cultura de Ansilta,* San Juan, Instituto de Investigaciones Arqueológicas y Museo.
1985   *La cultura de Los Morrillos,* San Juan, Instituto de Investigaciones Arqueológicas y Museo. (With contributions from C.T. Michieli and M. Pastore.)

GARDNER, G.A.
1931   *Rock Paintings of North-West Córdoba,* Oxford: Clarendon Press.

GAY, CARLO
1967   Oldest Paintings in the New World. *Natural History,* vol. 76, no. 4: 28–35, New York, American Museum of Natural History.
1971   *Chalcatzingo. American Rockpaintings and Petroglyphs,* Graz, Akademische Drucks und Verlagsanstalt.

GONZÁLEZ, ALBERTO REX
1960   La estratigrafía de la gruta de Intihuasi (Prov. San Luis, R.A.) y sus relaciones con otros sitios precerámicos de Sudamérica. *Revista del Instituto de Antropología,* vol. I: 5–302, Córdoba, Universidad Nacional de Córdoba.

GONZÁLEZ, CELIANO
n.d.   *Petroglifos de la provincia de El Oro.* Ambato (Ecuador), Editorial Pío XII.

GONZALEZ ECHEGARAY, J., and FREEMAN, L.G.
1981   Máscara del santuario de la cueva del Juyo. *Altamira Symposium,* 251–264, Madrid, Ministerio de Cultura.

GORDON, AMERICO
1980   Cura Cahuiñ, una visón nueva de los petroglifos del Llaima. Boletín del Museo Nacional de Historia Natural (Santiago, Chile), vol. 37: 61–74.
1985   El símbolo de los petroglifos "caras sagradas" y el culto al agua y de los antepasados en el Valle El Encanto. *Estudios en Arte Rupestre,* 265–278, Santiago.

GRABERT, H., and SCHOBINGER, J.
1969–1970   Petroglifos a orillas del río Madeira (N.W. del Brasil). *Anales de Arqueología,* vol. 24–25: 93–111, Mendoza, Universidad Nac. De Cuyo.

GRADIN, CARLOS J.
1973   La piedra pintada de Mamuel Choique (Prov. Río Negro). Relaciones, SAA, vol. VII: 144–158.
1979   Los grabados rupestros de la Angostura de Gaiman (Provincia del Chubut). In *Miscelánea de Arte Rupestre de la República Argentina,* 151–171. Monografías de Arte Rupestre, Arte Americano, no. 1, Barcelona, Diputación Provincial de Barcelona.
1983   El arte rupestre de la cuenca del río Pinturas, Provincia de Santa Cruz, Argentina. *Ars Praehistorica,* vol. II: 87–149, Sabadell (Barcelona): Ed. AUSA.
1984   Breve síntesis del arte rupestre de la Patagonia. In *Culturas Indígenas de la Patagonia.* (Segunda exposición del ciclo "Las culturas de América en la época del Descubrimiento"): 45–50, Madrid, Instituto de Cooperación Iberoamericana.
1988   Arte rupestre de la Patagonia: nuevo aporte para el conocimiento de la bibliografía. En *Nuevos estudios del arte rupestre argentino:* 5–35. Contribuciones al Estudio del Arte Rupestre Sudamericano, no. 2. La Paz, Sociedad de Investigación del Arte Rupestre de Bolivia.

GRADIN, CARLOS J., and AGUERRE, ANA M.
1983   Arte rupestre del área "La Martita," Sección A del departamento Magallanes, Prov. Santa Cruz. *Relaciones SAA,* vol. XV: 195–223.

GRAHAM, JOHN
1982   *Ancient Mesoamerica; Selected Readings.* Mountain View: T. H. Peek.
GRAHAM, MARK M. (Editor)
1993   *Reinterpreting Prehistory of Central America.* Niwot: University Press of Colorado.
GRAMAJO DE MARTINEZ MORENO, AMALIA, and MARTÍNEZ MORENO, H.
1988   *El arte rupestre del territorio santiagüeño,* Santiago del Estero (Argentina), Editorial El Liberal.
GRANDA PAZ, OSVALDO
1986   *Arte rupestre Quillasinga y Pasto,* Pasto (Colombia), Ediciones Sindamanoy.
GRANT, CAMPBELL
1965   *The Rock-Paintings of the Chumash,* Berkeley & Los Angeles, University of California Press.
1967   *Rock Art of the American Indian,* New York, Thomas Y. Crowell.
1983   *L'arte rupestre degli indiani nord-americani,* Milano, Jaca Book. (Serie "Le Orme dell'Uomo.")
GRANT, CAMPELL, BAIRD, J. W., and PRINGLE, J. K.
1968   *Rock Drawings of the Coso Range (Inyo County, California),* Maturango Museum, Publication no. 4, China Lake (California).
GREENLEE, BOB
1995   *Life among the Ancient Ones: The Accounts of an Anasazi Archaeological Research Project.* Boulder: Hardscrabble Press.
GREER, JOHN W.
1990   Rock Art Site on the North Side of the Sierra Gorda of Central Mexico, Querétaro and Guanajuato, *Bollettino* CCSP, vol. 25–26; 150–157.
GREGORY, DAVID A. (Editor)
1997   *Excavations in the Santa Cruz River Floodplain: The Middle Archaic Component of Los Pozos.* Tucson: Desert Archaeology. Series: Anthropological Papers; No. 20.
GRIFFIN, JAMES B., MELTZER, DAVID, SMITH, DRUCE, and STURTEVANT, WILLIAM
1988   A Mammoth Fraud in Science, *American Antiquity,* vol. 53, no. 3: 578–582, Washington D.C., Society for American Archeology.
GRIFFIN, JOHN W.
1988   An Unusual Shell Pendant. *The Florida Anthropologist,* vol. 41, no. 1: 28, Tallahassee, Florida Anthropological Society.
GROVE, DAVID C.
1970   *The Olmec Paintings of Oxtotilán Cave, Guerrero, Mexico,* Studies in Precolumbian Art and Archeology, no. 6, Washington D.C., Dumbarton Oaks.
1984   *Chalcatzingo: Excavations on the Olmec Frontier,* London, Thames and Hudson.
1999   *Social Patterns in Pre-Classic Mesoamerica: A Symposium at Dumbarton Oaks, 9 & 10 October, 1993.* Washington, DC: Dumbarton Oaks.
GRUHN, RUTH
1983   Projections of Gé Social Structure in the Rock Art of Northern Minas Gerais, Brazil: An Hypothesis, *Revista de Arqueologia,* vol. 1, no. 1: 40–45, Belém, Museo Paraense Emilio Goeldi.
1989   The Pacific Coastal Route of Initial Entry: An Overview. Abstracts of the First World Summit Conference on the Peopling of the Americas: 6–7. Orono (Maine), Center for the Study of the First Americans.
1999   *Social Patterns in Pre-Classic Mesoamerica; A Symposium at Dumbarton Oaks, 9 & 10 October, 1993.* Washington, DC: Dumbarton Oaks.
GUARALDO, ALBERTO
1987   Incisioni rupestri eterogenee nel Totonacapan centrale (Messico, costa del Golfo). Communication presented at the Valcamonica Symposium 87, organized by the Centro Camuno di Studi Preistorici.
GUFFROY, JEAN
1980   Les pétroglyphes de Checta (Departement de Lima).

Actes du XLII *Congrès International des Américanistes* (Paris, 1976), vol. IX–B: 337–350, Paris, Societé des Américanistes.
GUIDON, NIÈDE
1975   *Peintures rupestres de Varzea Grande, Piauí, Brésil.* Cahiers d'Archéologie d'Amérique du Sud, 3, Paris, Ecole des Hautes Etudes en Sciences Sociales.
1980   Definição e delimitação do estilo Varzea Grande, XLII C.I.A., vol. IX–B: 391–407.
1985   A arte prehistórica da área arqueológica de São Raimundo Nonato: síntese de dez anos de pesquisas, *Clio,* no. 7 (Serie Arqueológica, 2): 3–80.
1986   A sequência cultural da área de São Raimundo Nonato, Piauí, *Clio,* no. 8 (Serie Arqueológica, 3): 137–144.
1989   Tradições rupestres da area arqueológica de São Raimundo Nonato, Piauí, Brasil, *Clio,* Serie Arqueológicas, no. 5: 5–17 y 18 láminas.
1991   *Peintures préhistoriques du Brésil. L'art rupestre du Piaui.* Editions Recherche sur les Civilisations, Paris.
HAMBLETON, ENRIQUE
1979   *La pintura rupestre de Baja California,* México, Fomento Cultural Banamex.
HARTE, NEVILLE A.
n.d. (circa 1961)   *Panorama of Panama Petroglyphs,* Curundu (Panama, Canal Zone), author's edition.
HEDGES, KEN
1988   On the Rock Art of Nevada and Southern California. Abstracts of the First AURA-Congress, Darwin (Australia).
HEIZER, ROBERT F., and BAUMHOFF, MARTIN A.
1962   *Prehistoric Rock Art of Nevada and Eastern California,* Berkeley, University of California Press.
HEIZER, ROBERT F., and CLEWLOW, C. W.
1973   *Prehistoric Rock Art of California* (2 vols.), Ramona (California), Ballena Press.
1984   *Herança. A expressão visual do brasileiro antes da influencia do europeu,* Organized and edited by J.R. Valença and B. Furrer, São Paulo, Empresas Dow.
HEREDIA, MARIA DE LOS ANGELES, and RIVERA, CLAUDIA
1991   Los petroglifos de Achocalla, depto. de La Paz, Bolivia. *Boletín,* no. 5: 57–75, La Paz, SIARB.
HERNÁNDEZ LLOSAS, MARÍA ISABEL
1992   Secuencia rupestre Humahuaca y arqueología regional. *Boletín* SIARB, no. 6: 29–40, La Paz.
HERNÁNDEZ REYES, CARLOS
1973   Pinturas rupestres del valle del Mezquital y de la Teotlalpan, *III Simposio Internacional Americano de Arte Rupestre* (1970): 77–83, México, C. Hernández Reyes, ed.
HERRERA FRITOT, RENÉ
1939   *Informe sobre una exploración arqueológica a Punta del Este, Isla de Pinos,* realizada por el Museo Antropológico Montané de la Universidad de La Habana, La Habana (Cuba), Publicaciones de la Revista de la Universidad.
HESTER, JAMES A.
1966   Late Pleistocene Environments and Early Man in South America, *The American Naturalist,* vol. 100, no. 914: 377–388.
HILDEBRAND, ELISABETH R. VON
1975   Levantamiento de los petroglifos del río Caquetá entre La Pedrera y Araracuara, *Revista Colombiana de Antropología,* vol. 19: 303–370, Bogotá.
HISSINK, KARIN
1955   Felsbilder und Salz der Chimanen-Indianer, *Paideuma,* vol. 6: 60–80, Frankfurt a.M., Frobenius Institut.
HONEA, KENNETH
1976   *Early Man Projectile Points in the Southwest.* Albuquerque: Museum of New Mexico Press.
HOOVER, ROBERT L.
1973   Incised Steatite Tablets from the Catalina Museum, *The Masterkey,* vol. 47, no. 3: 106–109, Los Angeles, Southwest Museum.
HOSTNIG, RAINER
1988   Caza de camélidos en el arte rupestre del departamento

de Apurimac. *En Llamichos y Pacocheros: pastores de llamas y alpacas,* 67–76, Cuzco, Ed., Jorge A. Flores Ochoa.

1989   Una nueva localidad de arte rupestre en Apurimac (Perú): Llamayoc, *Boletín* SIARB, no. 4: 46–52.

HRDLICKA, ALES

1918   *Recent Discoveries Attributed to Early Man in America.* Washington, DC: Government Printing Office.

1918   *Skeletal Remains, Suggesting or Attributed to Early Man in North America.* Washington, DC: Government Printing Office.

1982   *Early Man in South America.* Saint Clair Shores: Scholarly Press.

HURAULT, JEAN, FRENAY, P., and RAOUX, Y.

1963   Pétroglyphes et assemblages de pierres dans le Sud-Est de la Guyane Française, *Journal de la Societé des Américanistes,* vol. 52: 157–166, Paris.

HYSLOP, JOHN

1975   The Petroglyphs of Cerro del Chivo, *Archaeology,* vol. 28, no. 1:38–45.

1976   Ichucollo petroglyphs (Peru), *Bollettino* CCSP, vol. 13–14: 215–217.

IBARRA GRASSO, DICK EDGAR

1967   *Argentina indígena y prehistoria americana,* Buenos Aires, Editorial TEA.

IBARRA GRASSO, D.E., and QUEREJAZU LEWIS, ROY

1986   *30.000 años de prehistoria en Bolivia,* La Paz-Cochabamba, Los Amigos del Libro.

IMBELLONI, JOSÉ

1943   The Peopling of America, *Acta Americana,* vol. I, no. 3: 309–330.

ISBELL, WILLIAM H.

1997   *Mummies and Mortuary Monuments: A Postprocessual Prehistory of Central Andean Social Organization.* Austin: University of Texas Press.

IZUMI, SEIICHI, and TERADA, KAZUO

1972   *Andes 4: Excavations at Kotosh, 1963 and 1966,* Tokyo, University of Tokyo Press.

JACKSON, A. T.

1938   *Picture-Writing of Texas Indians,* Bureau of Research in the Social Sciences, Study no. 27, Austin, University of Texas Press.

JACKSON, PETER

1982   The Petroglyphs of the River Vaupés, Colombia. *Bollettino CCSP,* vol. 19: 83–96.

JORDAN, PAUL

1999   *Early Man.* Stroud: Sutton Publishing.

JOYCE, THOMAS A.

1969   *South American Archaeology.* New York: Hacker Art Books.

KELLER, CHARLES M.

1973   *Montagu Cave in Prehistory: A Descriptive Analysis.* Berkeley: University of California Press. Series: University of California Publications in Geological Sciences; Vol. 28.

KEYSER, JAMES D.

1990   Rock Art of North American Northwestern Plains: An Overview, *Bollettino CCSP,* vol. 25–26: 99–122.

KIDDER, A. V., and GUERNSEY, S. J.

1919   *Archaeological Explorations in North-Eastern Arizona,* Bureau of American Ethnology, Bulletin 65, Washington D.C., Smithsonian Institution.

KIRKLAND, FORREST, and NEWCOMB, W., Jr.

1967   *The Rock Art of Texas Indians,* Austin, The University of Texas Press.

KLEIN, OTTO

1972   *Cultura Ovalle. Complejo rupestre "Cabezas-Tiara." Petroglifos y pictografías del "Valle del Encanto," prov. Coquimbo, Chile,* Valparaíso, Universidad Técnica "Federico Santa María."

KOCH-GRÜNBERG, THEODOR

1907   *Südamerikanische ·Felszeichnungen,* Berlin, Ernst Wasmuth A.G.

KOZLOWSKI, JANUSZ, and BANDI, HANS-GEORGE

1992   El problema de las raíces asiáticas del primer poblamiento de América. *Espacio, Tiempo y Forma,* Serie I (Prehistoria y Arqueología), t. V: 15–72. UNED, Madrid. (Versión ligeramente actualizada para la parte americana de un artículo originariamente publicado en el *Bulletin de la Societé Suisse des Américanistes,* no. 45, Ginebra, 1981).

KRAFT, J. C., and THOMAS, R. A.

1976   Early Man at Holly Oak, Delaware, *Science,* vol. 192: 756–761.

KRICKEBERG, WALTER

1949   *Felsplastik und Felsbilder bei den Kulturvölkern Altamerikas, mit besonderer Berücksichtigung Mexicos,* vol. I, Berlin, Palmen-Verlag (vormals Dietrich Reimer).

1968   Idem, vol. II *Felsbilder Mexicos,* Berlin, Dietrich Reimer.

KRIEGER, ALEX

1964   Early Man in the New World. In *Prehistoric Man in the New World,* 23–81, Chicago (J. Jennings and E. Norbeck, editors). Castilian edition: *El hombre primitivo en América,* with introduction and notes by L. A. Orquera, Buenos Aires, 1974, Ed. Nueva Visión.

KSICA, MIROSLAV

1974   *Umeni Stare Eurasie. (Die Kunst des alten Eurasiens),* Brno (Checoeslovaquia). [Exposition catalog.]

LAMING, ANNETTE, and EMPERAIRE, J.

1956   Découverte de peintures rupestres sur le hautes plateaux du Paraná. *Journal de la Societé des Américanistes,* vol. 45: 165–179, Paris.

LANGE, FREDERICK W. (Editor)

1995   *Paths to Central American Prehistory.* Niwot: University Press of Colorado.

LARICHEV, VITALY, KHOL'USHKIN, URIY, and LARICHEVA, INNA

1992   The Upper Paleolithic of Northern Asia: Achievements, Problems and Perspectives. III: Northeastern Siberia and the Russian Far East. *Journal of World Prehistory,* vol. 6, no. 4: 441–476. Plenum Press, New York and London.

LATHROP, D. W.

1977   *Ancient Ecuador; Culture, Clay and Creativity.* Chicago: Field Museum of Natural History.

LAYTON, THOMAS N.

1976   Stalking Elephants in Nevada, *Western Folklore,* vol. 35, no. 4: 250–257, California.

LINARES MÁLAGA, ELOY

1973   *Anotaciones sobre cuatro modalidades de arte rupestre en Arequipa,* Huancayo, Universidad del Centro de Perú.

1975   Cuatro modalidades de arte rupestre en el sur del Perú. *Dédalo,* vol. 21–22: 47–116, São Paulo: Museu de Arqueologia e Etnología.

1988   Arte mobiliar con tradición rupestre en el sur del Perú, *Rock Art Research,* vol. 5, no. 1: 54–66, Melbourne, AURA.

LORENZO, JOSÉ LUIS

1968   Sur les pièces d'art mobilier de la préhistoire mexicaine. In *La Préhistoire: problèmes et tendances,* 283–289, 5 láms, Paris, Editions du CNRS.

LORING, J. MALCOLM, and LORING, LOUISE

1983   *Pictographs and Petroglyphs of the Oregon Country,* (2 vols.), Monograph XXIII, Institute of Archaeology, University of California, Los Angeles.

LOSADA GÓMEZ, HELENA

1980   *Placas grabadas prehispánicas de Argentina,* Bibliotheca Praehistorica Hispana, vol. XIX, Madrid, Instituto Español de Prehistoria.

LUNARDI, FEDERICO

1943   Los misterios mayas del valle de Otoro (Honduras). *Revista Geográfica Americana,* vol. XX, no. 118: 11–24, Buenos Aires.

LYNCH, THOMAS

1983   The Paleo-Indians. In *Ancient South-Americans:* 87–137.

San Francisco (Ed. J. Jennings). (An expanded version of "The South-American Paleoindians," appearing in an earlier edition of the same book, 1978.)

LYUBIN, V. P.
1991   *The Images of Mammoths in the Paleolithic Art. Soviet-skaya Archeologia,* 1991/1: 20–42, Moscow.

MACGOWAN, KENNETH
1990   *Early Man in the New World.* Magnolia: Peter Smith.

MACNEISH, RICHARD S.
1973   *Early Man in America: Readings from* Scientific American. New York: W. H. Freeman.
1994   *Pendejo Pre-Clovis Proofs and Their Implications. Manuscrito presentado para las Actas de la Reunión Internacional sobre el Poblamiento de las América* (December 1993). FUNDHAM, São Raimundo Nonato (Brasil).

MALLERY, GARRICK
1893   *Picture-Writing of the American Indians,* Bureau of American Ethnology, Annual Report no. 10, Washington D.C., Smithsonian Institution.

MARKGRAF, VERA, and BRADBURY, J. PLATT
1982   Holocene Climatic History of South America, *Striae,* vol. 16, 40–45.

MARTÍN, GABRIELA
1975   Estudios para una desmitificación de los petroglifos brasileños. Papeles del Laboratorio de Arqueología de Valencia, 11: 487–505, Universidad de Valencia.
1988   Prehistoria del Nordeste de Brasil: estado actual de la investigación. Archivio de Prehistoria Levantina, vol. XVIII: 49–79. Diputación Provincial de Valencia.
1989   A subtradiçió Seridó de pintura rupestre préhistorica do Brasil. *Clio,* Serie Arqueológica, no. 5: 19–28.
1990   O adéus a Gruta do Padre, Petrolandia, Pernambuco. *Clio,* Serie Arqueológica, no. 6: 31–67. (Con la colaboración de Jacionira Rocha.)
1992   Arte prehistórico en el Nordeste del Brasil, *Homenaje a Miguel Tarradell,* Barcelona, Ed. Curiel.

MARTÍNEZ DEL RÍO, PABLO
1953   *Los orígenes americanos.* (3a edición), México.

MASSONE, MAURICIO
1982   Nuevas investigacione sobre el arte rupestre de Patagonia meridional chilena. *Anales del Instituto de la Patagonia,* vol. 13: 73–94. Punta Arenas (Chile). (Versión resumida en *Estudios de Arte Rupestre,* 205–223, Santiago, 1985.)

MATILLÓ VILA, JOAQUIN
1973   *Ometepe, isla de círculos y de espirales,* Managua, Centro de Investigaciones Rupestres.

MEADE, EDWARD
1971   *Indian Rock Carvings of the Pacific Northwest,* Sidney (British Columbia), Gray's Publishing Ltd.

MEDINA, ALBERTO, VARGAS, RUPERTO, and VERGARA, CIRO
1964   Yacimientos arqueológicos en la cordillera de la provincia de Talca, Chile. In *Arqueologia de Chile Centrál y áreas vecinas* (III Congreso Internacional de Arqueología Chilena): 219–234, Santiago.

MEGGERS, BETTY J.
1972   *Prehistoric America,* Chicago, Aldine-Atherton.
1992   *Jomon-Valdivia Similarities: Convergence or Contact?* New England Antiquities Research Association. NEARA Journal, vol. 27: 23–32.

MEGGERS, BETTY, EVANS, CLIFFORD, and ESTRADA, EMILIO
1965   *Early Formative Period of Coastal Ecuador: the Valdivia and Machalilla Phases.* Smithsonian Contributions to Anthropology, vol. 1, Washington D.C.

MEHRINGER, PETER J.
1989   Of Apples and Archaeology. *Mammoth Trumpet,* vol. 5, no. 2: 1–5, Orono (Maine), Center for the Study of the First Americans.

MEJIA XESSPE, TORIBIO
1968   *Pintura chavinoide en los lindes del arte rupestre* (Folleto), Lima.

MENGHIN, OSVALDO F.A.
1952   Las pinturas rupestres de la Patagonia. *Runa,* vol. V: 5–22.
1957   Estilos del arte rupestre de Patagonia. *Acta Praehistorica,* vol. I: 57–87, Buenos Aires, Centro Argentino de Estudios Prehistóricos.
1957 b   Vorgeschichte Amerikas. In *Abriss der Vorgeschichte,* 162–218, Munich, Oldenbourg.
1964   Eine bolivianisch-chilenische Gruppe von Felsgravierungen. *Festschrift für Adolf E. Jensen,* 379–384, Munich, Klaus Renner.

MENGHIN, OSVALDO, and GRADIN, CARLOS J.
1972   La Piedra Calada de Las Plumas (Chubut). *Acta Praehistorica,* vol. XI: 13–63, Buenos Aires.

MENTZ RIBEIRO, PEDRO A.
1969–1970 Incrições rupestres no vale do río Caí, Rio Grande do Sul, Brasil, *Anales de Arqueología y Etnología,* vol. 24–25: 113–129, Mendoza.
1973   Novos petroglifos no encosta centro-oriental da Serra Geral, Rio Grande do Sul, Brasil, Museu do Colégio Mauá, Antropología, 2: 1–28, Santa Cruz do Sul (Brasil).
1978   A arte rupestre no Sul do Brasil. *Revista do CEPA,* no. 7, Santa Cruz do Sul, Centro de Estudos e Pesquisas Arqueológicas.

MENTZ RIBEIRO, PEDRO A., MACHADO, ANA LÚCIA, and GUAPINDAIA, V. L. C.
1987   Projeto arqueológico de salvamento na região de Boa Vista, Territorio Federal de Roraima, Brasil, Primeira etapa de campo (1985), *Revista do CEPA,* vol. 14, no. 17: 3–78, Santa Cruz do Sul.

MENTZ RIBEIRO, PEDRO A., and TORRANO RIBEIRO, CATARINA
1985   Levantamentos arqueológicos no municipio de Esmeralda, Río Grande do Sul, Brasil. *Revista do CEPA,* vol. 12, no. 14: 51–123, Santa Cruz do Sul.

MENTZ RIBEIRO, PEDRO A., TORRANO RIBEIRO, CATARINA, and BECERRA PINTO, FRANCISCO C.
1989   Levantamentos arqueológicos no territorio federal de Roraima, 3a etapa de campo (1987), *Revista do CEPA,* vol. 16, no. 19: 5–47, Santa Cruz do Sul.

MICHAELIS, HELEN, and WEINERTH, CATHERINE
1984   UCLA Rock Art Archive Unpublished Documents. A Catalog. Institute of Archaeology, Occasional Paper no. 12, Los Angeles, University of California.

MILLIMAN, JOHN, and EMERY, K.O.
1968   Sea Levels during the Past 35,000 Years, *Science,* vol. 162, no. 3858: 1121–1123.

MIOTTI, LAURA
1991   Manifestaciones rupestres de Santa Cruz: la localidad arqueológica Piedra Museo, *El arte rupestre en la arqueología contemporaéna:* 132–138, Buenos Aires.

MONZÓN, SUSANA
1980   Préhistoire du sud-est du Piaui (Brésil), *Objets et Mondes,* vol. 20, no. 4: 153–160, Paris, Musée de l'Homme.
1987   *L'art rupestre Sud-Américain. Préhistoire d'un continent,* Monaco, Le Rocher.

MORSS, NOEL
1954   *Clay Figurines of the American Southwest.* Papers of the Peabody Museum of American Archaeology and Ethnology, Harvard University, vol. XLIX, no. 1, Cambridge, Massachusetts.

MOSTNY, GRETE
1964   Los petroglifos de Angostura. *Zeitschrift für Ethnologie,* vol. 89, no. 1: 51–70, Braunschweig.

MOSTNY, GRETE, and NIEMEYER, HANS
1983   *Arte rupestre chileno,* Serie El Patrimonio cultural Chileno, Santiago, Ministerio de Educación.

MUÑOZ, GUILLERMO
1991   *Estructura cultural de conservación del arte rupestre en el altiplano cundiboyacense (Colombia).* Information presented by the Grupo de Investigación de la Pintura Rupestre Indígena, Bogotá.

MUNSON, PATRICK J.
1990   *The Prehistoric and Early Historic Archaeology of Wyandotte Cave and Other Caves in Southern Indiana.* Indianapolis: Indiana Historical Society.

NAVAMUEL, ERCILIA
1986   Atlas Histórico de Salta, Salta (Argentina), Edición particular.

NEYRA AVENDANO, MÁXIMO
1968   Un nuevo complejo lítico y pinturas rupestres en la gruta SU-3 de Sumbay, *Revista de la Facultad de Letras,* no. 5: 43–75 and 37 figures, Arequipa, Universidad Nacional de San Agustín.

NIEMEYER, HANS
1968   Petroglifos del río Salado o Chuschul (San Pedro de Atacama, Prov. de Antofagasta, Chile). *Boletín de Prehistoria de Chile,* no. 1: 85–92, Santiago, Universidad de Chile.

1976   La cueva con pinturas indígenas del rio Pedregoso (Depto. Chile Chico, Prov. Aysén, Chile). *Actas del IV Congreso Nacional de Arqueología Argentina,* Parte I: 339–353, San Rafael (Mendoza).

1985   El yacimiento de petroglifos Las Lizas (Región de Atacama, Prov. Copiapó, Chile), *Estudios en Arte Rupestre,* 131–171, Santiago.

NIEMEYER, HANS, and SCHIAPPACASSE, VIRGILIO
1981   Aportes al conocimiento del período Tardío del extremo norte de Chile: análisis del sector Huancarane del valle de Camarones, *Chungará,* vol. 7: 3–103, Arica, Universidad del Norte.

NIEMEYER, HANS, and WEISNER, LOTTE
1972–1973 Los petroglifos de la cordillera andina de Linares (Prov. Talca y Linares, Chile). *Actas del VI Congreso de Arqueología Chilena,* 405–470, Santiago, Universidad del Chile.

NOGUERA, EDUARDO
1972   Antigüedad y significado de los relieves de Acalpizcan, México, *Anales de Antropología,* vol. IX: 77–94, México, UNAM.

NOVOA ALVAREZ, PABLO
1985   Pinturas rupestres del Territorio Amazonas de Venezuela, *Revista de Arqueología,* no. 55: 36–45, Madrid, Zugarto Ediciones.

NUÑEZ, LAUTARO
1976   Geoglifos y tráficos de caravanas en el desierto chileno, *Homenaje al R.P. Gustavo Le Paige:* 147–201, Antofagasta, Universidad del Norte.

1989   Hacia la producción de alimentos y la vida sedentaria. En *Culturas de Chile: Prehistoria:* 81–105, Santiago, Editorial Andrés Bello.

NUÑEZ, LAUTARO, and SANTORO, CALOGERO
1988   Cazadores de la puna seca y salada del área centro-sur Andina. *Estudios Atacameños,* no. 9: 11–60, San Pedro de Atacama, Universidad del Norte.

NUÑEZ, LAUTARO, VARELA, J., CASAMIQUELA, R., SCHIAPPACASSE, V., NIEMEYER, H., and VILLAGRAN, C.
1994   *Cuenca de Taguatagua en Chile: el ambiente del Pleistoceno Superior y ocupaciones humanas.* Revista Chilena de Historia Natural, vol. 67: 503–519. Santiago.

NUÑEZ JIMÉNEZ, ANTONIO
1959   *Facatativá, santuario de la rana. (Andes Orientales de Colombia),* La Habana, Universidad Central de Las Villas.

1975   *Cuba: dibujos rupestres,* La Habana, Editorial de Ciencias Sociales.

1986   *Petroglifos del Perú,* 4 volúmenes, La Habana, Editorial Científico-Técnica, PNUD/UNESCO.

1986 b Arte rupestre de Cuba; las pictografías de las cueva del Indio y de los Portales en la Sierra de Cubitas. *Bollettino CCSP,* vol. 23: 123–132.

1986 c *El arte rupestre cubano y su comparación con el de otras áreas de América.* Primer Symposium Mundial de Arte Rupestre, La Habana.

ORLOFF, NADINE
1982   Découverte d'un site à gravures rupestres dans la Sierra de Nayar (Méxique), *Journal de la Societé des Américanistes,* vol. 68: 7–25, Paris.

ORQUERA, LUIS ABEL, and PIANA, ERNESTO L.
1986–1987 Composición tipológica y datos tecnomorfológicos y tecnofuncionales de los distintos conjuntos arqueológicos del sitio Túnel I (Tierra del Fuego), *Relaciones SAA,* vol. XVII, no. 1: 201–239.

ORTIZ DE ZÁRATE, GONZALO
1973   Grabado rupestre de Sinaloa. III *Simposio Internacional de arte rupestre americano,* 73–75, México, Carlos Hernández Reyes, editor.

OYUELA-CAYCEDO, AUGUSTO (Editor)
1998   *Recent Advances in the Archaeology of the Northern Andes; In Memory of Gerardo Reichel-Dolmatoff.* Los Angeles: University of California, Los Angeles, Institute of Archaeology. Series: Monograph; No. 39.

PAGÁN PERDOMO
1978   *Nuevas pictografías en la isla de Santo Domingo. Las Cuevas de Borbón,* Santo Domingo, Museo del Hombre Dominicano.

PARDO, LUIS A.
1942   Los petroglifos de La Convención. *Revista del Instituto Arqueológico,* Nos. 10–11: 1–30, Cuzco (Reprinted in *Historia y arqueología del Cuzco,* 2: 599–630, Cuzco, 1957).

PARENTI, FABIO
1993   *Le gisement préhistorique du Pleistocène Supérieur de Pedra Furada (Piauí, Brésil).* Considerations chrono-stratigraphiques et implications paleoanthropologiques. Documents Lab. Géol. Lyon no. 125; 303–313, Lyon.

PARKMAN, E. BRECK
1981   The Status or Rock Art Research in North-Western California, *Rock Art Research,* vol. 6, no. 1: 69–71, Melbourne, AURA.

PARNES, MILTON, and MENDONÇA DE SOUZA, ALFREDO
1971   *Relatório das pesquisas arqueológicas no Ceará,* Centro de Informação Arqueológica.

PARRY, WILLIAM J.
1987   *Chipped Stone Tools in Formative Oaxaca, Mexico: Their Procurement, Production and Use.* Ann Arbor: University of Michigan, Museum of Anthropology. Series: Memoirs Series, Prehistory & Human Ecology of the Valley of Oaxaca; No. 20, Vol. 8.

PASSOS, J. AFONSO DE MORAES B.
1980   Algumas inscrições rupestres em Mato Grosso, Brasil, Sítio do Morro da Rapadura, *Actes du XLII Congres Int. des Américanistes* (1976), vol. IX-B: 369–380, Paris.

PEDERSEN, ASBJORN
1970   El arte rupestre del Parque Nacional Perito Moreno (Prov. Santa Cruz, Patagonia, Argentina). *Valcamonica Symposium,* I: 443–460, Capo di Ponte (Italia).

PÉREZ DE BARRADAS, JOSÉ
1941   *El arte rupestre en Colombia,* Madrid, Consejo Superior de Investigaciones Científicas.

PESSIS, ANNE-MARIE
1989   Apresentaçaõ gráfica e apresentação social na Tradição Nordeste de pintura rupestre do Brasil, *Clio,* Serie Arqueológica, no. 5: 11–17.

1999   "The Chronology and Evolution of the Prehistoric Rock Paintings in the Serra de Capivara National Park, Piauf, Brazil." In *Dating and the Earliest Known Rock Art,* ed. M. Strecker and P. Bahn, pp. 41–47. Oxford: Oxbow Books.

PIA, GABRIELLA ERICA
1987   *Asentamientos y pinturas rupestres en el Oriente Bolviano,* La Paz, Instituto Nacional de Arqueología.

1987 b Le pitture rupestri preistoriche nell'Oriente Boliviano e il loro significato popolazionistico e ambientale. La grande parete di Ur III. *Rivista di Antropologia,* vol. LXV: 347–364, Roma, Istituto Italiano di Antropologia.

1988   Los distintos momentos estilísticos encontrados en las pinturas rupestres de las áreas de Roboré, Santiago y San

José en el Oriente Boliviano, *Boletín SIARB*, No. 2: 40–52, La Paz.

PIMENTEL, VICTOR
1986   *Felszeichnungen im mittleren und unteren Jequetepeque Tal, Nord-Peru. Petroglifos en el valle medio y bajo de Jequetepeque, norte del Perú*, Materialien zur Allgemeinen und Vergleichenden Archäologie, vol. 31, Munich, C.H. Beck.

PIÑA CHAN, ROMAN
1955   *Chalcatzingo, Morelos*, México, Instituto Nacional de Antropología e Historia.
1989   *Gli Olmechi. La Cultura Madre*, Milano, Jaca Book (Series: "Corpus Precolombiano").

PINDELL, JAMES L. (Editor)
1998   *Paleogeographic Evolution and Non-Glacial Eustacy; Northern South America*. Tulsa: SEPM (Society for Sedimentary Geology). Series: Special Publications; Vol. 58.

PIPPIN, LONNIE C.
1987   *The Prehistory and Paleoecology of Guadalupe Ruin, New Mexico*. Salt Lake City: University of Utah Press.

PODESTÁ, M. MERCEDES
1986–1987 Arte rupestre en asentamientos de cazadores-recolectores y agroalfareros en la Puna sur argentina: Antofagasta de la Sierra, Catamarca. *Relaciones SAA*, vol. XVII, no. 1: 241–263.
1990   Cazadores y pastores de la Puna: apuntes sobre sus manifestaciones de arte rupestre. Comunicación presentada al X Congreso Nacional de Arqueología Argentina, Catamarca.

POLITIS, GUSTAVO (Editor)
2000   *Archaeology in Latin America*. New York: Routledge.

POMPA Y POMPA, ANTONIO
1975   La pintura rupestre pre y protohistórica en México. *Dédalo*, no. 21–22: 23–28, São Paulo, Museu de Arte e Arqueologia.

PORRAS GARCES, PEDRO
1972   *Petroglifos del Alto Napo*, Guayaquil.
1985   *Arte rupestre del Alto Napo. Valle del Misagualli*, Quito, P. Universidad Católica del Ecuador.

PORTER, STEPHEN C.
1988   Landscapes of the Last Ice-Age in North America. In *Americans before Columbus: Ice-Age Origins*: 1–24, Ethnology Monographs, 12. Pittsburgh, Dept. of Anthropology, University of Pittsburgh.

PORTUGAL ORTIZ, MAX
1989   Estilo escultórico Chiripa en la península de Santiago de Huata. *Textos Antropológicos*, Año 1, no. 1: 45–78, La Paz, Universidad Mayor de San Andrés.

PRIETO, RICARDO JUAN
1992   Geoglifos del río Jáchal, Provincia de San Juan. Instituto de Investigaciones Arqueológicas y Museo, *Publicaciones*, no. 19: 1–9, Universidad Nacional de San Juan, Argentina.

PROUS, ANDRÉ
1977   *Les sculptures zoomorphes du sud brésilien et de l'Uruguay*, Cahiers d'Archéologie d'Amérique du Sud, 5, Paris, Ecoles des Hautes Etudes en Sciences Sociales.
1986   L'archéologie au Brésil: 300 siècles d'occupation humaine. *L'Anthropologie* (Paris), vol. 90, no. 2: 257–306.
1989   Arte rupestre brasileira: uma tentativa de classificação. *Revista de Pré-Historia*, vol. 7: 9–33, São Paulo, Instituto de Pré-Historia, Universidade de São Paulo.
1994   *L'art rupestre brésilien: bilan et perspectives*. I.N.O.R.A. (International Newsletter on Rock Art), no. 9: 18–22, Foix (Francia).
1999   "Dating the Rock Art in Brazil." In *Dating and the Earliest Known Rock Art*, ed. M. Strecker and P. Bahn, 29–34. Oxford: Oxbow Books.

PROUS, ANDRÉ, and DE PAULA, F.L.
1979–1980 L'art rupestre dans les régions explorées par Lund. (Centre de Minas Gerais, Brésil). *Arquivos do Museu de Historia Natural*, vol. IV–V: 311–334, Belo Horizonte, Universidade Federal de Minas Gerais.

PULGAR VIDAL, JAVIER
1962   *Primera exposición nacional de quilcas*, Lima, Universidad Nacional Mayor de San Marcos.

QUEREJAZU LEWIS, ROY
1984–1985 El arte rupestre prehistórico en la zona andina de Bolivia. *Ars Praehistorica*, vol. II–IV: 233–244, Sabadell (Barcelona), Ed. AUSA.
1991   Rock Art in Santa Cruz, Bolivia, *Latin American Indian Literatures Journal*, vol. 7, no. 1: 126–141, McKeesport, State University of Pennsylvania.

QUIRARTE, JACINTO
1973   *Izapan-Style Art: A Study of its Form and Meaning*. Washington, DC: Dumbarton Oaks. Series: Studies in Pre-Columbian Art & Archaeology, No. 10.

REEVES, BRYAN, POHL, J., and SMITH, L.
1986   The Mission Ridge Site and the Texas Street Question. In *New Evidence for the Pleistocene Peopling of the Americas*, 65–80 (A. Bryan, ed.), Orono (Maine).

REICHE, MARIA
1968   *Geheimnis der Wüste. Mystery on the Desert. Secreto de la Pampa*, Nazca (Perú), Stuttgart (Alemania), Author's edition.

RIESTER, JURGEN
1981   *Arqueología y arte rupestre en el Oriente Boliviano*, Cochabamba-La Paz, Editorial Los Amigos del Libro. (The section on cave art was originally published in *Zeitschrift für Ethnologie*, vol. 97, no. 1: 74–102, Berlin, 1972.)

RIVERA CASANOVAS, CLAUDIA, and MICHEL LÓPEZ, MARCOS
1995   *Arte rupestre en el Valle de Cinti*, Chuquisaca, Bolivia. SIARB, Boletín no. 9: 56–77, La Paz.

RIVET, PAUL
1943   *Los orígenes del hombre americano*, México: Fondo de Cultura Económica.

ROHR, JOAO ALFREDO
1969   Petroglifos de ilha de Santa Catarina e ilhas adjacentes. *Pesquisas*, Antropologia, no. 19: 1–30, São Leopoldo, Instituto Anchietano de Pesquisas (Brasil).

ROOSEVELT, ANNA (Editor)
1997   *Amazonian Indians from Prehistory to the Present; Anthropological Perspectives*. Tucson: University of Arizona Press.

ROOSEVELT, ANNA
1999   "Dating the Rock Art at Monte Alegra, Brazil". In *Dating and the Earliest Known Rock Art*, ed. M. Strecker and P. Bahn, 34–40. Oxford: Oxbow Books.

ROOSEVELT, ANNA C., HOUSLEY, R. A., IMAZIO DA SILVERIRA, M., MARANCA, S., and HOHNSON, R.
1991   Eighth Millennium Pottery from a Prehistoric Shell Midden in the Brazilian Amazon. *Science*, vol. 254: 1621–1624.

ROPER, DONNA C.
1989   Red Ochre Use on the Plains During the Paleoindian Period. *Mammoth Trumpet*, vol. 5, no. 3: 1–6. Center for the Study of the First Americans, Orono, University of Maine.

ROUSE, IRVING
1949   Petroglyphs. *Handbook of South American Indians*, vol. 5: 493–502, Washington D.C., Smithsonian Institution.

RYDÉN, STIG
1944   *Contributions to the Archaeology of the Río Loa Region*, Göteborg, Ethnografiska Museum.

SANTORO, CALOGERO, and DAUELSBERG, PERCY
1985   Identificación de indicadores tempo-culturales en el arte rupestre del extremo norte de Chile. In *Estudios de Arte Rupestre*, 69–86, Santiago, Museo Chileno de Arte Precolombino.

SAWYER, ALAN R.
1966   *Ancient Peruvian Ceramics: The Nathan Cummings Collection*. New York: Metropolitan Museum of Art.

SAYRES, MEGHAN N.
1997   *Petroglyphs and Rock Art*. Emeryville: Avalon Travel.

SCHAAFSMA, POLLY
1971   *The Rock Art of Utah, from the Donald Scott Collection,* Papers of the Peabody Museum, vol. 65, Cambridge (Mass.): Harvard University.
1980   *Indian Rock Art of the Southwest,* School of American Research. Albuquerque, University of New Mexico Press.

SCHINDLER, HELMUT
1978   Felsritzungen am Oberlauf des Río Apaporis, *Ethnologische Zeitschrift Zürich,* vol. I: 45–60, Berna, Verlag Peter Lang.

SCHMITZ, P. I., BARBOSA, A. S., RIBEIRO, M. B., and VERARDI, I.
1984   *Arte rupestre no centro do Brasil. Pinturas e gravuras da pre-historia de Goiás e oeste de Bahía,* Instituto Anchietano de Pesquisas, São Leopoldo (Brasil), UNISINOS.

SCHMITZ, P. I., RIBEIRO, M. B., BARBOSA, A. S., BARBOSA, M. O., DE MIRANDA, A. F.
1986   *Caiaponia. Arqueologia nos cerrados do Brasil central,* Instituto Anchietano de Pesquisas, Publicaciones avulsas, no. 8, São Leopoldo, UNISINOS.

SCHOBINGER, JUAN
1956   El arte rupestre de la provincia del Neuquén. *Anales de Arqueología y Etnología,* vol. XII: 115–227, Mendoza, Universidad Nacional de Cuyo.
1962   Representaciones de máscaras en los petroglifos del occidente argentino. *Anthropos,* vol. 57: 683–699, St. Augustin (Alemania); Anthropos Institut.
1963   Nuevos petroglifos de la provincia del Neuquén, *Anales de Arqueología y Etnología,* vol. 17–18: 151–171, Mendoza.
1982   *¿Vikingos o extraterrestres? Estudio crítico de algunas teorías recientes sobre el origen y desarrollo de las culturas precolombinas,* Buenos Aires, Huemul-Crea.
1982 b Los petroglifos del Cerro Tunduqueral, Uspallata, Prov. Mendoza, Argentina. *Ars Praehistorica,* vol. I: 123–139, Sabadell (Barcelona), Ed. AUSA.
1985   Relación entre los petroglifos del oeste de la Argentina y los de Chile. In *Estudios de Arte Rupestre:* 195–203, Santiago, Museo Chileno de Arte Precolombino.
1983–1985 Algunas observaciones terminológicas sobre la prehistoria americana. *Anales de Arqueología y Etnología,* vol. 38–40: 7–28, Mendoza.
1988   *Prehistoria de Sudamérica: Culturas Precerámicas,* Madrid, Alianza Editorial (Alianza-América no. 15).
1988 b El arte rupestre del área subandina. Casos interpretables como expresión de vivencias shamá nicas. *Contribuciones al Estudio del Arte rupestre Sudamericano,* no. 2: 36–53. La Paz, SIARB. (Similar text in *L'Anthropologie,* vol. 92, no. 1: 361–370, Paris, 1990.)
1994   *La Reunión Internacional sobre el Pòblamiento Americano* (São Raimundo Nonato, Brasil, Diciembre de 1993). SIARB, Boletín no. 8: 32–36, La Paz.
1999   "Argentina's Oldest Rock Art." In *Dating and the Earliest Known Rock Art,* ed. M. Strecker and P. Bahn, 53–65. Oxford: Oxbow Books.

SCHOBINGER, JUAN, and GRADIN, CARLOS J.
1985   *Cazadores de la Patagonia y agricultores andinos. Arte rupestre de la Argentina,* Madrid, Ediciones Encuentro (Series: "Las Huellas del Hombre"). There is also an Italian edition, *Arte rupestre argentina,* and a French one, *Art de la Patagonie et des Andes,* by Editoriale Jaca Book, Milán.

SCHROEDER, SUSAN
n.d.   *Indian Women of Early Mexico.* Norman: University of Oklahoma Press.

SCHUBERT, CARLOS
1998   *Glaciers of South America.* Denver: U.S. Geological Survey. Series: U.S. Geological Survey Professional Paper; Satellite Image Atlas of Glaciers of the World; Vol. 1386-I.

SELLARDS, ELIAS H.
1941   Stone Images from Henderson County, Texas. *American Antiquity,* vol. 7, no. 1: 29–38, Menasha, Society for American Archaeology.

1986   *Early Man in America: A Study in Prehistory.* Westport, CT: Greenwood.

SELSAM, MILLICENT E. (Editor)
1984   *Stars, Mosquitoes and Crocodiles: The American Travels of Alexander Von Humboldt.* New York: HarperCollins.

SILVA CELIS, E.
1963   Los petroglifos de "El Encanto" (Florencia, Caquetá). *Revista Colombiana de Antropología,* vol. XII: 9–80, Bogotá, Instituto Colombiano de Antropología.

SILVERMAN, HELAINE, and BROWNE, DAVID
1991   New Evidence for the Date of the Nazca Lines. *Antiquity,* vol. 65, no. 247: 208–220, Oxford, Antiquity Publications.

SMITH, GERALD
1983   Geoglyphs, Rock Alignments and Ground Figures. In *Ancient Images on Stone. Rock Art of the Californians,* 84–95, Los Angeles, University of California.

SOCARRÁS MATOS, MARTIN
1985   La cultura de Los Círculos Concéntricos: computación aborigen, *Santiago,* no. 59: 73–80, Santiago de Cuba.

SORENSON, JOHN L., and RAISH, MARTIN H.
1990   *Pre-Columbian Contact with the Americas Across the Oceans. An Annotated Bibliography,* 2 volumes, Provo, Utah, Research Press.

SOUSTELLE, JACQUES
1984   *Los Olmecas,* México, Fondo de Cultura Económica (Edición francesa, Paris, 1982).

SPAHNI, JEAN-CHRISTIAN
1976   Gravures et peintures rupestres du désert d'Atacama (Chili). *Bulletin,* no. 40: 29–36, Societé Suisse des Américanistes, Ginebra (Suiza).

STEINBRING, JACK
1999   "Early Rock Art of Mid-Continental North America." In *Dating and the Earliest Known Rock Art,* ed. M. Strecker and P. Bahn, 5–14. Oxford: Oxbow Books.

STEINBRING, JACK, DANZIGER, EVE, and CALLAGHAN, R.
1987   Middle Archaic Petroglyphs in Northern North America. *Rock Art Research,* vol. 4, no. 1: 3–16, and vol. 4, no. 2: 150–161. Melbourne, AURA.

STEWARD, JULIAN H.
1929   *Petroglyphs of California and Adjoining States.* University of California Publications in American Archaeology and Ethnology, vol. 24, no. 2: 47–238 and engraved plates 22–94. Berkeley, University of California Press.
1937   Petroglyphs of the United States, *Smithsonian Report for 1936:* 405–425, Washington, D.C., Smithsonian Institution.

STONE, ANDREA
1987   Cave Painting in the Maya Area. *Latin American Indian Literatures Journal,* vol. 3, no. 1: 95–108, Beaver Falls, Geneva College.
1995   *Images from the Underworld: Naj Tunich and the Tradition of Maya Cave Painting.* Austin: University of Texas Press.

STONE, DORIS (Editor)
1984   *Pre-Columbian Plant Migration from Lowland South America to Mesoamerica.* Cambridge: Peabody Museum of Archaeology & Ethnology, Harvard University, Publications Department. Series: Peabody Museum Papers; vol. 76.

STRECKER, MATTHIAS
1982   *Rock Art of East Mexico and Central America: An Annotated Bibliography.* Second revised edition. Monograph X, Institute of Archaeology, University of California, Los Angeles.
1986   Documentación e investigación de las pinturas rupestres de Laja Mayu, Betanzos, Depto. Potosí, Bolivia. *Prehistóricas,* no. 1: 43–48, La Paz, Universidad Mayor de San Andrés.
1987   *Arte Rupestre en Bolivia.* Contribuciones al Estudio del Arte rupestre Sudamericano, no. 1. La Paz, SIARB.

SUJO-VOLSKY, JEANNINE
1975   *El estudio del arte rupestre en Venezuela,* Caracas, Universidad Católica Andrés Bello.

SWAUGER, JAMES L.
1974   *Rock Art of the Upper Ohio Valley.* Graz (Australia), Akademische Druck und Verlagsanstalt.

TAVERA-ACOSTA, B.
1956   *Los petroglifos de Venezuela* (with a foreword by Miguel Acosta Saignes). Caracas, Universidad Central de Venezuela.

TRATEBAS, ALICE M.
1999   "The Earliest Petroglyph Traditions on the North American Plains." In *Dating and the Earliest Known Rock Art,* ed. M. Strecker and P. Bahn, pp. 15–27. Oxford: Oxbow Books.

TUOHY, DONALD R.
1969   A "Wounded Elephant" and Three Other Petroglyphs in Northern Washoe County, Nevada. *The Nevada Archeological Survey Reporter,* vol. III, no. 1: 9–12. Carson City (Nevada), Nevada Archeological Survey.

VALENCIA RUBY DE, SUJO-VOLSKY, JEANNINE (in collaboration with Rafael Lairet and Patrick Aliñana)
1987   *El diseño en los petroglifos venezolanos,* Caracas, Fundación Pampero.

VASTOKAS, J. M., and VASTOKAS, R. K.
1973   *Sacred Art of the Algonkians: A Study of the Peterborough Petroglyphs,* Peterborough (Canada), Mansard Press.

VASTOKAS, J. M., and VILHENA VIALOU, AGUEDA
1984   Un nouveau site préhistorique brésilien daté: l'abri á peintures et gravures Ferraz Egreja (Mato Grosso). *L'Anthropologie,* vol. 88, no. 1: 125–127, Paris.

VIALOU, DENIS
1989   Une rencontre de préhistoriens. In *France-Brésil: Vingt Anos de Coopération:* 89–93, I.H.E.A.L., PUG.

VIGNATI, MILCIADES ALEJO
1950   Estudios antropológicos en la Zona Militar de Comodoro Rivadavia, I. *Anales del Museo de La Plata* (Nueva Serie), Sección Antropología, no. 1: 7–18, La Plata.

VILHENA VIALOU, AGUEDA, and VIALOU, DENIS
1988–1989   Art rupestre dans des abris-habitats préhistoriques du Mato Grosso, Brésil. *Ars Praehistorica,* vol. VII–VIII: 347–356, Sabadell (Barcelona), Ed. AUSA.
1989   Abrigo pré-histórico Santa Elina, Mato Grosso: habitats e arte rupestre. *Revista de Pré-Historia,* vol. 7: 34–53, São Paulo.

VIÑAS, R., SARRIÁ, E., RUBIO, A., and DEL CASTILLO, V.
1984–1985   Repertorio temático de la pintura rupestre de la Sierra de San Francisco, Baja California (México). *Ars Praehistorica,* vol. III–IV: 201–232, Sabadell, AUSA.

VIÑAS, RAMON, SARRIÁ, E., RUBIO, A., DEL CASTILLO, V., and PEÑA, C.
1986–1987   El santuario rupestre de la Cueva de la Serpiente, Arroyo del Parral, Baja California Sur (México). *Ars Praehistorica,* vol. V–VI: 157–204, Sabadell, AUSA.

WALLACE, WILLIAM J.
1985   A Last Look at Malaga Cove. In *Woman, Poet, Scientist: Essays in New World Anthropology Honoring Dr. Emma Louise Davis:* 134–144, San Diego, Ballena Press-Great Basin Foundation.

WATSON, PATTY J.
1992   *The Prehistory of Salts Cave, Kentucky.* Springfield: Illinois State Museum Society.

WEBER, GERTRUD, and STRECKER, MATTHIAS
1976   *Petroglyphen der Finca Las Palmas (Chiapas, Mexico).* Akademische Druck und Velagsanstalt, Graz (Austria).

WELLMANN, KLAUS, F.
1976   *Muzzinabikon. Indianische Felsbilder Nordamerikas aus fünf Jahrtausenden,* Akademische Druck und Verlagsanstalt, Graz (Austria).
1979   *A Survey of North American Indian Rock Art,* Akademische Druck und Verlagsanstalt, Graz.
1981   Rock Art, Shamans, Phosphenes and Hallucinogens in North America. *Bollettino* CCSP, vol. XVIII: 89–103.

WERLHOF, JAY C. VON
1965   *Rock Art of Owens Valley, California.* Reports of the University of California Archaeological Survey, no. 65, Berkeley, University of California Archaeological Research Facility.
1988   *Spirits of the Earth: A Study of Earthen Art in the North-American Deserts.* Vol. I: *The North Desert,* El Centro (California): Imperial Valley College Museum.

WILLEY, GORDON R.
1966–1971   *An Introduction to American Archaeology* (Vol. I, North America; vol. II: South America). Englewood Cliffs (New Jersey), Prentice-Hall.

ZAMBRANO, JOSÉ ANTONIO
1985   *La zona arqueológica de Tula,* México, Editorial del Magisterio "Benito Juárez."

ZAVALA RUIZ, ROBERTO
1978   *Guía de las Grutas de Loltun, Oxkutzcab, Yucatán,* México, Instituto Nacional de Antropología e Historia.

Abbreviations:

Boletín SIARB:	Boletín de la Sociedad de Investigación del Arte Rupestre de Bolivia, La Paz (Bolivia).
Bollettino CCSP:	Bollettino del Centro Camuno di Studi Preistorici, Capo di Ponte (Brescia, Italia).
Clio:	Revista Clio, Centro de Filosofia e Ciencias Humanas, Universidade Federal de Pernambuco, Recife (Brasil).
Relaciones SAA:	Relaciones de la Sociedad Argentina de Antropología, Buenos Aires.
Runa:	Runa. Archivo para las Ciencias del Hombre. Instituto de Ciencias Antropológicas, Universidad Nacional de Buenos Aires.

Index

Numbers in bold indicate volume; page numbers followed by "c" and "n" indicate caption and note.